To Win and Die in Dixie

The Birth of the
Modern Golf Swing
and the
Mysterious Death of
Its Creator

To Win and Die in Dixie

STEVE EUBANKS

Ballantine Books · New York

ESPN
BOOKS

Published in the United States by ESPN Books, an imprint of ESPN, Inc., New York, and
Ballantine Books, an imprint of The Random House Publishing Group,
a division of Random House, Inc., New York.

BALLANTINE and colophon are registered trademarks of Random House, Inc.
The ESPN Books name and logo are registered trademarks of ESPN, Inc.

LIBRARY OF CONGRESS CATALOGING-IN-PUBLICATION DATA
Eubanks, Steve.
To win and die in Dixie : the birth of the modern golf swing and
the mysterious death of its creator / Steve Eubanks.
p. cm.
Includes index.
ISBN 978-0-345-51081-5
1. Edgar, James Douglas, 1884–1921   2. Golfers—England—Biography.
3. Swing (Golf)   I. Title
GV964.E28E84 2010
796.352092—dc22
[B]   2009052591

Printed in the United States of America on acid-free paper

www.ballantinebooks.com
www.espnbooks.com

2 4 6 8 9 7 5 3 1

FIRST EDITION

Book design by Mary A. Wirth

To Liza

Contents

Author's Note

This is a true story. All the people and events in this book are real. There are no composite characters or time compressions. The dates and places are accurate, as are all references to books, magazines, and newspapers of the period. Like all writers of narrative nonfiction, I struggled with how to handle dialogue and capture the feelings and actions of people in the first two decades of the twentieth century. The racial references are painfully true to the period, and whenever possible, I used contemporary source information—transcripts, letters, diaries, written reports, first-person accounts, and so forth—for the dialogue as well as the thoughts and feelings of the characters. When that source material was not available, I relied on oral histories, some passed down through two generations. Just how accurate those conversations are after ninety years of retelling is anybody's guess; but in the absence of other materials, family histories are the best one can expect.

PART ONE

A Man in the Road

James Douglas Edgar.

This is a man who will one day be the greatest of us all.

—Harry Vardon

Newspapering was a young man's game. At least that was what Comer Howell told himself as he rolled his shoulders, put one foot on the running board, and unlatched the door of his Type 59 Cadillac. It was an odd and incongruous thought given that Comer was barely out of his teens and flush with promise. He had already studied abroad at Oxford and was only a few credits shy of a degree from the University of Georgia, but the pangs of another exhausting day reporting news for the *Atlanta Constitution* coupled with the suffocating heat of a Georgia summer night had zapped his vigor and left him feeling much older than his years.

With a tall, lean physique, a chiseled jaw, and perfectly slicked hair, he bore a remarkable resemblance to California's latest moving picture sensation, an Italian named Rudolph Valentino. But Comer was no "Latin Lover" and certainly no play actor. With his chin high, a watch chain dangling from his vest pocket just so, the fingers of a hand relaxed in the pocket of his trousers, Comer looked like what he was: one of the *Northsiders,* the proper Atlantans who lived in the large neoclassical, Tudor-Jacobean, or colonial revival homes along the wooded northern hills of the South's fastest-growing city. Atlanta had geographical as well as social demarcations. The hilly north side of town where oaks, magnolias, and dogwoods shaded the manicured lawns was the province of the right families, many wealthy, all white. The pine-laden flatlands grew progressively darker. The east side of town housed clusters of Orientals, Japanese and Chinese, who had migrated to the region as agricultural and railroad workers, and the southern enclaves were majority negro: areas someone like Comer Howell rarely visited, and never at this time of night.

He had removed his four-button jacket, a staple of the sacque suit, but too hot for August, even at midnight. He'd also loosened the silk tie, removing the clip and unfastening the collar of his white shirt, a faux pas bordering on scandalous in a town where lingering Edwardian mores required professional men to change clothes several times a day depending on the activity. Comer's father certainly would have frowned on his casual appearance, but the elder Howell would just have to understand.

The thought of explaining his present wardrobe to anyone, especially his father, caused Comer's shoulders to slump. He worked at the family newspaper and lived under his father's roof (one of the largest Victorian dwellings on the north side) in the warm comfort of family largesse, but with those trappings came the heft of the Howell name. Maybe it was just the lateness of the hour: with Monday about to slip into Tuesday and his eyes burning from cigarette smoke and the strain of putting another day's newspaper to bed, Comer couldn't wait to get his car rolling uptown. Cadillac was one of the first automobiles with a venting system that blew air directly into the passenger compartment, and the Type 59, with its innovative tilted windshield, provided as comfortable an experience as one could find on the road. By all rights he was too young to be driving a luxury automobile, especially at a time when most Georgians still owned horses, or at least a mule, but along with the responsibilities of upholding the family reputation, being a Howell in Atlanta carried certain perks. Comer refused to feel guilty for indulging a few extravagances.

Of course, if he were such a big deal, why was he leaving the office at this hour, especially after going to press with such burning stories as the one about an eighty-year-old Atlantan who had fallen from a ladder in his yard?

He opened the door and waited on the running board while his passengers plopped into their seats. No matter the hour, Comer would never breach his Southern manners by sitting down before his guests. Lloyd Wilhoit, the city editor, got in first. He was a crusty, authoritarian man whose perpetual frown blended with his cheeks until one fleshy crevice became indistinguishable from the next. His demeanor didn't brighten as he climbed into the back seat of Comer's car for a ride home. No one told Wilhoit to sit in the back: it was just assumed he would want to be chauffeured.

Paul Warwick, a senior reporter and a man with enough clout at the paper that even Wilhoit left him alone, sat in the front. They were grizzled veterans of the news business, real reporters who ground out stories like meal from a stone, and men who viewed Comer as a nice kid, but the boss's son, not their equal. That didn't stop them from hitching a ride after a long night, especially since Howell had the nicest car in the newsroom.

Boss's son: the moniker could burrow a hole through the sternest of young psyches. No matter what he did or how hard he worked, Comer seemed destined to be known as Clark Howell's son. His dad had taken over as owner, editor, and publisher of the *Atlanta Constitution* in 1901, just a few months after Comer was born, and in the two decades since, the paper had grown into one of the most respected news organs in the nation. Of course Comer had had nothing to do with that success, which meant he had more to prove. Co-workers always looked askance at a young heir. It was common in any job, but it was especially brutal in a cut-throat business like the news.

As if Clark Howell's shadow were not large, Comer's grandfather, Captain Evan Park Howell, had been a war hero, the kind of man other men spoke of with faraway looks in their eyes. After serving in Virginia under Stonewall Jackson and leading a Confederate artillery battery during Billy Sherman's romp through Atlanta, Captain Howell had worked as the sole reporter at the *Atlanta Intelligencer*. He hadn't done it for money. The family sawmill on Howell Mill Road had become a gold mine as the town Sherman torched rose from the ashes. Lumber couldn't be cut fast enough, and the Howell Mill became one of the city's primary suppliers. Wealthy and a war hero, Captain Howell, known as E.P. among his friends, dabbled in law and politics, being elected state senator twice, but his true passion was the paper: reporting, editing, and publishing news of the New South. So, in 1887, E. P. Howell bought controlling interest of the *Atlanta Constitution* and assumed the mantle of editor-in-chief. Comer's family had controlled things ever since.

Unspoken resentment hung like summer mist about Comer's two passengers that night. After all, how were a city editor and a senior reporter supposed to treat a Howell? In addition to being their boss, Comer's dad had once been president of the state senate and a candidate for governor. Newspapermen running for political office was quite common, since the public saw them as intelligent and informed citizens, as well as some of the wealthiest. The man who had beaten Clark Howell in that governor's race, Hoke Smith, had once owned the *Atlanta Journal*, the rival paper to the *Constitution*.

While Comer never lived in the governor's mansion and never ran anything more complicated than a weekly bridge game, he did live a life most reporters could not fathom. He wore black patent leather shoes to work, and two-toned wingtips with his casual attire at a time when many Georgians went shoeless. He also owned brogues with fringed tongues for the occasional retreat to Augusta, Thomasville, or the Jekyll Island Club. His tuxedo, a fifty-dollar extravagance, had been custom-tailored in New York along with several of his golf coats and knickerbockers. He didn't play much golf, but he kept the clothes on hand in case he got called for a game at Brookhaven or the Atlanta Athletic Club at East Lake, clubs his family had belonged to from their inception.

Comer went to all the right parties. His acquaintances, romantic and otherwise, were esteemed Southerners, and his accent was just so: proper Victorian grammar delivered in an adagio rhythm with the r's rolled into ah's; none of the banjo-twanging phrases of the hillbillies, or guttural vowel swallowing of the field hands. He was the consummate gentleman. Even his name reeked of status: Hugh M. Comer Howell, his father's family name plus the full name of his maternal grandfather, who was himself the famous late president of the Georgia Central Railroad. Little wonder other reporters at the paper had trouble warming up to him.

Comer worked as hard as anyone, staying late, taking piddling assignments, and pecking out un-bylined tripe on the latest socialite wedding— *"officiating the service was the honorable reverend . . ."*—or listening to endless blather at City Hall. Today's inanity had included paragraph upon paragraph about traffic safety. The Junior Chamber of Commerce had declared the second week of August as "Traffic Safety Awareness Week," in an attempt to draw attention to the maimings and deaths on the city's streets. It was no doubt a worthwhile cause. According to the *New York Times,* one person was killed by a car every forty-two minutes in America, an epidemic that showed no signs of abating. Unfortunately, by eleven o'clock on a Monday night, Comer couldn't have cared less. He was hot and exhausted, and longed for nothing more than a few hours alone in his Chippendale walnut bed.

He would decide how to respond to the contempt he sensed from Wilhoit and Warwick tomorrow. Fair or not, nepotism always left a stain. To combat it, Comer had to become the best reporter in the city. He needed nitty-gritty newspapering, something that would make Comer Howell the talk of the town for his efforts, not his name. Right now, though, he needed sleep. A dark, quiet house awaited him on Wesley Avenue, and he had a darn nice motorcar to transport him there: emerald green with a sturdy arched grille, sleek curved running boards, and twelve-spoke wheels, a machine worth more than most people at the paper made in a year, a point no one mentioned, but another source of unspoken tension among his passengers.

Conversation was light. They were too tired and the night was too hot for chitchat. August was always the most oppressive month, but this one had been especially stifling, and nightfall brought no relief. The air felt like molasses, and the smells of sawdust and tar, "the aroma of progress" as politicians called it, were enough to turn the stomach. Once they got rolling the breeze cooled things down a bit.

That all changed as they rolled through the 500 block of West Peachtree Street.

Wilhoit saw it first.

"Comer, stop the car! A man in the road!" he shouted.

Jerking the wheel toward the center of the street, Comer hit the brakes and the car wobbled to a stop. Thankfully there was no traffic. Comer whipped the car around at the Fifth Street intersection.

Then he saw it, too, a motionless figure facedown near the curb, legs sprawled, and a head cocked at a strange angle near the gutter. At first Comer thought it was a scarecrow or one of those mannequins that Gavan's used to display their thirteen-dollar men's suits, but as the headlights hit the figure, Comer saw the puddle, black and glistening.

It was a man. There could be no mistake. He wore cuffed trousers and a white shirt, and lay in a pool of blood.

They froze. As much as Comer, Wilhoit, and Warwick believed themselves to be noble men of courageous stock, nobody felt compelled to rush forward. They climbed from the Cadillac slowly, haltingly. When a streetcar approached, they clamored over each other in an attempt to flag it down.

There weren't any passengers at midnight, so Wilhoit convinced the two conductors to help. Together, the five men inched toward the figure in the street, each fighting the urge to flee the scene as blood oozed from the lower extremities.

"He's still breathing!" one of the streetcar workers said.

This news jolted Wilhoit into action. He ran to a house on the other side of the street, the only one on West Peachtree with the lights on at that time of night. "I need to telephone an ambulance," he shouted.

Comer felt like his heart was going to leap out of his chest, but his legs seemed paralyzed. He couldn't look away from the blood as it shimmered in the glow of the new White Way streetlamps the city had installed. The orbs, five per pole, gave the growing pool a glistening sheen. Comer knew he couldn't stand there while this waxy-looking man expelled his last breath. The figure appeared so unnatural, like a mime or an actor in makeup.

When Comer finally moved, he slipped, only then realizing the blood had enveloped his feet. Comer leapt onto the sidewalk, his breath shallow. He sprinted to the nearest boardinghouse, opened the screen and banged on the door.

"Let me use your telephone!" Comer shouted. "A man has been hit by a car!"

Why he'd used those words wouldn't occur to him for some time. Comer had no idea what had happened in the street. Nobody did. But Traffic Safety Awareness Week continued to weave through his subconscious. Comer had learned a lot about auto accidents in the last two days: like the fact that, so far in 1921, thirty-eight Atlanta souls had been called home in traffic-related incidents, the fifth-highest death toll among cities of 100,000 residents or more. He also knew that cars were multiplying like rabbits. Henry Ford's Model T factory on Ponce de Leon Avenue had been churning out vehicles in Atlanta since 1915. A year after Ford came to town, the city had 6,000 automobiles chugging up and down its streets. George Hanson had added to the congestion by opening his Hanson Six plant, calling Atlanta "The logical automobile center of the Great Southeast." Now there were close to 25,000 cars in town, and the death toll continued to climb. It shouldn't have surprised anyone. The automobile itself was only a few years old, and motor vehicle dexterity was still a generation away. Most roads hadn't been upgraded from their horse-and-buggy conditions, and Georgians certainly weren't accustomed to fast, powerful machines on their streets. Dozens of people had died by walking in front of cars they had seen. They had simply underestimated the closing speed of a Model T. Shouting that the man in the street had been hit by a car was a reflex, a verbal vomit in the midst of a crisis. At the time Comer didn't give it a second thought. There were far more pressing concerns, like getting an ambulance to the scene. He had no idea how crucial his words would later become, or how much he would regret having uttered them. At that moment, he just wanted to do something, anything, to help.

He banged on the door again. "Please, help," he yelled. "We need an ambulance."

Then he heard a crash like one of the windows being blown out. *What on earth?* Running out front, Comer saw a young man, not much older than himself, dressed in nightclothes and leaning over the body. He glanced to his right and saw that rather than come to the door, the man had jumped out the front window leaving the screen in a mangled heap near the curb.

Bedclothes Man fell to his knees in the sticky black pool. Undaunted by the vast amount of blood, he cradled the pale head of the victim in his lap. To Comer's shock, the bleeding man was still alive and trying to speak. Bedclothes Man leaned down, putting his ear almost against the man's barely moving lips. An inaudible whisper escaped between raspy and ever slowing breaths. Then all movement stopped.

The bleeding man died in the lap of a friend who showed no shame in weeping like a baby in the middle of the street.

"Who is he?" Wilhoit asked after Bedclothes Man got control of himself.

"Edgar," the man said.

"Edgar who?"

Bedclothes Man shook his head. "Douglas Edgar," he said in a decidedly British accent distinct to some region in the North of England. "James Douglas Edgar."

"Why do I know that name?" Warwick asked.

The man in bloody bedclothes looked up, cocked his head, and said: *"'Cos he's the greatest golfer in the world."*

The statement was far from hyperbole. For starters, the man in his bedclothes was himself a professional golfer, an Englishman named Tommy Wilson who had come to America to serve an apprenticeship under his mentor, J. Douglas Edgar. The two had known each other since Wilson was a boy. Wilson had caddied for Edgar and then become his assistant at the Northumberland Golf Club in Gosforth on the outskirts of Newcastle-upon-Tyne. After the war, when Edgar had moved to Atlanta to become the professional at Druid Hills Golf Club, Wilson had followed him.

It was no surprise that Wilson held his mentor in such high esteem. The two were apparently living together, so the young man's emphatic statement about Edgar being "the greatest golfer in the world" could have been discounted. But Wilson was not alone in his opinion. In the small but vibrant universe of golfers, J. Douglas Edgar was generally acknowledged as one of the finest players in the game, mentioned as a favorite in almost every tournament he entered, and often photographed for pretournament publicity as one of the "leading contenders" no matter how important the event. Photos of Edgar with Harry Vardon and Ted Ray, two golfing giants of the late nineteenth and early twentieth centuries, littered major golf magazines, and no less an expert than Bernard Darwin, the dean of a niche profession that would later become known as golf writing, said, "I watched a good deal of Edgar's play and never wish to see anything more consistently brilliant."

Darwin wasn't the only scribe singing Edgar's praises. In 1920, *Golf Illustrated* magazine, the dominant American golf publication at the time, rhetorically asked, "Did it occur to you that J. Douglas Edgar has an uncanny way of winning championships?" And editors at *The Official Organ of the Professional Golfers of America,* the precursor to *PGA Magazine,* wrote that "When the records for 1920 are all compiled, it can be seen that [Jock] Hutchison, [J. Douglas] Edgar, and [Walter] Hagen have accounted for the majority of the main events this year."

Even Vardon, the greatest golfer in the world at the turn of the twentieth century, and the only man in history to win six British Open Championships, said of Edgar, "This is a man who will one day be the greatest of us all." That would have been a nice compliment from anyone, but Vardon rarely handed out officious accolades. During the height of his playing career he beat half his fellow competitors through sheer intimidation, often pretending other players simply did not exist. Vardon, who played against Walter Hagen, and lived long enough to see Bobby Jones, Gene Sarazen, and a young Byron Nelson, was known to have used the word "greatest" in reference to only two players: Bob Jones, of whom he said, "With a few more years in the game, he will be one of the greatest golfers in the world," and J. Douglas Edgar.

In the years that followed, others gushed about Edgar's abilities. Tommy Armour, winner of the British Open, U.S. Open, and PGA Championship, who would become known as the Silver Scot, said, "He was undoubtedly the greatest of them all, and taught me the most." Several of the lessons Edgar taught Armour occurred during head-to-head contests where Edgar thumped Armour handily.

Then there was O. B. Keeler, a columnist for the *Atlanta Journal* who became famous as Bobby Jones's friend and personal scribe. Keeler wrote that Edgar was "a strange and fascinating little man. . . . And let me tell you, when he was right, I never have seen the golfer who could keep step with him." Keeler never wrote a careless word, so it is safe to assume that he put Jones among those who could not keep step with a "right" Edgar.

As late as 1947, noted journalist Ray Haywood wrote in *Golfing* magazine that "Douglas Edgar, a name known only to the older golfers, was the world's greatest golfer—amateur or professional—bar none. . . . Edgar can't be compared shot for shot with [Byron] Nelson. His time was much earlier—fortunately, perhaps, for Nelson. He can be compared with Jones, however. Jones was Edgar's pupil." It was true: the greatest amateur golfer in history, Bobby Jones, while struggling through his formative years as a teenager, learned from Edgar, and in fact, came out of the only slump he ever experienced in his career after spending countless one-on-one hours with Edgar.

Anyone with a passing interest in golf knows Bobby Jones. The same cannot be said of Douglas Edgar. However, Haywood witnessed Edgar firsthand; he saw Jones win his championships; he watched Nelson, Ben Hogan, and Sam Snead; and he put Edgar at the top of the heap.

In the decades immediately following his death, Edgar was considered the father of the modern golf swing, a savant who was the first to employ many of the principles considered to be fundamental in later years. In describing his swing and the types of shots he played, Darwin, Keeler, and Grantland Rice all used words like "unique," "unusual," and "not seen before." Ninety years later, the motions Edgar prescribed can be found in almost every golf instruction book in print, and his "unique" swing is now the model for most professionals. Edgar also coined many phrases that remained in use ninety years after his death, and he created one of the first mass-produced golf training aids, his "gate to golf," a device that has been copied thousands of times.

A contemporary sportswriter named Angus Perkerson wrote: "Edgar knows golf; he knows he knows it, and that convinces him that he is equal to the best. Why shouldn't he feel that way, having won over Harry Vardon and Ted Ray?"

Yet, like a photo left out in the sun, memories of J. Douglas Edgar have faded over the years. During Jones's reign as the game's greatest player, and on through the early years of Byron Nelson and Gene Sarazen, references to Edgar's influence were common, but by the early 1950s, he was more of an afterthought, marked mainly by a passing "Oh, remember Douglas Edgar?" By the 1970s, he had become a historical footnote, the answer to a trivia question for only the most obsessed golf aficionados. By

1980 the silver platter Edgar won in a Southeastern regional qualifier for the Wanamaker Championship had become the J. Douglas Edgar trophy, given to the winner of the Winter Eclectic competition at Gosforth Golf Club in northeast England (prompting many of the event's winners to say things like "Who the devil is J. Douglas Edgar?"). The occasional "whatever happened to" article popped up every five or six years throughout the 1980s and into the early 1990s, but for the most part, Edgar all but evaporated from golf's collective consciousness. By the turn of the twenty-first century, even officials at the USGA, the PGA Tour, and the Royal & Ancient Golf Club at St. Andrews said, "Who?" when asked about Edgar.

But despite his slip into relative obscurity, one unassailable fact solidifies Edgar's claim on history: ninety years after his death, he still held the oldest unbroken record in American professional golf.

None of that mattered a wit to Detective J. W. Lowe (pronounced *Lao*), who caught the call and was the first investigator on the scene as crickets and tree frogs announced August 8 giving way to August 9. Lowe had never heard of J. Douglas Edgar—golf was not a game for peace officers, especially in a city like Atlanta where country club membership was a symbol in a hierarchy that did not include civil servants. The detective had heard of Comer Howell, though. Everybody in town knew the Howells. Lowe was somewhat surprised to see such a prominent citizen out in the middle of the night, especially given the gruesome scene in the street.

"When did the ambulance arrive?" Lowe asked.

Wilhoit responded. He seemed to have recovered more than the others. "Too long," he said. "I called the Grady ambulance first. It didn't come."

"How long?" Lowe asked.

"Twenty minutes," Wilhoit said. "Then I called Patterson Ambulance. It got here in about five minutes, but it was too late."

From the quantity of blood on the scene, it wouldn't have mattered if the ambulance had been around the block. Mr. Edgar appeared to have bled out in spectacular fashion, a sure sign that an artery had burst. Lowe had once investigated a brawl where the victim had been struck in the neck with the sharp edge of a shovel. The initial blood spurt in that one had been nearly twenty feet. By the time the heart gave way there was a washtub of blood around the body. Still, the ambulance story would not make the powers at Grady Memorial happy, especially since the man who'd called for their services was the city editor of the *Constitution*.

"Mr. Howell," Lowe said, turning his attention to Comer, who stood on the curb with his shoulders hunched and his hands in his pockets. "You told Mr. Wilson here that you believed Mr. Edgar had been struck by a motorcar?"

Lowe had already examined the Cadillac. If this had been a hit-and-run, Comer's vehicle was not involved.

Comer appeared to be in shock. His face was almost as pale as the corpse. In a voice as fragile as a canning jar, he explained to Lowe that he had just spouted the first thing that came to mind, that the assumption of a hit-and-run was pure speculation given that the body was in the road. He didn't mention his subconscious preoccupation with Traffic Safety Awareness Week. The fewer words he had to utter the better. Comer wasn't sure how long he could stand there without getting sick or fainting.

Lowe made no judgments about the story. He took statements from Wilhoit, Warwick, the roommate, Wilson, and the men from the streetcar. All the accounts seemed to line up. Still, no one had any idea what had happened to Mr. Edgar, or why.

"We found his hat," Comer offered.

"Oh?"

Wilhoit produced a light tweed touring cap, clipped in the front, the kind worn by gentlemen on the golf course, or so Lowe assumed.

"It was in the street, ten yards that way." Wilhoit pointed down West Peachtree back toward town.

More nods and notes. There was no blood trail, no skid marks, no stream of tattered clothing, none of the things normally found around hit-and-run accidents. A few hours later one of Edgar's shoes would be discovered, a golf shoe, fully laced and tied, in a bush near the boarding-house door. It would be one of many clues to materialize in the coming days. At that moment, however, Lowe didn't have much. It was time to knock on doors. Somebody somewhere had to have seen or heard something. His first order of business was to talk to everyone who lived in the immediate vicinity.

Still standing on the curb and staring at the black pool where the body had been, Comer concentrated on his breathing. His gut flipped, and he was afraid to move his feet for fear of falling down. In the blink of an eye, he'd gotten his wish. A front-page, multiple-column, multiple-day story with numerous angles and all sorts of intrigue—just the kind of thing that would allow him to carve his own mark on the family paper—had fallen, quite literally, at his feet. This was the kind of unbelievable luck reporters dreamt about; the gruesome and untimely death of the world's greatest golfer, not in some obscure locale, but right in front of him on West Peachtree Street! It was a story Comer could convey with the vivid clarity only an eyewitness could offer. He would be asked about it at parties for years. *What really happened, Comer? Did he actually die right in front of you? The world's greatest golfer, a thing like that! What do you think killed him?* He would be the social centerpiece at every function in town.

As he gazed at Douglas Edgar's blood, the streetlights still twinkling off the pool like stars in a cloudless country sky, those thoughts made Comer's stomach lurch. Suddenly, everything seemed upside down. He didn't know it at the time, but his life was about to change forever. At that moment, he knew only one thing with absolute certainty: what he had wanted—what he had longed for out of life only an hour ago—was not what he would want from now on.

CHAPTER 2

A busy morning on Peachtree Street
in the 1920s.

J. Douglas Edgar, golf professional at Druid Hills Golf Club and one of the best known golfers in the world, was struck by an unidentified automobile at the corner of Fifth and West Peachtree streets late Monday night and died on the way to the hospital after being picked up by a passing automobile.

—*Atlanta Constitution,*
August 9, 1921

Despite his exhaustion, sleep found Comer Howell in reluctant fits. A light breeze through the open windows of the sleeping porch didn't help, as he had lost the wrestling match with the sheets for most of the night. Watching a man die had that effect, or so he assumed. Comer had never held death in such intimate proximity. He had seen the dead, sure—no one survived the flu epidemic of 1918 unscathed, and, of course, there had been the odd passing of a family member while Comer and his brothers stood vigil—but nothing like this. Unlike his grandfather, who had witnessed men cut down by Union muskets and swords, Comer had come of age in a time of peace with prosperity waiting in the wings. The fever of the postwar depression was breaking, or so everyone said. The economy hadn't quite turned the corner, but recovery was in sight. The 1920s teemed with potential. Investors were heading back to Wall Street, and, on a local level, Citizens & Southern Bank had started an optimistic campaign to entice depositors to think five years down the road. Men of Comer's generation felt confident that they were living in an enlightened age, a time when eugenics would cull the morons and miscreants from their midst, and the League of Nations, spawned by the defeat of the Huns, promised to make war a thing of the past.

Tragedy on a local level was another matter entirely. Fresh memories, particularly of the blood, loomed large in Comer's mind. Suddenly life—not his life, but life in general—seemed bleaker, or at least more fragile.

Even Comer's older half-brother, Clark Howell, Jr., had a more hardened perspective. Clark had seen blood spilled in the War to End All Wars. Now Major Howell, as Clark was known, was in Washington, D.C., working for the *Constitution,* covering matters that would shape the world, while Comer continued to slog through endless hours at Atlanta City Hall. Clark was the oldest child; the son who carried their father's name, and first in line to take over the paper. Comer didn't realize it—and why would he, since he'd never had any real sibling feuds with his brother—but those facts had been tender on his personal fire, the fuel behind his instinctive need to overachieve. Now, in one fateful night, that fire had given way to a deflating wave of melancholy. Clark would have reacted better, Comer told himself, or at least differently. What would his brother have done if it had been he who had found a dying man in the street?

Comer closed his eyes and tried to change the scene, but the vision of Douglas Edgar wrenching out one last whisper continued to visit him in the morning as it had throughout the night. He'd been awake for hours, but by the time he rolled out of bed, a baking sun had already turned the morning dew into wafts of rising steam. He picked up the late-morning edition of the *Constitution* and read a front-page story on Edgar, a story replete with errors, a collection of grand mischaracterizations that Comer knew would tear through Atlanta like a summer storm. The first sentence said: "J. Douglas Edgar, golf professional at Druid Hills Golf Club and one of the best known golfers in the world, was struck by an unidentified automobile at the corner of Fifth and West Peachtree streets late Monday night and died on the way to the hospital after being picked up by a passing automobile."

Edgar had died in the street. He had been taken to the hospital all right, only it had been in an ambulance that was in no hurry.

Then there was this paragraph: "Mr. Edgar was a native of Scotland, having come to Atlanta eight years ago from St. Andrews, Scotland. He was about 40 years of age. A pathetic touch is added to the fatal occurrence by the fact that his wife and children are expected to arrive in Atlanta next week from England, a date to which it is said that he had long looked forward to."

Comer could barely remember hearing anything over the thumping of his heart, but he had heard Tommy Wilson tell Detective Lowe that Edgar was from Newcastle. Unless the British had moved the border, Newcastle was in England, not Scotland. He also remembered hearing Wilson say that Edgar was thirty-six years old, not forty, and that he had been in Atlanta since 1919: two years, not eight.

When the subject of the wife and children had come up, Wilson had said they were still in England. That meant that while still a "pathetic touch," unless the family had access to some super-powered cruise ship, they most assuredly were not expected in Atlanta next week. Transatlantic travel was a seven- to ten-day affair with another two days to get from New York to Atlanta by train. Even if Wilson had just failed to mention the family's travel plans, which didn't seem likely, there was no way they would make it in the time frame reported by the *Constitution*.

It was, however, a later paragraph, the one dealing with cause of death, that made Comer break out in a sweat.

"The driver of the automobile that struck the dead man has not been found. Persons living in the vicinity where the accident occurred stated that they thought they had heard a dull crash and groans, and one person stated that he had seen a car dash down Fifth Street. No accurate description of the car could be obtained and the police at once began a search for the death car and its driver."

Death car! Comer prayed that there was more evidence of a traffic accident than what he had witnessed at the scene, that the hit-and-run and rogue "death car and its driver" were more than fantastic theories based on speculation that he himself had injected into the dialogue.

Comer could hear the chatter up and down the streets now. *Yes, it was a motorcar that never slowed down, or so I heard. Poor man was scooped up and rushed to the hospital, but died in the rear seat. Mangled beyond recognition: horrible business that.* Street corners, coffee shops, offices, and clubs were no doubt agog with renditions of last night's events, none of them accurate, but all hardening in resolve with each retelling. Word of mouth was still the most popular way of receiving information in the South. A thousand Atlantans owned large, boxy electronic receivers, but the region was still seven months away from having its first commercial radio station. Ironically, the race into that new medium was another blood feud between Clark Howell's *Constitution* and the *Atlanta Journal*. Even though Hoke Smith had long ago sold his interest in the rival newspaper, the intense competition that had festered in the governor's race carried over into a war between the papers, one that lasted long after Smith sold out. On the radio front, as happened too many times for the Howells' liking, the *Journal* won the race. The morning of March 15, 1922, the *Journal*-owned WSB became the South's first radio station, and the bulky toys that had been little more than useless purveyors of static burst to life with a clear jazz rendition of "The Light Cavalry Overture." Two days later, the Howells would enter the multimedia market with the 220-watt WGM. Broadcasting from the Georgia Railroad & Power Building, the first sounds out of Clark Howell's station would be a newscast, an attempt to show that, unlike the *Journal*, the *Constitution* and its owners would use their broadcasting license to educate and inform. But that was next year's news. In the summer of 1921, the only transmitted information came through telephone, telegram, and old-fashioned street-corner conversations, an activity Georgians attacked with vigor.

Despite what the Yankee aristocracy thought, more than 85 percent of white Georgians, male and female, over the age of ten could read, and over half of their negroes were literate. The written word occupied an exalted pedestal. Whether it was the *Farmers and Consumers Market Bulletin* or the collected speeches of Henry Grady, Southerners viewed printed text, especially the stories in their newspapers, as gospel truth. When they, through phone calls, church gatherings, or casual conversations at the feed store, retold those stories, the words became the property of the teller, and as such, solid as granite. Another day or two of gossip, and questioning any aspect of the Edgar story would be akin to calling a man a liar.

Maybe an eyewitness had been found after Comer left the scene. As much as he wanted this to be true, it seemed unlikely. Lowe and several uniformed men had canvassed the area and come up with little. The only reliable source had been a widow named Miss L. S. Warren, who lived directly across West Peachtree from the incident. Miss Warren had been the one to call the police, since it had never occurred to Comer or his cohorts to make that call after phoning the ambulances.

"I heard some sort of ruckus, I don't know what all, just a commotion that startled me awake," she had told Lowe after getting properly dressed at almost one A.M.

"Could it have been a car hitting a person in the street?" Lowe had asked, leading her in the direction of an auto accident, Comer feared, because of what he had yelled to Tommy Wilson earlier.

"It could have been," she'd said somewhat hesitantly. "But I've never heard such a thing before, so I could only guess as to what it must sound like."

The only sound she had recognized was a motorcar speeding away. "It was running rapidly, and from the sound it seemed to be a high-powered car," she had said.

This revelation did nothing but reinforce the hit-and-run theory. After all, Edgar was found in the street, bleeding and dying, and traffic safety was on everyone's mind. Miss Warren hearing an automobile speed away fit perfectly into the "death car" narrative, which appeared to be taking on a life of its own.

· · ·

Comer finished his coffee, dressed, and drove the Cadillac downtown toward the *Constitution* offices. Within minutes he was weaving along Peachtree Street, Atlanta's main artery. The most famous road in the state, Peachtree was a serpentine corridor that had once been an Indian trail running along the first ridge of the Appalachian foothills. Even though "Peachtree" would become synonymous with the city and state, the name was a malapropism. A section of the original trail had once been the demarcation line between the territories of the Creek Indians to the south and the Cherokees to the north. The unofficial border had been a large "pitch tree" where "pitch tree creek" ran into the Chattahoochee River. In what amounted to a game of Whisper Down the Lane, white settlers passed down the oral history until "pitch tree" became "Peachtree." By 1814 the transformation was complete. Fort Peachtree was erected on the site of the old pitch tree to protect local settlers during the War of 1812, and the city's main thoroughfare would forever bear the name of a tree that never grew there.

Now the street looked like a river weaving through a canyon of elevator buildings, constructed in the Chicago style, along with a smattering of picturesque High Victorian structures from the Reconstruction. Model Ts lined up like black boxes on both sides of the road, and the sidewalks bustled with railroad and insurance men wearing bow ties and flat-brimmed boaters. No architectural or industrial theme sprang out of Atlanta. The main commerce was transportation—railroad and automobiles—which meant the city existed to move people and things from one place to another. Atlanta was a pass-through, with everyone, even those who weren't going anywhere, moving at a breakneck pace.

When Comer reached the paper, he avoided conversation and parked himself behind his desk where he reread this morning's story. "Thomas Williams, assistant at Druid Hills, was prostrated with grief. He and Mr. Edgar had been companions for years," the paper said.

Wilson. Tommy Wilson, not Williams. For goodness' sake, how could they get so many things wrong?

The piece continued: "[Edgar] had been in ill health for some time and only a month ago returned from England where he spent several months in an effort to recuperate."

As was his habit, Comer took out a pocket-sized notebook and pen. He wrote: "Illness?" and "Just returned after several months?" In addition to taking copious notes, Comer always jotted down stream-of-consciousness questions as he was reading or listening. It could be annoying. He would be engaged in social conversation when, without so much as an "excuse me," he would turn away and start scribbling questions. Lectures, interviews, dinner parties: the notebook was never far from his side.

He kept the pen ready as he read: "L. L. Shivers, prominent Atlantan, it seems, was the last of Mr. Edgar's friends to talk with him."

Comer wrote: "L. L. Shivers—Lester Shivers?" Lester Shivers was an executive with Carter Electric Company, a lighting distributor with a retail store at 63 Peachtree Street, only a few blocks from the paper. The company also had a major warehouse operation in Savannah. Comer knew Lester Shivers well enough. He was definitely the kind of man who would accept Comer's call.

"[Shivers] had played golf with Mr. Edgar during the afternoon, and the two men had gone to Mr. Shivers' for dinner," the story continued. "After dinner, said Mr. Shivers, they played bridge for a while. At about 11:30, continued Mr. Shivers, he took Mr. Edgar to the corner of Fifth and West Peachtree, where Mr. Edgar alighted to go into his home. This was the last Mr. Shivers saw of him. It is believed that the death car appeared almost immediately after this."

If the paper couldn't get Tommy Wilson's name right, Comer had little confidence in the details of Edgar's last moments. Without much preamble, he went to a telephone and rang Main 6172, the number for Carter Electric. Within minutes he had Lester Shivers on the phone.

After the normal pleasantries and the obligatory questions about the family, Comer asked about the events of last night.

"Horrible," Shivers said. "I can't describe how grief-stricken we are. Am I to understand that you were the one who discovered Douglas in the street?"

Comer confirmed that, yes, he, along with Wilhoit and Warwick, had, indeed, been the first to stumble upon Mr. Edgar. He didn't convey the grizzly details. Shivers's voice quivered with distress. There was no reason for Comer to add to the man's pain.

"We played golf earlier in the day. Brookhaven, with Howard Beckett, the pro there, and Darkie Wilson," Shivers said.

"Darkie?" Comer said.

"Yes, Tommy Wilson, Douglas's apprentice. Douglas always called him Darkie. He brought it from Newcastle—the name. His skin darkens quite easily in the sun. In a town like Newcastle, I guess Tommy was considered dark. Douglas always smiled when he said it."

Unsaid but understood was the fact that Newcastle had no negroes, so the nickname Darkie, while appropriate and accurate in northeast England, carried a whiff of ironic humor in Atlanta, a joke Edgar must have enjoyed.

"He had not been to my home since returning from England," Shivers continued. "I invited him to supper, and he accepted. Then he and Mrs. Shivers and my daughter, Caroline; you remember Caroline?"

Comer said he did, in fact, remember the young Miss Shivers, unmarried and living on her own in town, or so he'd been told by more matchmakers than he cared to remember.

"The four of us played bridge until around nine o'clock. Caroline had to leave us then. I didn't want her traveling down town much later into the night. That being the case, Douglas stayed on and we played a three-handed game for another hour. Then he and I talked until around eleven-thirty. He could not have been happier. I believe he had things worked out. He wanted to take a streetcar back to the boardinghouse he was sharing with Darkie. I said, 'Nonsense, old boy, you'll ride with me.' He persisted, but I wouldn't hear of it. I drove him back to Fifth and West Peachtree. He got out and leaned on the door of my car and we talked for a few more minutes. Then he bade me good night, and started across the street. I drove away."

His voice tailed off. Then he said, "I was just about to retire when I received the call that he'd been struck by a car."

So the rogue car theory had become fact within minutes of Comer leaving the scene. That didn't take long.

"Do you have any news on the driver?" Shivers asked.

"The what?" Comer said before catching himself. "No. No news I'm afraid."

He thanked Shivers for his time, offered his best to the missus and Caroline, and went straight to his notebook where he wrote, "Believed he had things worked out?"

He tapped the pen on the paper. Then a question came to him as he replayed the time line in his head. If Caroline left the bridge table at nine, and Mrs. Shivers retired at ten, that left Lester and Edgar alone in the Shivers parlor for the better part of an hour and a half on a Monday night.

At the bottom of the page he wrote, "What do men discuss so late on a Monday?" a question he would later underline with a pencil.

The question he didn't write was "Why do you care so much, Comer?" For reasons he could not explain, Comer felt compelled to help in this case. And, also for reasons he could not pinpoint, he needed to learn more about the life of J. Douglas Edgar.

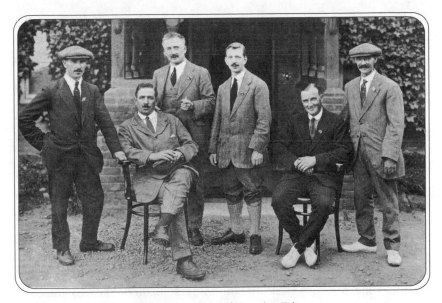

CHAPTER 3

The smiling face of Douglas Edgar
(seated at right) posing with a group of players
from the North of England.

It was while I was just a boy that a gentleman asked me why I didn't take up golf. I told him I wanted to do something else with my life besides hit a little ball around. He teed up a ball and told me to have a try at it. I missed it seven times and then I decided to prove to myself that I could learn this game.

—J. Douglas Edgar

The Edgars were Geordies, a fierce and independent lot from the northeastern edge of England within sight of Hadrian's Wall. A working-class area filled with farmers, coal brokers, and shipbuilders, natives were known for their wit and veracity as well as their healthy distrust of southerners. That was nothing new. For centuries a tempestuous peace had existed between those who lived in what the British called "the North of England," and the ladies and gentlemen in the south. Londoners looked down their noses at the industrial north, while Geordies considered those hailing from south of Birmingham to be erudite snobs.

A similar cultural divide separated Northerners and Southerners in America, only with inverted geography. For decades before and after the American Civil War, Northerners dismissed Southerners as gun-loving ignoramuses living in grim hovels, "a beautiful woman with a dirty face," as Lady Astor would later call Georgia's crown jewel of a city, Savannah. By the same token, American Southerners loathed Yankees for their holier-than-thou hypocrisy. The social construct in England was the same with the north and south reversed.

Even the name, Geordie, had derogatory connotations in the south. No one was sure where it originated, or if it described the people or their accent (a syncopated meter closer to the rhythmic clips of Edinburgh than the word-heavy yaws heard south of Cambridgeshire), but that didn't stop southerners from using "Geordie" as a pejorative, like "rube" or "redneck." One etymological theory had the word coming from the Geordie brand of lanterns used in the nearby coal mines. That made as much sense as anything. Newcastle was so synonymous with coal that it spawned one of the more common expressions in the English language: "carrying coals to Newcastle," which means a redundant action, like "selling ice to Eskimos."

Dumping the city and its residents into the "coal" box, however, ignored one of England's more fascinating cultural tapestries. In the late nineteenth and early twentieth centuries Newcastle was home to the region's largest shipbuilding operation and many of the country's first commercial printers. Grey Street, the main thoroughfare a block from the train station and within sight of the Tyne River, was a model of neoclassical architecture and a vast intellectual nerve center. Literacy flourished. The town's literary and philosophy society became known for their formal debates and enormous volume of books, a vast collection that predated the London Library by half a century.

With Socratic jousting going on in Latin on one side of town and coal being transported on the other, the perfectly coiffed and permanently soiled comingled at the Town Moor, a large green lung in the heart of town. It was Newcastle's equivalent of Central Park, an area jealously protected by the Freemen of the City, and the place where Geordies got their first taste of golf.

Actually, the first recorded round came in 1646 when Charles I whacked a featherie around a Newcastle field where the Scots held him prisoner. After that the game vanished for two centuries until the Freemen of the City formed the City of Newcastle Golf Club in 1891. The original petition, filed on June 10, 1891, read: "We the undersigned acknowledging the rights of the Freemen of the City over the pasturage of the Town Moor beg that permission be granted to us, to make say, nine or more holes in the turf that is the depth of the turf only, and measuring four inches in diameter in or about the valley leading down from the Fever Hospital. It is also essential to roll the turf for a space of, say, nine feet on each side of the holes. For the granting of which privileges we are willing to pay such nominal sum of money as may be agreed upon."

Greens nine feet in diameter would have been thimble-sized even in the nineteenth century, especially so close to St. Andrews where some of the putting surfaces butted up against the acre mark. Thankfully, the completed course was a lot nicer than what the Freemen outlined. The architect was none other than Old Tom Morris, the scion of St. Andrews and four-time winner of the Open Championship. Still burly at age seventy and wearing a wiry white beard that covered his leathery neck, Morris raised a hickory-shafted cleek like Moses parting the waters and declared that, in time, his latest creation "will be one of the finest inland courses in the Kingdom."

Not bloody likely, as the locals might have said. The land, while perfect for picnics and dog walks, had neither the features nor character to become more than what it was on opening day: a pedestrian, modest course. It would remain just that for many years, primarily because the

Freemen failed to word their petition to provide for future modifications: a bunker here, a new tree there, maybe damming a tributary to add a pond or two. By law, they couldn't even grow adequate rough.

Nobody thought about such far-flung problems on opening day, however. After lacing the ceremonial first tee shot down the fairway, Old Tom retired to a lavish luncheon and some malt refreshments in the clubhouse, a 120-year-old windmill that had been used to grind snuff and cornmeal until the members spent five thousand pounds remodeling it. For its new purposes the windmill housed a billiard room, club room, locker room, and the most luxurious accommodation of the period, indoor toilets.

The mayor and several aldermen accompanied Old Tom to lunch, along with several original members: two surgeons, a couple of merchants, a shipbuilder, artist, engineer, ironmonger, architect, and solicitor. They were also joined by Councilman Baxter Ellis of the Town Moor Management Committee, who continued to express his earnest desire "that the recreation of this new enterprise should be of a kind in which no animosity should spring from the ranks."

Golf should be for the people, Ellis argued. Let the game remain an upper-class trophy in the south. In the north, golf should stick to its roots. The Scots, who laid claim to inventing the game, believed in keeping it open to everyone. It wasn't until the "white settlers," as the Scots called the English, moved in with their club system that golf became a game for landowning gentlemen. Most citizens of Newcastle wanted the course open to any and all.

A couple of drinks into the luncheon, Mr. J. W. Pease offered a toast where he thanked everybody from the most obscure alderman to the mayor. In response the mayor said, "I am, indeed, quite pleased that a better feeling prevailed in the council about outdoor pastimes," an oblique reference to fears that the town's park would become a private retreat for the well-heeled.

It didn't. The golf course, although maintained by the members, remained open to the public. This led to more than a little grumbling. The members didn't mind paying the bills and sharing the grounds with local riffraff—most citizens showed proper deference, cleaning up after themselves and stepping aside to let members play through—but the cow chips were too much. According to city ordinance, cattle owned by the Freemen—two cows ("*too coos*" in the local dialect) per Freeman—were allowed to graze throughout the moor, including on the golf course. A local rule provided relief from the malodorous droppings, but that did little to assuage rankled feelings. Players still had to retrieve their balls after all.

The members slogged along for six years until a group finally decided that enough was enough. They split from the City of Newcastle Golf Club and formed another club north of town on a beautiful rolling plat with plenty of grass, yawning hardwoods, a meandering stream, breathtaking views, and not a cow to be seen. The land was in the middle of a two-and-a-half-mile tri-oval horseracing track, but that was an asset, not a liability. It was perfect. When Northumberland Race Park moved from the Town Moor to High Gosforth Park, the golfers followed close behind. Owners of the track thought the new club was a great idea, since they hosted only three major race weeks a year: the Easter Meet, Race Week, and the Autumn Race, and a golf course would provide a steady income stream the other forty-nine weeks of the year. So, like bitter Baptists splitting from the flock to form a new congregation, a renegade group of disgruntled City of Newcastle Golf Club members gathered at the County Hotel on January 24, 1898, and unanimously resolved: "We hereby form a club, limited by guarantee, to be called the Northumberland Golf Club."

Now Newcastle had two courses, and a nasty cold war brewing between them.

A precocious thirteen-year-old named Douglas Edgar watched all this preening and posturing with detached amusement. Despite his youth, Doug, as everyone called him, felt quite comfortable listening to the musings of older men. The third of John and Ann Edgar's four children, Doug was the brightest of the bunch by a good margin. His schoolmistress knew he had an extraordinary IQ, but she wasn't convinced that was a good thing. Doug was so bright that he finished his studies quickly, leaving plenty of time for all the mischief that drips from the pockets of thirteen-year-old boys.

He spent a lot of time at the Town Moor where he became a keen observer of human nature, and an ingenious entrepreneur. Tipping his hat to the ladies and complimenting their appearance, Doug quickly picked up on any aspect of their looks that appealed to them—*"A canny pair of shoes them, missus, an a bonny hat tha', too! Gans nice wi' the colour of ye dress an all."* Then he would volunteer to help passersby with their dogs, or offer to carry bags for a gentleman. A few steps into the chore, his trick hip, the one that did, legitimately, catch every so often, would miraculously buckle. The boy would crumble in pain. But, no, no, he could still carry the package; he would just limp along behind. This was always good for a shilling or two. Regulars grew wise to the scam, but they continued to play along. You had to admire the kid's gumption.

With a little money in his pocket, Doug realized how lucky he was to spend his days aboveground. Compulsory education went into effect in 1882, two years before Doug was born, which meant children had to remain in school until age fourteen. After that, boys from the middle or lower classes, boys like Doug, put the books away and strapped themselves behind a plow, or put on gloves and headed to the docks, or, worse yet, grabbed a Geordie lantern and slipped into the blackness of a mine. John Edgar worked as a "foreman land drainer," a job that would be called "soil conservation manager" today. His father, Edward Edgar, had been a farmer and, in his spare time, a prodigious inseminator. John was one of nine siblings, all of whom had grown up in a cottage at 45 Seventh Avenue. When you threw in grandparents, a cousin, and two domestic servants, the modest dwelling housed fifteen people. When he reached adulthood, John married the maid, Ann Douglass, and they moved to Heathery Lane, Northumberland, where they had a daughter, Margaret, who would become a seamstress; a son, John Jr., who would also grow into a land drainer; the baby, Thomas; and Doug, who conned people out of coins in the park while searching for life's true calling.

Young Doug found his love in the unlikeliest of places: near the windmill of the City of Newcastle Golf Club. One day he offered to carry a Scottish gentleman's clubs to the course. Caddying had never occurred to him, and he wouldn't have been very good at it. His right hip was bothersome, even in his youth. The drama in the park might have been award-winning, but real problems existed. Hauling two fully stocked golf bags, one on each shoulder, all day would have given him trouble. He could, however, be a porter for a quarter mile or so.

On the way to the clubhouse, the gentleman asked Doug, *"Hae ye ever played at golf?"*

"Na, sir," Doug said with a smile. *"Not my game like."*

"How do ye kne? Ye should least give it a try 'fore ye fooz it, do'n ye think?"

"Aye, Ah suppose so, sir," Doug said out of politeness. Agreeability could be worth an extra bob or two. *"Ah just think Ah want to do summit mair wi' me time, summit challengin'."*

The gentleman threw his head back and laughed so hard his shoulders shook. When he caught his breath he said: *"Mair challengin'?"*

Doug didn't know how to respond, but he didn't have to. The man stopped, reached into his golf bag, and extracted a ball and a middle spoon (the 1890 equivalent of a three- or four-hybrid). He pounded the turf into a small mound creating a makeshift tee. Then he placed the ball on the tuft, handed Doug the club and said, *"Aer ye goo then. Play away."*

This was an unexpected challenge, one Doug felt uncomfortable accepting, but the gentleman was still wearing a broad smile, which was a good sign. The more Doug kept him engaged and entertained, the more this excursion would be worth. Besides, the ball was just sitting there. How hard could it be?

Grabbing the club like a cricket bat, he was surprised by how small and soft the leather handle felt in his hands. He looked at the ball and positioned his body to strike it, taking a wide stance and raising the club above his shoulder as he had on the occasions when his older brother had bowled to him. On those occasions, standing in front of a makeshift wicket, Doug had imagined himself as legendary batsman Walter Read scoring 338 against Oxford. With a golf club, however, he had no frame of reference, no image to emulate. So he took what he imagined was a good golf swing, and missed the ball by three inches.

The gentleman chuckled and said, *"Hae another goo."*

Doug flushed with anger. Then he widened his stance and took another vicious swing. This time he missed by six inches.

He didn't have to be told to try a third time, or a fourth, or a fifth. With each whiff, he said to himself, *Right, then, pay attention, boy. Watch the ball and smack it away. It's sitting still! Hit it!*

His sixth attempt came closer, but the club still swished through nothing but air. On the seventh swing, determined to get the club down to the sphere's mocking perch, Doug took a vicious lunge, and slammed the dirt a foot behind the ball.

His point made, and perhaps fearful that the kid might snap the hickory shaft of his favorite club, the gentleman picked up the ball, took his bag, and said, *"Ye can live a loon life 'fore ye find somethin' mair challengin'."* And with that, he was gone.

Doug stared at the knob where the ball had been and tried to wrap his mind around what had just happened. How could he have missed the damned thing? It was sitting there like an egg in a nest. Anyone could have struck it, or so he assumed. At first he felt embarrassment, then anger, but later he was intrigued. This golf was something different, something he felt compelled to master. He'd finally, after thirteen years of life, been presented with a worthy challenge. He would not rest until he proved to himself that he could conquer this confounding game.

It wasn't until later in the day that another realization hit him: the gentleman had gotten away without tipping him a farthing.

Despite his fascination, golf did not come easy to Doug. He did, indeed, learn to make contact with the ball, but the game turned out to be a lot tougher than he'd imagined. By the time he turned fifteen, his curiosity had blossomed into a full-blown obsession. He spent every spare minute on the grounds of the City of Newcastle Golf Club armed with a collection of cast-off clubs and balls that had been abandoned in the high grass and cow piles around the course. Doug devoted hours to learning the swing, watching the best players in the area and trying to mimic their movements. He practiced at night in the darkness of his bedroom, hoping that by depriving his eyes of light, he might develop the proper feel. When the sun was out, he would swing in front of anything that provided a reflection: mirrors, windows, doors. Shopkeepers in town had to shoo him away as he swung his imaginary club, blocking the views of legitimate patrons. Even his mother, while patient and encouraging, would often yell, *"James Dooglas, to bed with ye!"* when the thumps of another practice swing echoed through the house.

He won a couple of tournaments at the Workingmen Golf Club, which reinforced his desire to make golf his life's calling. Doug would strive for the rest of his days to find the perfect swing. But unlike the gentlemen of the upper class, men with titles in front of their names and haughty suffixes after them, playing golf under the puritanical umbrella of amateurism was not an option. Doug had to make a living. The only way to do that and feed his fixation was to become a golfing professional.

Turning pro was an easy decision for Doug, even though doing so ensured him a lifetime of second-class citizenship. Golf pros, while admired for their playing abilities, fell a notch below blacksmiths and roofers in the pecking order of professional tradesmen. They were the game's stake horses, the men who were fed and kept in corner golf shops where they built clubs like woodsmen or cobblers. On race days, they were brought out so lords and ladies could watch them run. The rest of the time, the golf pro was expected to give lessons, play a good game, build clubs, and attend to the needs of his members without ever darkening the door of the clubhouse. In "open" tournaments, pros were the bottom rung of competitors. Only amateurs were given access to locker rooms and lavatories. If the pros were lucky, they got a shed where they could change their shoes and dry off after a rainstorm. Even scoreboards discriminated. Amateurs were given the title "Mr." in front of their names, while professionals were afforded no such courtesy.

The pro could be the object of great interest, however. Challenge matches were as big as boxing contests, and gambling was ferocious. From the public's perspective, the biggest events were not the championships, which attracted a few hundred curious spectators, but the four-ball and singles matches where gamblers and bookies lined every fairway. Money flew like heather in a storm and galleries looked more like the crowd around a dice table than anything associated with the genteel amateur game. In an 1875 match pitting the Morrises, Old Tom and his son Tommy (the only man to win the Open Championship four consecutive times), against the Oggs, Willie and his brother Mungo, every gambler in Edinburgh turned out, and every shop in North Berwick, the village that hosted the match, shut down. Events such as these were nineteenth-century pay-per-view spectacles with crowds as bawdy and bare-boned as a modern football crowd. And the men who called themselves golf professionals soaked up every minute of it. They thanked their lucky stars to be able to eke out a living on the links instead of the shipyards.

As a teenager Doug couldn't wait to be part of the show. He didn't mind that he would never have "Mr." next to his name—far from it—he had a chance to spend his life playing a game! Oh, sure, most of his time would be spent sanding and polishing golf clubs and driving nails through the soles of shoes, but he would be around the game that had swallowed his every thought. That alone was worth any sacrifice. Doug also saw golf as more than a vehicle to keep him out of the mines; he viewed it as a road to glory and riches. The most famous Englishman without a noble title was a twenty-nine-year-old golf pro named Harry Vardon, a poverty-hardened, lowly educated scrapper from Jersey who was on his way to becoming the first worldwide sports celebrity. In Vardon, Doug saw a sports version of Horatio Alger. The son of an out-of-work carpenter, Harry had sold seaweed fertilizer for twelve cents a pound before becoming a caddy at the Royal Jersey Golf Club. Then his parents bound him over as a houseboy to keep him from starving to death. From there he tried gardening before finding golf. Now, in the summer of 1899, he was a three-time Open Champion, and more admired in England than Prince Edward. Doug loved golf, but he also saw the game as a way to break away from his homeland's rigid class structure. He would never be Lord Edgar or even Mr. Edgar, but he could be like Harry Vardon. And in Doug's eyes, being Vardon was far, far better.

He knew he had a lot to learn and a long road to travel, so he signed on to be the apprentice of John Caird, the pro at the City of Newcastle Golf Club. In a small golf shop next to the windmill, he spent most of the day whittling club shafts from hickory and wrapping their ends with tanned strips of soft leather.

J. W. Frazer, a member at City of Newcastle Golf Club, remembered Doug from that time. "Douglas Edgar—what pleasant and interesting memories that name brings," Frazer said. "Back in the years when I was much younger, in the full enjoyment of early manhood, and Douglas Edgar was a boy, working on golf clubs in the little workshop attached to the modest clubhouse, I remember him at the time as a clean-cut, good-looking youngster, rather on the delicate side; always willing, naturally obliging, and never without that ready, charming smile. All the members took a great personal interest in Douglas."

Caird took great interest in him as well, seeing something special in the boy—not a natural athletic gift like that of Vardon or John Henry Taylor, the Devon pro who had already won the Open Championship twice and seemed poised to take the title several more times, but something more subtle and nuanced, a "feel" for the game, like an artist's vision for a canvas. Doug instinctively knew how to add depth and color to the basics of the swing.

The boy certainly worked hard enough. He practiced every spare daylight hour, trying new and different swings and putting himself in all manner of bad spots on the course, so he could figure out how to recover from trouble. *"Ah've got te kna' Ah can get mesel' out o' the bad positions if the ball divin't gan where Ah want it te,"* Doug said.

Caird was pleased.

Then one afternoon Caird called his apprentice in from the course. *"Dooglas, we're cluesin' the shop tomorrow,"* he announced.

"Are we? There's nowt wrang, is there?" Doug said.

Caird shook his head. *"No, nothing wrang. We won't be opening e'tall. Ah have a match at Northumberland."*

Doug looked wounded. He figured Caird didn't trust him to run the shop on his own.

The pro let the boy worry for only a second. *"You'd be comin' to watch,"* he said.

Doug perked up. *"Me! Never, really! Who'd ya be playin'?"*

"Ah'll be partnering with Charles Ridley," Caird said. *"We are playin' Harry Vardon."*

Every leading golfer in the area traveled to Northumberland Golf Club for the match. The paddocks of the racecourse had been cleared to make room for bicycles and carriages as spectators traveled from as far away as Edinburgh. They didn't come to see John Caird, who, despite being a fine golfer, had played his last round at the Town Moor in front of a hare and a couple of crows. His partner, Charles Ridley, was the best playing member at Northumberland, someone who regularly broke ninety on the difficult course, but not the kind of player who attracted much of a gallery. Everyone was there to see Vardon.

The front stretch of the racetrack ran parallel to the first fairway and Doug elbowed his way through the crowd to get a good view. When he got his first glimpse of Vardon he was struck by the man's size. In photographs Harry looked like an average chap, not much different from Doug's own father, but in person Vardon resembled a lumberjack. His forearms were the size of Doug's calves, and his shoulders were as wide as a doorway. If Old Tom Morris had looked like Moses, Vardon looked like Atlas with a mustache. The only thing missing was the globe.

The big man laced an opening tee shot 190 yards down the first fairway and the crowd went wild. Vardon shot 77 in the first round, Ridley had 84, and Caird had 89. Because Vardon was taking on both players, his score being pitted against the best-ball score of the other two, he was only one-up at the lunch break, but in the afternoon, he shot a 37 on the outward nine, and then made four straight fours to close out the match five-and-four.

Doug watched every shot in awe. The golf was spectacular, but so was his looming dread. As he walked back home that night, only one thought occupied his mind: there was no way he would ever be as big and strong as Vardon. No Edgar male had reached the six-foot mark, and while there were no weaklings in the bunch, no man in his family had ever been mistaken for a physical specimen. Vardon had overpowered the Northumberland course, sweeping John Caird and Charles Ridley up in his wake, something Douglas Edgar knew he could never do.

If he was going to be the best golfer in the world, there had to be another way.

CHAPTER 4

Hugh M. Comer Howell (second from left)
was always the most handsome and easygoing of
the four Howell brothers.

One Killed—Eight Injured. This is safety first week. Yet, in spite of the fact
that every one is putting forth every effort to minimize accidents, the above
heading featured the first day's news. And such is life. The unexpected
happens. Every precaution and every preparation oftentimes fail to bring
about security from suffering and pain. But it is well to realize that when
things break wrong, you have a friend. So, why not make one now. A four-
percent savings account is your best friend in a time of need.

CENTRAL BANK AND TRUST CORPORATION,
Advertisement in the *Atlanta Journal*
sixteen hours after Edgar's death

A negro was killed the same night as Edgar, shot in the head by Officer E. C. Stegall of the Atlanta Police Department. According to Officer Stegall's written account, the negro had been "out of his mind on the hooch." Upon being called to investigate reports of a tall one skulking around a neighborhood between Decatur and Gilmer streets, Stegall found the culprit in the alley off Piedmont Avenue. Supposedly the man motioned "in a threatening manner" as if he intended to shoot Stegall. No gun was found, and no further accounts of the shooting appeared in print. It was as if no one gave the dead man another thought.

Edgar was another matter. Within twelve hours of the golfer's death, a time frame when the body was still lying on a rectangular marble slab in the Patterson funeral home, Atlanta mayor James Key proclaimed, "We're going to get that driver!" Police Chief James Beavers, seizing on the outrage, asked the Police Commission to fund twenty-five additional officers to combat traffic carelessness. "No mercy will be shown to automobile speeders, or to persons driving cars while intoxicated," Beavers said. "They will get the limit."

Intoxication, itself, had been illegal since Prohibition went into effect in 1920, a fact Beavers failed to mention. But, no matter: the point was to show strength and commitment, and get the public behind him. Beavers issued a general order on Tuesday morning directing all officers to show zero tolerance for speeding, reckless driving, and operating a motorized vehicle while impaired. "Officers shown to be lax in their enforcement of these ordinances will be suspended summarily," Beavers said.

Less than twenty-four hours after his death, Edgar was being used as a political tool, a hammer to get more police officers on the streets. There had been only one fatality, Edgar, but Beavers and others quickly pointed to the total of six auto accidents on that Monday. Mrs. Alice Martin Carr, who lived at number 8 Marietta Place, had gotten things rolling. As she was driving her husband's Model T down Curran Street near Turner Place, a young boy had darted out in front of her. She hit the brakes and whipped the wheel to the left, but clipped the boy, eight-year-old Harry Riche, with the running board. The boy was treated for minor cuts and bruises at Grady Hospital and released before supper. No charges were filed against Mrs. Carr.

A little later in the day, William Leake took a carload of friends, including Mr. and Mrs. Richard Starnes, Andrew Campbell, and Mr. Francis Morgan, up Peachtree Street. At the Collier Road intersection, Leake accidentally hit the accelerator instead of the brake, and his Model T plowed into the passenger-side door of a Wise Cleaning truck. Leake suffered a broken shoulder. His passengers suffered cuts and bruises. The truck driver was unhurt, but the truck caught fire and was completely destroyed.

The biggest nonfatal catastrophe occurred at the corner of Forsyth Street and North Boulevard when, according to that afternoon's *Journal,* "a Montag Company truck driven by Joe Price, a negro, ran amuck, and struck four cars. The negro was arrested on charges of drunkenness, reckless driving, and operating an automobile while intoxicated. The truck first struck the automobile of G. H. Holiday, president of the Atlanta Dental Supply Company, then swerved sharply and struck the machine driven by Greely Whatley, a negro, of 333 Fulton Street. It then caromed off and side-swiped two other automobiles which were following up the street. The truck finally came to a stop when it crashed into a telephone pole. The occupants of the four vehicles were uninjured."

Mayhem continued into the evening. George Huggins of Brown's Mill Road rear-ended a car at the intersection of Trinity Avenue and Prior Street. Huggins was bruised, and his son, George Jr., left his two front teeth embedded in the dashboard. The owner of the other car, S. C. Scarborough of Ellenwood, escaped unscathed. Again, no charges were filed.

The final accident to be logged before Edgar's death came around dusk when George Strickler of Oakdale Road struck one Carrie Colquitt, a negress, with his motorcycle. The woman suffered a broken arm, but police determined the accident was unavoidable. They made no case against Mr. Strickler.

By the hottest hours of Tuesday afternoon Comer Howell had decided that the traffic accident meme concerning Edgar had to be true. Everyone from the mayor to the police chief to Edgar's friends, of which there seemed to be plenty, were repeating it with such a foregone sense of authority that Comer figured it had to be verifiable. Maybe the coroner had told his colleagues that the cause of death was obvious. Or maybe the physician who examined Edgar had let it be known that only a car could have caused the man's injuries. Surely there was more to it than the speculation Comer had been a part of ginning up on the street last night. There had to be evidence.

Even Tommy Wilson had bought the story. Comer called Darkie from the office, first to see how he was doing, but also to apologize for the sloppy job the *Constitution* had done in getting his name (and almost everything else) wrong in the morning edition.

"I canna believe he's deed," Wilson said. *"He was so happy. To be knacked down by a car like tha' . . . I just canna ger it straight in me head."*

A more seasoned reporter would have probed deeper to find out what portion of the story Tommy couldn't get straight in his head, but Comer let it go. Tommy's voice sounded like a quivering reed.

"Ah know'd 'im since Ah was nine year auld," Wilson continued. *"He showed us everythin'. Ah didn't kna' wat a golf club woz afore Ah know'd 'im. He was the best marra Ah had. Nee one ever wanted betta'."* Then, through tears, Wilson said, *"Ah have to gan send Mrs. Edgar a telegram. Ah dinn't kna' wat to say about it. Ah just dinn't kna."*

Comer didn't know what to say about it either. It was an awful situation, one where he felt at once helpless but also compelled to press ahead. As someone who was there, someone who had spent most of last night reliving those dark minutes on West Peachtree Street, Comer needed to know the truth. And he needed to know more about Edgar. Maybe learning about the man would add some order and reason to his death. For updates on the case, he needed to talk to Detective Lowe, but to get a clearer picture of the man's life Comer had to rely on Edgar's friends. The writings of O. B. Keeler were as good a source as any.

Oscar Bane Keeler was an affable old cuss according to the men who knew him; a welcome presence in every clubhouse and locker room in the South, with a chair waiting for him at any card table in Atlanta. At thirty-seven years old, Keeler had the look of an elder statesman: tall and lean with a square jaw, quick smile, and brilliant eyes behind the round lenses of his ubiquitous Ben Franklin glasses. He dressed well—high-collared three-piece suits, a watch chain draped from a vest pocket, and a clean straw boater that never ruffled his hair—and no one questioned that Keeler was the South's best sports columnist (a sore subject at the *Constitution* since Keeler wrote for the *Journal*). His baseball and football prose was as eloquent as anything printed on the subjects. But golf was his passion. A fair player who carried a single-digit handicap during his best days, Keeler not only captured the nuances of the game and its players, he saw golf as one of mankind's better angels, a revealer of character, and a microcosm of the toils and triumphs of the human spirit. Horton Smith, the man who would later win the very first Masters tournament, called him "one of the finest characters associated with golf," and Lee Read, secretary of the Southern Golf Association, would say: "Keeler is to golf what fertilizer is to grass, and I doubt if anyone has spread more of it."

He was also an unabashed ambassador for Atlanta and the South, even though he was a native of Olympia, Washington. Like a lot of columnists of that age, Keeler didn't hesitate to inject himself into the story, and felt no professional obligation to distance himself from his subjects. He spent years mentoring and promoting a young Atlanta woman golfer named Alexa Stirling. Now he was taking an avuncular interest in the city's newest teen sensation, a rather ordinary, somewhat pudgy kid named Bobby Jones.

This second week of August, however, Keeler was not thinking about his young stars. Like many in the golfing community, he grieved. "Golf lost one of its greatest exponents and one of its preeminent teachers, and the world of sport lost a great sportsman, when J. Douglas Edgar, English golf professional at the Druid Hills club, was struck down and killed by some mad speed fiend in a motor car last night in front of his home on West Peachtree," Keeler wrote.

Somehow Comer felt heartened that Keeler believed it to be a hit-and-run. The crafty columnist, while often zealous in his language, was never careless, so Keeler's stamp of approval on the cause of death felt reassuring. Comer couldn't help but think about how great it would be if Keeler wrote for the *Constitution*. The Howells had had Henry Grady, one of the greatest writers, editors, and orators in America at the turn of the twentieth century, and the *Constitution* had published the Uncle Remus stories of Eatonton, Georgia, native Joel Chandler Harris—*"Bimeby, one day, arter Brer Fox bin doin' all dat he could fer to catch Brer Rabbit, en Brer Rabbit bin doin' all he could fer to keep 'im fum it, Brer Fox say to hisse'f dat he'd put up a game on Brer Rabbit, an he ain't mo'n got de wuds out'n his mouf twel Brer Rabbit come a lopin' up de big road, lookin' dez es plump, en ez fat, en ez sassy es a Moggin hoss in a barley-patch"*—but Grady and Harris were dead and gone. Now it was the *Journal* that printed literary prose.

In addition to Keeler, it had just hired Comer's family friend Margaret Mitchell to write first-person essays on the lives and remembrances of surviving Civil War veterans. A feisty, independent young woman, some found Peggy off-putting, but Comer, unlike a lot of people at the *Constitution,* thought she had potential to become one of America's great writers.

Keeler was one of the best now, and today's column felt personal. "Douglas Edgar came to Atlanta less than three years ago—came to America then—and in that short period he had made himself an amazing reputation as a tournament golfer, and as an instructor, and had won for himself a great list of friends and admirers attracted by his personality as well as by his remarkable golfing attainments," Keeler wrote. "When he was 'right' no golfer I have ever seen equaled him in absolute command of the ball, and mastery of the finer points of the game. At East Lake last fall in the Southern Open, playing on the longest course in the country and one of the most difficult, and playing the first two rounds in a cold gale of wind, he shot seventy-two holes without a six in his entire score, a record, I believe, for steadiness. His last round was a 70, three under par; with as brilliant an exhibition of golf as Dixie ever saw.

"It was not alone as a golfer that Edgar was a valued friend and citizen," the column continued. "He was well educated and a splendid talker. He had served in the British army. He was intelligent and thoughtful."

Edgar was also Keeler's teacher, and a fellow mentor to Bobby Jones. The two men had talked a lot about Jones, both sharing an unbridled enthusiasm for the kid's potential. They had spent time together away from golf as well. Keeler introduced Edgar to baseball—they attended numerous Atlanta Crackers games at Ponce de Leon Park—and they shared a love of boxing, often sitting together at local bouts.

"His theories of golf were intensely interesting," Keeler wrote. "As a teacher, I suppose his position was unique—certainly his pupils say so. His emphasis was on the 'mental attitude.' He would say, 'Have your mind right and swing through the gate,' and he allowed his pupils to have their own ideas in stance and grip as long as there was nothing impossible about them."

The reader was offered a good sense of Keeler's personal sadness as he closed the column. "Atlanta golfers—American golfers—grieve today for the untimely passing of a great example and exponent of the game," he wrote. "And those who knew him grieve more deeply for a friend and comrade."

In what seemed like callous editing on someone's part, the *Journal* ran its standard "Gossip of Sportdom" column right beside Keeler's emotional eulogy. The thrice-weekly column, written by an insufferable boor and gadfly named Morgan Blake, rambled more aimlessly than that Montag truck driven by the negro Joe Price. It might not have been so bad, but the subject of the column was local golf. Rather than lead with Edgar, Blake prattled on about a match between the team of Bobby Jones and Jess Daniel against Frank Ogg and Bob Schwab at Ingleside Golf Club. "Bobby Jones played his usual wonderful game Monday up to the greens, but his extremely bad putting lost him the chance to lower the course record," Blake wrote. "During the afternoon Bob missed about ten four-foot putts. His first round was 39, and his second 42."

On and on it went. "The topography of the Ingleside course is an appeal to the esthetic in any man, and even the writer, while dubbing his way around it as he does on all courses in all countries and in all climates, was so impressed with the beautiful scenery that he actually enjoyed the round." Now that the reader knew how worldly Blake was, the columnist spent another three paragraphs fawning over the people whose largesse made his lifestyle possible. "The hospitality of the Ingleside club members was of a kind to warm the cockles of one's heart," he penned. "To show how kind were our hosts, Messrs. Kingdom and Guntz refused to laugh a single time at the weird performance of John J. Dubb. And Mr. Guntz even went so far as to remark on several occasions that Mr. Dubb's shot might have been worse. This is the acme of politeness and kindheartedness."

It wasn't until the fifteenth paragraph that Blake got around to mentioning Edgar. "Sunny-hearted Douglas Edgar is dead, killed by an automobile driven by an alleged human who didn't even stop his car after running over one of his fellow men," Blake wrote. "That this fine fellow should meet such a cruel end is hard to realize. He was just in the prime of his manhood, of compelling and attractive personality, and in the few years he has been in Atlanta he had won hundreds of close friends.

"As to his golfing ability and his wonderful success as a teacher of the game he loved, we need not comment. In all parts of the world where golf is played Edgar was known and accredited as one of the real stars of the game. The men and boys he had taught and helped in their games believed that there were none like him."

· · ·

"How good was he?" Comer asked the gentleman on the other end of the phone line. The man's name was James Frazer, an Englishman who had lived in Moncton, New Brunswick, Canada, since before the war. Frazer had been a member at the City of Newcastle Golf Club, and Northumberland Golf Club, and had watched Edgar grow up in the game. He was also, himself, a Geordie, and while the accent wasn't as thick and pronounced as that of Darkie Wilson, it still sounded more like a combination of German and Irish than anything heard in Britain. It took Comer a second to put his mind in translation mode. Once he sorted through the soft r's, dropped t's, and elongated vowels, he took great interest in what Frazer had to say.

"Doug Edgar, oh, he was quite a golfer that one," Frazer said. "We members at the club always expected great things out of him, but he was an exceedingly unlucky player in those days. When a prize seemed to be lying as easily as his club in his hands, a hopeless lie from an excellent shot dropped him a stroke or two, which is often the difference between a winning and losing score. Time was stronger than bad luck, though.

"I'll give you two instances coming within my personal experience. One Sunday evening I asked him to join in a round and play the best ball of a friend's and mine on my home course. As he had already played two rounds that day, carrying his own clubs—the Sabbath preventing the engagement of caddies—he said he felt really too tired to attempt it. But after a little persuasion, he agreed to go round with us, playing only his mid-iron. The bogey of the course was then, I believe, 79, and it was no easy bogey. He went round in 72! I never saw a more perfect piece of golfing, and I have seen most top-notchers."

Comer smiled at Frazer's tale, especially his old-style use of the word "bogey." Prior to 1890, there was no standard scoring measurement in golf, because none was needed. For the first three hundred years of its existence, golf was a match play game where one or two players played directly against one or two other players. Whoever had the lowest score on a particular hole won that hole. The person who won the most holes won the match. If your opponent made a six and you were already playing your seventh shot, you picked the ball up and moved on. The popularity of Britain's Open Championship changed all that. Stroke play, where many competitors play against each other, became the vogue after Tommy Morris won three consecutive Open titles. Clubs throughout the country began hosting their own stroke play events. The problem was handicapping. In individual matches, it had never been a problem: better players simply gave strokes to less-skilled competitors, but in stroke play a standard unit of measure had to be established.

The Coventry Club solved the problem by establishing an imaginary player named "Bogey" who always posted a perfect round. So perfect was "Mr. Bogey" that he would later morph into "Colonel Bogey" and be used as an icon of courage in the British military, much like the "Uncle Sam Wants You" campaign in America. For years "bogey" in golf was synonymous with "error-free," the standard everyone strived to achieve. That changed as athletes and equipment improved and scores began falling below the bogey standard. The biggest change had been the advancement of the golf ball. An Ohio bicycle manufacturer named Coburn Haskell had created a ball from a solid core that he wrapped with small rubber bands. He held the ball together with a cover made from hard-molded Indian tree rubber. Suddenly, the average or below-average player could hit the Haskell ball farther than the best players in the world could have ever launched the old featheries. Even the gutta-percha ball, which had been the standard for the latter half of the nineteenth century, yielded to the Haskell. Scores plummeted. By 1920 "par" had become the standard, and "bogey" was one shot worse than error-free.

Mr. Frazer's fond use of the word "bogey" showed him to be a man from a different time, one who seemed to yearn for days long passed.

"The second example I can give you was on a seaside course at Newbiggin, in Northumberland, also on a Sunday," Frazer said. "Cold. A wet North Sea wind blowing gales across, typical of that time of year, Doug played in a long overcoat and shot 74. The bogey, if I'm not mistaken, was somewhere around 78. It would have been an exceptional performance under perfect conditions.

"I never saw him after coming to Canada. In fact, I never heard his name until he won our Open. You know, Vardon said he would be the greatest, or something to that effect."

"So I heard," Comer said.

"Tragic," Frazer said. "Have authorities progressed in finding the killer?"

Comer didn't know. That was his next call.

Detective Lowe wasn't very forthcoming, in part because of politics. Police Chief Beavers had deftly used the latest spate of traffic accidents to lobby for more officers. With that sort of coup in play, Beavers would frown on one of his detectives speaking out of school. Lowe didn't have a lot of news, anyway. Everyone, it seemed, had jumped on the hit-and-run bandwagon. A dozen people who lived on West Peachtree now claimed to have been awakened at midnight by sounds of a car, a thump, even groans in the street. Of course, none of them had bothered to step outside, or rush to the aid of a dying man. People who had never heard a train whistle at midnight now claimed to have been awakened by a man groaning more than a block away. Comer hoped he wasn't the only skeptic.

Lowe wasn't inconsiderate, but the case was taking its toll. He had just wasted several hours questioning a young man living at the YMCA. The man's car had been found on the street at Hemphill Avenue, half a mile from the crime scene. The boy seemed shiftless, a drifter of sorts, but after a little digging Lowe discovered that the kid had reported his car stolen earlier on Monday. It turned out the car couldn't have been involved. A neighbor had reported it abandoned on the street as early as ten o'clock, a time when Edgar was very much alive and in the company of Lester Shivers.

One disconcerting tidbit had come from a local streetcar motorman named Irvin Fisher who had been piloting the outbound West Peachtree streetcar in the hours before Edgar's death. According to Fisher, sometime between eleven-forty P.M. and midnight, three men had been standing on the southwest corner of West Peachtree and Fifth. "One of them wore a uniform, and the others were in short sleeves," Fisher had said. "They didn't look to be waiting [for a streetcar] since they were on the wrong side of the road for the town-bound car. And they didn't try to stop me."

Fisher also saw an automobile parked around the corner on Fifth Street. From his vantage point, he could not tell if anyone was in that car, but he was sure he hadn't seen Edgar or Lester Shivers. Comer was equally certain that he and his passengers had not overlooked three men standing on the corner of West Peachtree and Fifth.

He went back to his notebook and wrote: "3 men—W. Peachtree and 5?" and then: "Car at corner?"

Who were those men? What had they been doing at that hour? And where had they gone? There wasn't a soul anywhere in sight when Comer, Wilhoit, and Warwick discovered Edgar. Did three men loitering on the corner suddenly vanish into the summer night? And what about the car? If it had been theirs, why hadn't they been in it instead of stand-ing at an intersection?

Then, a far more important point dawned on Comer: was he the only person asking these questions?

Lowe promised to keep him posted and Comer hung up with a cold dead feeling in the pit of his stomach. Maybe it was lack of sleep, but he felt more anxiety than he had at any point since this affair started. It wasn't just the questions that remained unanswered, but the ones that, as far as he could tell, went unasked. Comer also couldn't shake the guilt he felt for being the first person to interject "auto accident" into the conver-sation. Since that theory had become a given in all corners, Comer wanted to have it verified before letting the matter rest.

He wasn't much of a telephone talker—not like some of his friends who couldn't pull themselves away from the boxes—but immediately upon disconnecting with Detective Lowe, Comer had the operator con-nect him with Main 5661, the number for Dr. George Noble, Jr., the physician who had signed Edgar's death certificate.

After the perfunctory questions about friends and family—yes, Comer's father and mother were fine, and, yes, his older brother, Clark, was busy as ever—the subject of Edgar came up. "There were no broken bones, and very few abrasions," Dr. Noble said. "He had a bruise on one ankle and a scrape on his right hand, but nothing severe. The cause of death was a small wound, about half an inch wide and three inches deep, that penetrated his left thigh approximately six inches above the knee." Noble could not verify the type of instrument, but he did say, "It was thrust at an upward angle into the femoral artery with some force."

No tattered clothing, no shattered bones, no deep or widespread bruising, just a small cut in his trousers, and a puncture wound that sev-ered a large, vital artery.

After thanking Dr. Noble and confirming that, yes, he would see him tomorrow at the coroner's inquest, Comer walked outside to get some fresh air. Peachtree bustled, as always, despite a temperature abutting the triple-digit mark. At 1,050 feet above sea level, Atlanta claimed a more temperate climate than other Southern cities. During the dog days it was hard to imagine how Hell could be any hotter. Georgia had the highest capital city east of Colorado, a trivial nugget that always seemed to find its way into dinner party conversation. Some natives also found a way to re-peat the old saw that Peachtree Street straddled the Eastern Continental

Divide. Comer had friends who would swear that if a drunken negro urinated in the middle of Peachtree, what ran to the east would end up in the Atlantic, and the dribbles that ran west would eventually find the Gulf of Mexico. A great story, and close, but not exactly true: the train station a half mile away sat on the actual Continental Divide, but such boasts, as inane and inaccurate as they might have been, went largely uncorrected. Atlantans did everything they could to promote their city. A little nudging of the truth in the name of boosterism wasn't all that bad—at least it hadn't been in the past.

As he stood on the sidewalk outside the *Constitution* offices, Comer watched the parade of Model Ts rumbling up and down the street, and he tried to imagine what would happen if a man were hit by one of them. The impact would certainly be traumatic. Assuming properly sized tires, the bumper of a stock Model T would catch a victim at knee height, no doubt breaking many bones. And then what? An automobile with a full head of steam couldn't stop instantly. A man struck by a speeding car would either be knocked backward several yards, or more likely tossed onto the hood. Either of those outcomes would leave cuts, scrapes, bruises, and more cracked and broken bones, not to mention a stream of torn clothing.

Comer watched the traffic for several minutes as he ran through every horrifying collision scenario his mind could conjure. None of them worked. No part of a moving automobile could have caused a half-inch-wide, three-inch-deep stab wound to the thigh and no other injuries. Even a glancing blow or a protruding piece of metal from a bumper or a sideboard would have ripped cloth and flesh.

Opening his mouth, Comer pulled his lungs full of humid summer air. His feet were suddenly heavier, and his abdomen started to ache. He wasn't a doctor, a coroner, or a detective, but one thing seemed clear: despite consensus to the contrary, it appeared highly unlikely that Douglas Edgar was killed by a hit-and-run automobile.

⚛ CHAPTER 5 ⚛

The compact and connected "Movement"
of J. Douglas Edgar.

When I first got *The Movement* I at once felt it to be what I had long been looking for, and after I had thoroughly tested it in my own game and more especially with pupils who had up to then "beaten me," I knew it was the goods.

—J. Douglas Edgar

The Northumberland Golf Club members didn't have a pro for a few years, but it wasn't for lack of trying. As early as 1898 they attempted to hire John Caird from the City of Newcastle Golf Club. That made sense. Caird was one of the best pros in the North of England, and Northumberland had evolved into the premier club in the area. Why Caird turned them down remains unknown. He did, however, recommend someone, and in the spring of 1904 the members of Northumberland retained eighteen-year-old Douglas Edgar as their first professional. No one made a fuss—in fact, no official record of Edgar's hiring exists—but he was mentioned in a 1904 "thank you" letter sent to C. J. Potter. That summer Mr. Potter had arranged for a pro named T. G. Renouf from Silloth-on-Solway (a small resort town on England's northwest shore) to partner with Edgar in a match against Caird and James Kay of Seaton Carew. Other than being the first written record of Edgar's new job, the match was unremarkable. "Shocking" weather blew a cold northeasterly rain into everybody's ears, but that didn't slow down the gambling. Money and alcohol flowed like the Tyne as Edgar and Kay beat Caird and Renouf two-up. Nobody broke 80.

In the years that followed, Edgar grew into a striking young man with high cheekbones and a twinkling smile, the kind of fellow who attracted friends with ease. Charming, charismatic, and just mischievous enough to earn a reputation in the region as "a bit of a lad," Doug became especially popular with the ladies. Men liked him, too. He was the kind of fellow everyone invited in for a drink, a bet, and a laugh. Northumberland seemed perfect for him. Not only could Doug step out of the pro shop and watch the ponies run, a hundred-yard jaunt from his workbench he could throw back a pint of bitter at Brandling House, an eighteenth-century manor with a popular post-race pub.

The only friend he failed to make was the game of golf itself. For the better part of a decade after coming to Northumberland, Doug drifted through golf mediocrity, never giving up on his quest to find the perfect swing, but never having much success. He tinkered with all the major theories, and became one of the more knowledgeable and popular instructors around (especially for aspiring female golfers), but he remained a modest player, nothing like Vardon, who had added another Open Championship to his résumé in 1903 as well as capturing the 1900 U.S. Open.

By the time Edgar took the job as pro at Northumberland, Vardon had become a superstar, the international face of the world's fastest-growing sport. He had golf balls and clubs named after him. There was a "Vardon golf coat" sold by E. W. Targett in London under the banner headline *"Harry Vardon won his Championships wearing my Golf Coats, and declares that 'for freedom of swing and comfort they are unequalled.'"*

"Our Harry," as he was known throughout England, was an Everyman icon. People bought Vardon statuettes (twenty-six pounds, five shillings in bronze; five pounds, five shillings in plaster). His likeness could be found on ads for Guy's Tonic, a *"nerve-toning and strength-giving restorative"* sold by chemists in shilling bottles. He also pitched Players Cut Navy Cigarettes—*"beautifully cool and sweet smoking."* In America Vardon was the spokesman for Bell-cap-sic Plasters: *"For aches, sprains, strains and weak places"*; and 3-in-One oil: *"the ideal golf club oil used and recommended by all champion players of this royal game."* People who wouldn't know which end of a golf club to hold recognized Vardon. He was synonymous with excellence, a hero for every commoner with a dream. He was also the perfect celebrity endorser.

His life story read like Kipling. Born on the isle of Jersey, Vardon had been introduced to golf at age seven when his family was evicted from their modest hut by a group of top-hat-and-pea-coat-wearing Episcopalians who needed land for the Royal Jersey Golf Club. It was the first of numerous indignities that forged Harry. His father, a carpenter who built wooden ships, pounded more drinks than nails once metal steamships did away with his industry. Harry caddied and sold golf balls he found in the weeds until age fourteen, when his mother packed his bundle and sent him off to work as the house servant of a local doctor. It was as close to indentured servitude as existed in the late nineteenth century. Not until he turned seventeen and became the gardener for a retired army major did Vardon become known for his golf. Major Spofforth, the captain of the Royal Jersey Golf Club, realized Harry was a ringer. The good major watched his gardener take a couple of swings and immediately took him as a partner. They won most of their matches. Prior to that, Vardon's only rounds had been trespasses when he and his brother slipped out at dusk or on moonlit nights to get in a few holes.

Harry would have excelled at any sport. Broad and strong with hands the size of mitts, he had the balance of a dancer, and the kind of eye-hand coordination that would have made him a champion cricketer, marksman, or lawn tennis player. He chose golf because it was the only game he had seen up close as a caddy. When he became a player, Vardon revolutionized golf by changing the mechanics of the game. Prior to Harry, players gripped the club with all ten fingers, often splitting their hands apart as if holding an ax. Through experimentation, Vardon realized that moving his thumbs down the shaft, gripping the club more in his fingers than his palms, and overlapping the pinky finger of the right hand with the index finger of the left, his big hands could work as a single unit, and he could generate a tremendous amount of clubhead speed with a light grip pressure. That discovery, forever known as the "Vardon grip," changed golf. Players who had taken short, choppy swings to hit low runners found the new grip allowed them to make long, full swings. The ball would fly great distances when struck with this new grip. It also allowed a skilled golfer to manipulate the ball left or right in flight. No one made the ball dance like Vardon. His skills were so precise that he could hit it high, low, left, or right without ever taking a divot. The club simply clipped the top of the grass and Harry's ball bored through the air like a rifle shot.

His skills were legend, but it was his competitive drive that made him the greatest player in the world at the turn of the twentieth century. Sportswriters referred to him as a "humble champion" and "a gentleman first," but they never had to play against him. Those who faced him knew Vardon as a master of silent intimidation. Never one to hang out with the boys or chat with his opponents during a round, he was one of the first golfing champions who understood that half the field could be beaten before the first shot was struck. By making himself larger than life, he drove many players to crumble in his presence. As for his humility, one need only look at Vardon's personal stationery to get a sense of his ego. Ornate and expensive, fully half the page was cluttered with printed images of his Open Championship medals, his U.S. Open plaque, and his German Open medal beside the bold headline, "H. Vardon, Golf ball and Club maker: The only golfer who has ever won the English, American, and German Championships."

Vardon was a great gentleman, generous and unfailingly cordial, but he was also the kind of competitor who would step on an opponent's neck once he got him down.

The whole of England loved him.

Meanwhile, on the 16th of January 1907, the not so famous but affable Douglas Edgar, then twenty-one, married Margaret "Meg" Coulson, the twenty-five-year-old daughter of a local grocer and the prettiest girl in town. The members of Northumberland passed the hat—"a maximum of two shillings and a sixpence"—to buy the couple a nice silver serving set. The Edgars moved into a lodge house at Fencer Hill Park not far from the club where Doug continued to toil in the game, while Meg began domesticating. In 1908 they had their first child, a daughter they named Rhoda.

It was after his daughter's birth that Doug's focus intensified. From the moment she was born and throughout the rest of his time with her, Doug would always whisper to Rhoda, *"Ah'll make ye the finest lady in the land. Ye will gan te the best schools, an', if ye choose, ye can be the best lady golfer in the world."* To follow through on that promise, Doug had to get better at his own game. And he needed to do it quickly.

In 1909, Doug laid bare his golf on a world stage, entering the Open Championship for the first time at Royal Cinque Ports in the southern town of Deal. A port village in Kent a few miles north of the Dover cliffs and the place where historians believe Julius Caesar first set foot on Britannia, Deal was as far away from Gosforth as you could get and still be in the same country. Edgar and a few of his members scraped together enough cash for the journey. It turned out to be an unwise investment.

Doug was so nervous he could barely breathe. He shot 81 in the morning followed by another bad but consistent round of 81 in the afternoon. After the first day's play, Doug trailed John Henry Taylor by fifteen shots. Other than the fact that the skies cleared and spectators could see France some twenty miles across the Channel, not much improved on the second day. Edgar shot 76 in the morning and 78 in the afternoon. He missed fairways, found bunkers, chipped poorly, and couldn't make a putt longer than a couple of feet. Taylor played brilliantly and won his fourth Open Championship by six shots over James Braid. Edgar limped in twenty-one shots off the pace.

Doug finished tied for twenty-first and didn't make a shilling. The only positive he could take home was the fact that he'd tied Vardon. Of course, Vardon was thirty-nine years old and suffering from tremors after a near-fatal bout of tuberculosis, so Vardon's poor performance was little consolation to Doug. Years later Edgar would write, "Sometimes people have said to me, 'Oh, it is all very fine for you, Edgar, you are a natural golfer.' Good Heavens! Never was there a more unnatural golfer; certainly not you, even if your handicap be eighteen. Some time or another I must have done everything wrong that it is possible to do. I have worked on countless different ideas, but like the explorer looking for gold have had, as it were, to sink numerous shafts before eventually striking lucky. In fact, my golfing career has been most laborious, and I can safely and truly say that if I could have seen ahead, I probably would not be a golfing professional."

His search for the secret to golf would often lead to some bizarre behavior. More than once he practiced his swing while looking in a tall pub mirror only to topple a table full of beverages. Local carriage drivers knew to keep an eye out for the crazy golf pro who stood in the road to see his reflection in large bay windows. One night when Rhoda was still an infant, Doug awoke from a dream, jumped out of bed, and began swinging the fireplace poker. After banging walls and furniture, Meg yelled, "Get back to bed, you fool!"

Still, nothing seemed to click. In the 1910 Open at St. Andrews, he carded rounds of 80, 81, 81, and 79 and finished twenty-two shots behind winner James Braid. A year later at Royal St. George's in Sandwich, south of London, Vardon came roaring back to form, winning his fifth Open Championship in a playoff over Frenchman Arnaud Massy, while Edgar shot 80, 82, 83, and 78. Doug finished tied for forty-seventh with a twenty-year-old kid from Chicago named Chick Evans.

He could handle being an afterthought to players like Vardon, Braid, and Taylor; those three were recognized around the world as golf's Great Triumvirate. He could even handle losing to someone like Ted Ray, the giant thirty-four-year-old Jerseyman with a physique that dwarfed even Vardon. But when he couldn't beat a skinny, big-eared American named "Chick," well, that was almost more than Doug could bear.

The struggles continued through 1912 when Ted Ray won the Open Championship at Muirfield and Vardon finished second. Braid finished third, and Edgar finished twentieth, twenty-two shots back. That September, Doug turned twenty-eight in the midst of a career crisis. He and Meg had two children now. Their son, Douglas Jr., whom Doug nicknamed "Burglar" for his ability to unlatch and crawl into cabinets, had been born in March of 1910. The budget was strained, and his performance in tournament play was a financial and psychological loss.

In addition to seeing himself as physically inferior to stronger and more naturally gifted athletes like Vardon and Ray, Doug's trick hip continued to give him trouble. Anyone standing close to him could hear joints pop whenever he bent over to take his ball out of the hole, and there were pangs with every backswing late in his rounds. The rotation of the backswing was akin to propping his right leg against a grinding wheel. If he couldn't figure out how to improve and get some relief for his aching hip, Doug resolved to join his brother in the farm business. It wasn't as absorbing and fun as being a golfer, but at least a man could raise a family as a foreman land drainer.

The hip wasn't Doug's only affliction—it wasn't even the most painful—it was just the one that could be pinpointed. Far more dangerous to his long-term well-being was his love of the bottle and the track. Doug was a social addict, a man who needed human engagement like a fiend needed opium. It didn't occur to him that a good part of his family's financial problems stemmed from his belief that today was the day he would win the big one; the ponies would break his way; he would, today, walk home a winner. The thrill of watching a pack of Thoroughbreds through the final gate was a drug he could not resist. But it wasn't just the races that occupied him. He got that same thrill betting on himself on the golf course. Win or lose (and in those days he lost more often than he won) he could never get enough of the gambler's high. Throw in a propensity to lap up any beverage in front of him and it was easy to see why the Edgars constantly teetered on the brink of ruin.

If Doug's compulsions had any positive benefit, it was his belief that he could, indeed, become the greatest golfer in the world. No matter how dire the situation, no matter how illogical his obsession, he knew in his heart that he was just one breakthrough away from becoming a champion. No one else believed it. Vardon, Braid, Taylor, and Ray had, between them, never said more than a handful of words to Edgar. Of that group, only Vardon, who had an uncanny memory, called Doug by name. Edgar was more than a nonfactor; he was a virtual nonentity. Even Meg questioned how much longer they could endure Doug's folly. But he knew he was close. There was "a movement" that he was close to finding, one that would change things forever.

Doug's sunny nature and lack of malice made his foibles hard to begrudge. He lived the life every man secretly wanted: throwing consequences to the wind and indulging his appetites with a smile and a wink. M. R. Philipson, a member at Northumberland at the time, described Edgar as "a very pleasant companion, always more apt to be laughing and joking and seldom dour. Edgar played golf with a smile and a jest, and lived his life the same way."

Joie de vivre offset a lot of sins, like the party he threw on Burglar's third birthday. It wasn't a birthday party per se—although the boy assumed the hoopla was for him. As it turned out, Doug had taken the better part of a month's pay and bet it on a horse named Sauce Pan. Right after the race Edgar was informed by telephone that Sauce Pan, at ten-to-one, had finished first.

"Right then, boys!" he shouted to everyone in earshot. *"Out we goo. It's to toon for a party."*

He took an advance from the club equal to his winnings, gathered Burglar on his shoulder, and Rhoda and Meg at his side, and threw a high-spirited shindig at the local pub, a group of raucous followers trailing him like gulls chasing crumbs. Drinks poured like a North Atlantic rain with Doug at the center of the party. Later in the evening, with most of his stash depleted and the party petering out from exhaustion, Doug picked up an evening paper and saw that he hadn't gotten the whole story. In his exuberance, he had hung up the phone before his informant could tell him that Sauce Pan had crossed the finish line first . . . and been disqualified.

A week later, in a quiet move that never made its way to the club minutes, the directors at Northumberland took over all of Edgar's accounts. The board would administer his affairs, keeping the family fed and placing Doug on a very short financial leash.

He was flat broke the day he found what he would call "The Movement." The discovery came on the High Gosforth Park Race Course. The club continued to be very good to him, and he had plenty of time to work on his game. A couple of months earlier the members had vacated their old barn of a facility and were using the track's weighing room and paddock while putting the finishing touches on a sparkling new clubhouse. They wouldn't move in until September 1913, which meant that other than the odd lesson, the pro had very little to do but practice and play.

Now, standing on a scruffy buffer of land between the third fairway and the gates of the back stretch, Doug tried to hit a few mashies around the gates—one curving to the left, and the other to the right. His hip gave him fits, so he didn't take full swings. In fact, he didn't move his hips on the backswing at all. The gates were not far away, so distance wasn't a concern. He only wanted to catch the ball solidly on the clubface without collapsing in pain. A full backswing wasn't necessary. On a lark, he decided to take an abbreviated swing, locking his upper arms against the muscles in his chest. He wanted to see how well he could hit it without turning his ailing hip on the backswing at all.

The moment the ball clicked, Doug knew it was solid. What he didn't know until a second later was just how remarkably he had hit it. Not only did the ball fly exactly as he had intended, it went farther than any shot he'd hit in a year. It had to be a fluke. He felt as though he'd taken the club halfway back, the length he might swing if he were hitting a modest pitch with a niblick. Certainly the shaft had come nowhere close to parallel with the ground. And the arms! His triceps had been locked to his rib cage as if he'd had a rope tied around his chest.

He dropped another ball on the turf and tried the same swing, restricting the hip turn on the backswing and keeping his upper arms in close contact with his torso. With a dramatic whip through the hitting zone, Doug hit another shot that soared as far and straight as any he had ever hit in his life.

Could this be? Could it possibly be this simple?

Doug tried the shorter, tighter swing again, and again, and again. Each swing produced a better shot than the one before, and with each shot, he learned something new. The restricted hip turn was not a detriment: it was the catalyst, the Rosetta stone that had finally decoded the golf swing for him. He had tried it only to minimize the pain. But by keeping his hips still on the backswing, he realized that he could coil his upper body around a steady base like drawing the string of a bow. When his shoulders unwound, the clubhead shot through the ball and sent it sailing with extraordinary distance and accuracy.

He felt a wave of excitement, but kept his feeling tempered. This type of swing went against every tenet of conventional wisdom. The hips were supposed to turn on the backswing. Golfers pulled the heel of the left foot off the ground as the lower body twisted and the arms lifted the club high above the head. All the greats had long flowing backswings. The shaft of the club always extended beyond parallel to the ground. That was where the power came from, or so everyone thought. The golf swing was a finely choreographed dance where every part of the body moved in precise sequence.

Vardon, whose words on golf echoed like the thunderous proclamations of Zeus, had said, "If you are standing properly, the procedure which produces a satisfactory shot is simply this: The clubhead starts first, the arms follow, and the body screws around at the hips with the head kept still until the instrument is in position behind the head. Coming down, the clubhead again starts first, the arms follow, and the hips unscrew until the ball is struck, and the pace which the club has been gathering on its downward journey produces what we call the follow-through.

"If you turn the hips correctly, the right leg will straighten as you take the club up. You could do with a wooden leg at the top of the backswing. As something must give to accommodate the turn of the body, the left knee bends. Consequently, the heel is raised from the ground, and as the body-turn continues the pressure on the left is supported by the inside of the front foot.

"Give the clubhead a start coming down before you begin to bring the arms around. And then hit."

Doug's new swing went against everything Vardon had said. He didn't screw the body around at the hips. In fact, he kept the hips as still as possible on the backswing. The right leg didn't straighten or turn to wood. In fact, Doug kept the right knee flexed and perfectly still. As a result the left heel barely moved, and the club, far from being "behind the head," finished the backswing in a two o'clock position slightly behind the right shoulder. The shaft never got parallel to the ground, much less beyond parallel as was the case with Vardon, Taylor, Braid, and Ray.

On the downswing, Doug's new swing was a complete reversal of Vardon's technique. Instead of giving the clubhead a good start and letting the arms follow with the hips unscrewing behind, Doug's downswing started with the hips rotating toward the target. This pulled the shoulders, arms, and then the club into the hitting zone. After that, the club moved through the ball on a distinct inside-out path, shooting it out with a velocity Doug had never before experienced. And, on his follow-through, the club went around his body to the left, with his hands never getting higher than his head, a complete reversal of the idea that a good golfer must extend the club down the target line as far as possible, finishing with the hands high.

He wasn't about to turn conventional wisdom on its ear because of a couple of well-struck mashies. Even after spending the rest of that day, and the next, and the next hitting great shot after great shot with the new swing, Doug kept his discovery to himself. After years of searching, of contorting himself like a circus freak, attempting to do things that his body simply was not capable of doing, it was hard for him to believe that he had finally stumbled upon "The Movement." Of course, he checked the swing in every mirror and window he could find, but he didn't mention his discovery to a soul, not even Meg. Goodness knows she'd had her fill of false hopes, being treated to no end of "eureka" moments over the years. None had panned out. But this one seemed different. Stable. Simple. Right.

A few years later Doug would write, "Looking back over a period of some years I feel I must have been like a man lost in a thick fog, walking round and round in a circle; or like a man looking for a secret door into an enchanted garden, many times getting near it, but never quite succeeding in finding it. In fact at one time I got so depressed and disgusted with my game that I very nearly abandoned it. That I stuck to it was chiefly due to a sort of inward feeling that there must be in this game some secret or key which, once found, would put me on the right road for the desired destination. I was never lucky enough to be shown it, and it was only after continuous search that I eventually chanced upon it."

A bad hip led to the birth of the modern golf swing, a swing so out of place in its day that the nicest thing people called it was "unusual." Today it is the swing seen on every tournament driving range in the world, the swing that has been taught by every top-shelf pro since World War II. It has been called "the coil" and "the X factor," the "swing connection," and the "one plane" swing. Doug simply called it "The Movement."

While he knew he was on to something, he could never have imagined that the simple principles he discovered at the High Gosforth Park

Race Course would become the cornerstones of golf instruction for the next ninety years. All Doug knew was that he could now manipulate shots at will, curving the ball in whatever ways he wanted. He also realized something far more profound: he had discovered a way to swing the club that would put him, modestly athletic Douglas Edgar, on par with men like Vardon, Braid, Taylor, and Ray.

He had, at long last, discovered the secret that would make him a champion.

As the legendary pro Tommy Armour would later write:

> Douglas Edgar was the father of the present-day method of hitting the ball. That was, in brief, the inside-out action, coupled with a movement that kept the right elbow much closer to the body than was vogue at the time. As years go by and I see his methods adopted by all the star golfers in this country, I often think how fortunate we were that he did not remain in England. Of course, if he had stayed there, they would have eventually laughed him out of the country with his ridiculous ideas, which were so directly opposite to the accepted theories of the great masters of the then world's capital of golf.
>
> However, Edgar came to America and this country, which was full of enthusiasm and youth and fired with ambition, took his ideas, dissected and boiled them down; found them to be correct and utilized and improved on them. The result is the complete dominance of this country in the game of golf.
>
> Of course, it was only after he had perfected the action that Edgar really began to make his own presence felt.

Years later, Edgar's friend and apprentice Tommy Wilson would say, *"If Edgar were alive the dayuh he'd make millions as a player, instructor an' writer. He wad make Ben Hogan's 'secret' gandie like a school girl's let's-go-trade."*

Of course, if he had remained in England, things might have turned out differently. He might have lived long enough to see all his dreams come true.

CHAPTER 6

The children—Rhoda and Douglas Edgar, Jr.—in 1921.

The news of the death of J. Douglas Edgar comes as a great shock to all golfers in this country, and especially to the golfers of Newcastle and the immediate district, amongst whom he was very well known.

—Newcastle Daily Journal

Twelve-year-old Rhoda Edgar learned of her father's death from a stranger. On Tuesday, August 9, 1921, she wore a flowered dress and buckled shoes as she walked along Killingworth Road past the Victory Inn, a cold, utilitarian, stone public house with windows disproportionately small for its size. As she reached the front of the inn, a scruffy teenage boy stuck his head out the door and shouted, *"Hey ye, Miss Edgar, du ya kna' tha' ya father's deed."*

Rhoda did not know her father was dead until that moment. She also had no idea that the heart of man could harbor such gleeful cruelty.

By the standards of northern England, the Edgars lived well. They were not rich, and, in fact, appearances exceeded their balance sheet. But they had a house and food and wore clean and relatively new clothes. They seemed untouched and unfazed by the bleak starvation that plagued much of postwar England. No dirty faces or tin can begging for them. They had traveled, lived in the Land of Plenty, America, where they had rubbed elbows with the famous and wealthy. This made them targets. The family of a "golf expert," as Doug had labeled himself, should not be living such a high life, or so went the thinking. The young man who took delight in telling a girl that her father was dead had just acted on an impulse shared by many Geordies. If the Edgars lived better than their neighbors, then it was the neighbors' job to knock them down a peg or two.

The young man's smile would scar Rhoda for the rest of her life. As she would tell her own children many decades later, "That was, for me, the day God died."

The entire family received word of Doug's death through less than ideal means. By the time Tommy Wilson's telegram made it to Meg Edgar, news had already spread like an oil spill. Before the Tuesday sun rose in Georgia, the *Newcastle Daily Journal* reported that "Mr. J. Douglas Edgar, international golf player, was killed by a motorcar at Atlanta on Monday, says a Reuter message. The police are searching for the driver of the car whose identity remains unknown. Mr. Edgar was professional for Druid Hills Golf Club. He was a native of Newcastle-on-Tyne where at present his wife and children are residing."

Just like that, the hit-and-run story went international. Papers in England, Scotland, Ireland, France, and Germany picked up and repeated it throughout the week. The *Newcastle Daily Journal* also heaped lofty but inaccurate praise on Doug's history as a player. "Edgar had a natural aptitude for the royal and ancient game, and he combined powerful hitting with good style," the paper said. "When still a youth, he was recognized as a player of no mean ability and promise. Edgar was undoubtedly in the first flight of the young school of professional golfers, and although he failed to get home in the American Open Championship and in the American Professional's Championship, he was always in the best of company. Those who knew him best saw no reason why he should not, in the future, attain the highest honours to be obtained in the United States and in other countries.

"He had all the attributes in his bag to do so. His standard of play was not reached by practice only; he made a deep study of the game in all its respects and had a theory that as a result of his studies, conducted on a scientific basis, he could convert the most unpromising material into a sound golfer. That such a promising career should have been cut short in so tragic a manner is a matter for universal regret."

The more he learned about Edgar, the more Comer Howell felt an odd sense of admiration for the man: odd in that Edgar was dead, and, from what Tommy Wilson and others said, he hadn't left much for his family. Still, Comer couldn't ignore the tinge of remorse, and the hint of jealousy he harbored for what Edgar had done.

Comer wasn't one of those people obsessed with golf. Like the rest of the Howells, he played the game badly. He didn't love it. He played because it was expected. His father had been one of the early members at the Piedmont Driving Club, the Atlanta Athletic Club, and the Capital City Club, and those memberships now hung like shiny baubles on the family Christmas tree. Every now and then Comer would comply with the social edicts of his name by putting on plus-fours and paying some ancestral son of the Dark Continent two bits to tote his golf bag while he swatted balls all over the course. What drew Comer to Edgar was not the golf—on that front, Comer could barely keep up his end of the conversation—but the way in which the man had reached the pinnacle of his chosen profession.

Succeed or starve was a feeling Comer had never experienced. He had always worked at the paper, going back to his days as a boy with a de-livery route. If he chose to do so, he could live off the proceeds of the fam-ily business for the rest of his life. In tough economic times—and, God knew, these were hard times—having such a path laid before you was a blessing. But Comer was marking time. Even the kids on the street cor-ners with their yellow Coca-Cola stands experienced the thrill of entre-preneurship. Barefoot boys were the company's vending machines in those days, and fistfights often broke out over rights to the busiest street corners. The kids knew the tingle that came with making a sale; they felt the anxiety of spending three cents a bottle on inventory in the hopes of selling enough five-cent "Co-Colas" (Coke would not become the com-mon name for the soft drink for some years) to turn a profit. Comer had never felt that tightness in his chest, the clammy palms and sharpened focus that came with having something meaningful on the line, just as he had never known the worth of making it on his own.

The fact that Edgar had fought and scrapped to become one of the world's top golfers fascinated Comer. From what Tommy Wilson said (and in contrast to what had been printed in the *Newcastle Daily Jour-nal*), Edgar had been anything but a gifted athlete. He was of average strength and gimpy in the hip. Despite those obstacles, Edgar never quit, because so doing would have meant going back to a life of sheep, cows, chickens, and what few crops he could pull out of the cold English ground. Comer found something compelling in the story of a man who, through nothing more than force of will, reached the zenith of his chosen profession. It reminded him of other stories—stories that had kept him starry-eyed as a boy sitting cross-legged in front of the fire.

Every Southern descendant of the Civil War had a story. A lot of Atlantans heard them firsthand as many Confederate veterans still lived in town. Most in their seventies, eighties, or nineties, the old soldiers told their tales with an added sense of urgency, lest anyone forget. The Howells were no different. Stories of Captain E.P. took a back seat only to the Scriptures in their home. Comer had been four years old when his grand-father had died, but Aunt Rosalie would never let the children forget what had happened.

Her stories always centered on her father's austere beginnings, how his grandfather and namesake, Evan Howell, had migrated from North

Carolina to Duluth, Georgia, because of the spring water, and how the family had cut and sold lumber, living a simple Christian life. Evan, it turned out, so vehemently opposed Southern secession that he tried to bribe his grandson into not joining the army, but E.P., a twenty-one-year-old hardhead and ardent Confederate, signed up immediately.

When word of hostilities at Fort Sumter reached Atlanta, E.P. hopped on his horse and galloped to the home of his girlfriend, Miss Julia Erwin, originally of Erwinton, South Carolina. Knowing that he would soon be off to war, E.P. implored Julia to marry him right then and there. They found a preacher, and were husband and wife within the hour. After the ceremony, such as it was, Julia realized she still had a thimble on her finger. She had been sewing when E.P. came knocking on her door.

Within days he was at Fort McAllister in Savannah and, later, Fort Pickens outside Pensacola. A few months later he was transferred to Virginia where he served under the command of Stonewall Jackson. Known as a natural leader (or at least fearless enough to give that impression), E.P. rose to the rank of lieutenant and then captain. He maintained a close bond with his men, though. After one brutal and seemingly useless march through the hills of northwest Virginia, the enlisted men elected Howell to ask General Jackson what on earth they were doing.

Howell walked into Jackson's tent, saluted, and said, "Sir, the men have sent me to ask if you would declare your intentions."

Stonewall didn't mince words. "Sir, when I have an inclination to inform you or your comrades of my purposes I will let you know."

E.P. would retell that tale for years, always with a hint of embarrassment in his voice.

The moxie he showed did not go unnoticed. When he was transferred to the Army of Tennessee, he led an artillery battery in the battles of Chickamauga and Atlanta. Rosalie told tales of him making sure his men always had food and shoes. She also told of how her father had purchased a negro in Savannah after the slave said to E.P., "You have a kind face. Won't you buy me?" According to his daughter, E.P. named the slave Caesar, and took him to Virginia as a body servant during the early years of the war. Caesar slept on the floor beside his master's cot until he caught pneumonia. Then E.P. gave up the cot and slept on the floor until Caesar died. According to Aunt Rosalie, E.P. bought another slave named Jerry, "who served him through the hard battles in North Georgia and through the Georgia campaign, and who was very devoted to his master."

Comer loved those stories. He also enjoyed going through the hat boxes and reading old letters his grandfather had written. Like the one to Julia dated July 28, 1864:

My Dear Wife,

I have not heard from you in several days owing to the fact, I presume, of the breaking up of the usual mail route by the Yankees. Your last letter dated the 18th, and I am now exceedingly anxious to hear from you again. But I am not at all certain that you will get this, nor am I certain that I will receive one from you in some time.

We are still standing quiet since our big fight on last Friday. We occupy ditches around town, the enemy just in front of us; sharp and shooting and cannonading now and then. The enemy shells the city once in a while, doing no other damage than to kill a few women and children. A lady was nursing her child in town the other day and a shell burst into the house, killing the child and the splinters from the house wounded the lady frightfully in the face.

Jerry wishes to be remembered to his family. I have one of Grandpa Howell's boys, "Tom," staying with me now. He is a fine negro, and waits on me well. He ran off and left his wife for fear the Yankees would get him and came to me. He is a very likable boy.

I wish so very much I could be with you to eat your nice okra soup and your corn. I do hope that the next summer will permit us to enjoy ourselves under our own vine and fig tree. And then our earthly happiness will begin. Or has it already commenced and will then only mature? If this writing is disagreeable to you, write me. Paper is so very scarce that it is necessary to make every piece count.

You asked me in your last letter if I would like to have a needle case. I would like very much to have a very small one fitted out with thread and buttons. Jerry will come to Erwinton, I guess, in the course of a month as I want to send one of my horses up, and he wants to go. Much love to all:

Your affectionate husband,
E. P. Howell.

The highs of victory from Chickamauga were gone by the time of that letter. Lookout Mountain had fallen, and then Missionary Ridge, the beginning of the end. Union troops under the command of "Uncle Billy" Sherman headed south like the Horsemen of the Apocalypse. E.P. and his company retreated to the area of Atlanta known as West End, where they waited on hell to befall them.

On August 4, 1864, E.P. wrote to Julia:

My Dear Wife,

    This is a rainy, disagreeable morning and I will try to make it agreeable by writing to you. We have not moved from our position on the west of Atlanta yet. We had a pretty heavy firing on our right and left yesterday, but today not a shot at us. The day before, they fired a few over our Batty. The enemy are evidently trying to turn to our left and stroke the Macon road below or about West Point.

    Such an ordeal I have seen the last five years. To think of it, we have been married going on four years. Well, I'll declare! Don't time fly. Why, it seems as if it were only last year that I was courting you, and yet how many scenes have crowded past since then? How very different is the grand panorama of human life looked at through the vista of the past than it is viewed as it slowly changes, dragged on by the weary present.

    From the sublime I will fall or rise to something.

    I want you to get a good receipt for making hard soap, nice soap. It is impossible to buy it now. Have me some made by the time Jerry comes. Also, try to have me two pairs of socks knit, long legs, and large enough.

    I hope the boy keeps well. Kiss him for me.

Your husband,

E. P. Howell

"The boy" was Clark, Comer's father, born in 1863 nine months after one of E.P.'s few trips home. Whether or not the socks arrived went unanswered. Weeks after the letter was written, Billy Sherman defeated the forces of General John Bell Hood and gained control of the former town of Terminus, now called Atlanta.

The Atlanta campaign had lasted all summer. E.P. had written to his wife in Erwinton because the Howell house had been one of the first to go up in flames, not because of its strategic value, but because it was there. Julia almost didn't make it out. With Union troops bearing down, she wrapped a large batch of biscuits in her apron, put the baby in a wagon, tied a cow to the back so they would have milk, and headed east to South Carolina. That story would be told many times to friends and family, a harrowing tale of escape from torch-wielding barbarians. For Comer, it was an intimate family remembrance. Years later, the world would know the story, too, only with different characters. Comer's family friend Margaret "Peggy" Mitchell recounted the tale of Julia's escape, complete with the cow and biscuits, in her novel *Gone with the Wind.* In fiction it was

Melanie tying the cow to the wagon as the O'Haras fled Tara. In real life, it was Julia Howell doing most of the heavy lifting.

When the war ended, E.P. and Julia returned to the family land and rebuilt, not just their home but their life. E.P. cut and sold lumber at a breakneck pace for two years, a time he would later call "the happiest of my life." In 1867 he took his first newspaper job at the *Atlanta Intelligencer,* and the rest was history. He served in the state senate, and was a Democratic delegate to every national convention between 1878 and 1892. He served on a committee appointed by President William McKinley to investigate the sale of bad beef to the army during the Spanish-American War. When Georgia decided to construct a state capitol building in Atlanta, E.P. headed the committee. The budget was a staggering one million dollars, but Captain Howell and his cohorts opened the doors one dollar under budget. A century and a half later the capitol would still stand as one of Atlanta's most recognizable landmarks.

Even in achieving all of his goals, Comer's grandfather never forgot to pay attention to the people around him. He hired Henry Grady after striking up a conversation with the reporter at a train station. Grady told E.P. that he was on his way out of town. The paper he worked for had closed, and he was off in search of greener pastures. The captain hired him on the spot, and then gave him a ride to his new office.

Comer admired his father more than any living human he knew. Clark Howell, a beefy man with stray whiskers of his unwieldy mustache sticking out like straw from a bale, had accomplished many amazing things, not the least of which was consolidating the family's interest in the newspaper. But E.P. had built it all from nothing. It was he who had known what it meant to succeed or starve. It had been E.P. who had felt the flutters, seen the horrors, and known the thrills.

He wasn't ready to put Douglas Edgar on the same pedestal as his grandfather, but Comer sensed a similar magnetism in the two, even though he hadn't known either of them in life. Like E.P., Doug Edgar had beaten the odds, ignored the critics, continued to pursue his dreams beyond the point of sense and reason, and, in the end, triumphed. Edgar had reached the pinnacle in an unforgiving game. It was a trait to be admired, regardless of a man's foibles.

· · ·

Tommy Wilson rubbed his hands together and stared at the floor in silence for long periods during their chat. *"We played before he died,"* he said, the Geordie accent softer as the shock of the last twenty-four hours eased. *"Douglas gave me two shots a side. Me partner an' Ah'd them two doon wi' three te play, an' suddenly Douglas woke up an' finished three, three, three te beat us."*

If Comer remembered the course correctly that was a birdie-eagle-par finish, which was not a bad way to close out a match.

Then, with a sad look in his eyes, Wilson said, *"He always sez he'd never let his boy be a golf pro."*

Comer let that statement hang in the air without comment. He knew about fathers following sons. Clark Howell had had the drive to run for governor. Comer still lived at home. Father-son topics were touchy, and Comer wasn't about to let this discussion veer into murky territory.

Wilson didn't mind. After a moment's reflection he finished the thought. *"He always said: 'Neigh the way I've suffered wi' it.' "*

Like Edgar, Comer loved boxing, and it occurred to him that the two of them might have run into each other. They had attended many of the same bouts. At the very least, Comer had probably passed Edgar in the crowds.

"He never missed a canny prize fight, except one," Wilson said. *"One night Tiger Flowers woz fighting another negro, an' he had tickets fre the two of us. But Ah got sick. Ah kept saying, 'Go on doon. Tell me how it ends.' But he wouldn't de it. He wouldn't leave me alone. He made soup an' heated some goose grease an' turpentine. He sez, 'We'll stay here an' read aboot it in the mornin'. They'll probably fight te a draw an' leave us disgusted anyways.' "*

"You say he didn't leave much wealth for his family?" Comer asked, trying to get at the heart of Edgar's successes.

Wilson shook his head. *"He spent money as fas' as he made it,"* he said. *"He wrote a book,* The Gate te Golf, *an' had a device, a genius contrivance te help golfers swing on the reet path."*

Comer had heard about the book and the contraption, but he didn't know much about either.

"It woz an incredible thing. He always sez he could get ye te swing 'through The Gate,' as he called it, ye could learn the secret te golf. He called it, The Movement." Then after another pause: *"He thought he'd make a*

million dollars on tha' book. But if he had, he'd hev spent three quarters of it before he got it. He woz like a child wi' money. He couldn't say ne te anybody."

A smile crossed Wilson's face as a fond memory popped into his mind. *"One night, after the spirits, he went into a car dealership an' ordered two eighty-five-hundred-dollar limousines,"* he said. *"The next day the dealer showed up at the club te deliver them. Doug woz in the back nursing a morning-after, so Ah'd te tell the dealer tha' we didn't have seventeen dollars, much less seventeen thoosand. Poor fellow woz crestfallen."*

Antics like that certainly did not sit well with proper Atlantans, most of whom adhered to rigid codes of conduct. No golf pro, a foreigner no less, would violate that structure. After the war—the Civil War, which, to Southerners, was the only war that didn't need a qualifier—the social fabric as well as buildings and infrastructure of the former Confederacy were in tatters. The only things strong men and women of the South didn't lose were their God, their families, their honor, and their code. Rituals kept the few remaining shards of old-world order from being swept up in the fast-changing dynamo that was the twentieth century. Edgar's behavior ran afoul of that code. He had no doubt rubbed a lot of people the wrong way. How many other auto dealers had he snookered? How many enemies had he made? These were not questions Tommy Wilson could answer, but they might be ones that shed light on why the man was dead.

Before twilight, Comer received his final visitor of the day: Howard Beckett, another golf professional, this one from the Capital City Club at Brookhaven, one of the country clubs that had welcomed the Howells to the membership rolls. Beckett had been a friend of Edgar's, someone who had partnered with him in many exhibitions and who had known him both as a peer and a comrade. He had also been the other pro in the group yesterday when Edgar played what turned out to be his last round of golf. To Comer's surprise, Beckett marched in and stood in front of him like a man in search of a fight.

"This was not an accident!" Beckett announced.

Comer had no idea what that meant, but Beckett was angry, so Comer wasn't sure how to proceed. Finally, he said, "How are you, Howard?" and things calmed down.

Beckett took a seat, went through the normal pleasantries, and got back to his original point. "I don't believe Edgar's death was an accident," he said, punching each word with a finger. "Nobody runs a man down and drives away like that without a purpose."

Comer should have been elated to have someone in front of him who was willing to entertain an alternative theory, one that involved nefarious intent, even though Beckett seemed perfectly happy with the hit-and-run story. He wondered why Beckett was so adamant. Did the pro know something that the investigators did not?

For the moment, at least, Beckett seemed content to share more tales of Edgar's zest for life. "He had a personality, that one," Beckett said. "He made himself hard to forget. He made you want to be around him. He attracted people just by showing up anyplace, with or without a golf stick in his hand."

Comer sat silently. Beckett had come to him, so Comer let the pro finish his thought.

"At his best, I'd say he was the best golfer in the world," Beckett continued. "But he had a lot of psychology about him. He had to feel right. When he did he took great delight in bringing it in. He could brood for days, and then he could talk to a pupil for hours and be the most charismatic person in the world.

"He loved his drink—thought Prohibition was stupid and didn't mind violating it. When he traveled, he always knew where to find a nip, even in towns he'd never visited. He just had a way about him. People took to him. He always got what he wanted."

On the drinking front Edgar was not alone. In the year and a half since conformation of the Eighteenth Amendment to the U.S. Constitution, commonly known as Prohibition, it had become one of the most violated laws in history. The law itself was simple enough: *"The manufacture, sale, or transportation of intoxicating liquors within, the importation thereof into, or the exportation thereof from the United States and all territory subject to the jurisdiction thereof for beverage purposes is hereby prohibited."* Alcohol as drink was illegal. According to Temperance Unionists, as well as Baptists, Methodists, Presbyterians, and Quakers, America would be a grander and more God-fearing place because of this action. Plus, it stuck a finger in the eye of Catholics, who were overrunning many of the nation's cities.

Many common people, hardworking men and socially stressed women of all races and classes, found the whole thing absurd.

In Georgia, bootlegging was nothing new. Southern Protestants had been railing against the sins of the bottle since John Wesley first mounted his pulpit in Savannah in the 1700s. Georgia and most of its neighbors were dry long before legislatures ratified Prohibition. Bootleggers had been plying their trade for decades. Corn, which was about the only crop that would flourish in the hard crimson clay north of Atlanta, became the primary ingredient for "moonshine," or simply "shine," as locals called it. Moonshiners ran their product down from the hills of Dawsonville and Dahlonega as fast as their Model Ts would carry it, supplying white Atlantans with all the liquid refreshment they could drink, and providing a depression-proof source of income for poor Appalachian families. Negroes had their own suppliers of peach liquor and muscadine wine. The Orientals kept to themselves, brewing their own lugubrious concoctions from rice. Orientals, particularly in the South, lived entirely separate lives from their white neighbors, so, for the most part, local police left them alone.

Edgar would not be the last Atlantan to violate the sumptuary laws, nor the last man in town to place an illegal wager. According to Beckett, ole Doug still loved the thrill of a bet. "He would bet on himself with outrageous sums," Beckett said. "I saw him wager two months' salary on himself to win. And he did! When he was right there was no stopping him. But there were times when the money he put at risk . . . well, it was a concern."

Like liquor, gambling was a damnable sin in Georgia. And just like finding a drink, a man with a nose for it could place a bet on almost anything. Money flew like confetti at the boxing matches Comer attended, and a "private club" could always be found to bet on horses, cards, dice, or baseball games. Challenge golf matches were a siren song for gamblers, and larger golf tournaments always included calcuttas where players were auctioned off like cattle, often with the players themselves standing on stage to gin up the bidding. As a recreational dalliance, a bet here and there was not inherently dangerous. There were bookies who, while not exactly wholesome, were at least honorable lawbreakers. But a gambler with a predilection for trouble could find it. If Edgar was one of those men, the list of potential suspects would be a long one.

Comer asked Beckett if he thought Edgar's drinking and gambling might have had anything to do with his untimely demise.

"Oh, no," Beckett said. "He was one of the happiest revelers a man could ever aspire to meet."

"What then?" Comer asked.

Beckett cocked his head as if this were the oddest question in the world. "Why," he said, "the women, of course."

CHAPTER 7

A smiling Doug Edgar and an
unidentified female fan.

Golf is truly a Goddess, and must be wooed accordingly, with
due meekness and humility, but at the same time with boldness
and determination. Truly, there is something inexplicable about
this Goddess whose devotees she alternately fills with ecstasy
and despair.

—J. Douglas Edgar

In the beginning, Doug kept his Movement to himself. But golfers throughout Northumberland realized he had stumbled onto something: A man who had struggled with his game for fifteen years did not suddenly beat all comers without some explanation.

"Hey, what'v ya done different, Doog?" Tommy Wilson asked.

Wilson had been a boy of no more than ten when he'd walked onto the grounds of Northumberland looking for work. Darkie had reminded Doug quite a bit of himself at that age: confident, outgoing, an easy conversationalist, and dirt poor. As such, the pro adopted Wilson as his caddy and, once the boy finished his compulsory education, an apprentice. Darkie became a fine clubmaker. He also learned to play a respectable game. For years, Wilson studied Edgar's swing, so he was one of the first to notice the changes in Doug's motion. The swing appeared shorter and rounder, arcing around Doug's torso rather than high above his head.

"Howay yu can tell me, man!" he said.

A crooked smile crossed Doug's face as he unveiled the gemstone he had unearthed. As he would later write: "What I have discovered is the underlying secret of success of all the greatest golfers, and even the worst golfers when they have unexpectedly made a good shot."

It was that, and quite a bit more. His newly minted motion generated incredible power in a compact swing. "For a straight shot," he wrote,

the clubhead does not travel along the line of direction, but crosses it in a curved arc. This statement may seem rather startling to some players and quite different from the principle they have hitherto acted upon. Precisely! There are so many golfers at the present time who are, so to speak, groping in the dark. They may have worked hard at the game and know a certain amount about it, but while they can probably play other games, such as lawn tennis, well, they have never "got away" with golf as they feel they should. Why? Because they have bothered and worried themselves over an infinity of details without getting to the root of the matter; they have, in fact, never got the grain sifted from the chaff.

The manner in which the clubhead meets the ball is the essential part of the golf swing. It is in the two or three feet immediately before and after impact where the real business takes place; it is there that the master-stroke is made and the duffer's shot marred.

It is not the position of the hands, wrists, elbows, body, etc. at the top of the swing that makes the shot, nor is it a wonderful follow-through. It must not be concluded, however, that the position of body and hands at the top of the swing is of no account. On the contrary, it is a matter of considerable importance, for only an artist can be hopelessly wrong at the top and yet be able to adjust himself in time.

However fine golf may be for the lucky few natural golfers, I think that for those who have acquired The Movement—and all can certainly do so by exercising self-control and by practice—golf is intoxicating. It has the exhilarating effect of champagne, without the after-effects.

The Edgar Movement was actually an elimination of movement from the conventional swing. By cutting down on the hip turn and restricting the length the club traveled on the backswing, he was able to store energy like a wound catapult; energy that would be unleashed at the moment, as he put it, "when the clubhead meets the ball." To help restrict the hips, he widened his stance a few inches beyond shoulder width, well beyond normal for the day, and splayed his left foot counterclockwise. Such simple adjustments caused the ball to spring off the club with jarring velocity.

Edgar used Darkie Wilson as his guinea pig, making sure his new swing was not an anomaly that worked only for him. When Wilson showed instant improvement, Doug literally leapt with joy, tapping his toes and heels on the hard Northumberland ground as he danced a jig in celebration. Now that he knew the new swing wasn't something only he could implement, he could teach it to all his students. "If you've got two arms, two legs, a heart and a head on your shoulders, I can make you play golf," he would say repeatedly.

A retired British colonel named Atkinson took him up on that challenge. Atkinson was sick of losing to another retired army officer named Bewick. "You are to teach me until I am able to beat Bewick," Atkinson said. "I must learn to play well enough to beat Bewick."

After two days of lessons Atkinson beat Bewick in a match that wasn't close. In a show of gratitude, Colonel Atkinson paid off all of Doug's debts, which had continued to mount even after the club tied him to a financial tether.

· · ·

Almost everyone Doug taught showed measurable improvement. Even members who would be called golfers only by the kindest of souls achieved a modest level of proficiency under Edgar's tutelage. However, The Movement shone brightest in Doug's own game. In the 1914 Northumberland and Durham Professional tournament, a regional event that attracted the best pros from throughout the North of England, and an event where Doug had struggled, he shot two rounds of 69 on the par 74 Burgham Park Golf Club, winning the event by ten shots.

Everyone was stunned. Those from outside Newcastle said, "Douglas Who shot what?" Closer to home, people who knew Edgar realized that this new discovery might actually be, as he put it, "the goods." Doug was finally shooting scores that caught the public's eye, beating players who had taken his money with depressing regularity back when he was swinging the club like everyone else.

Some skeptics figured the streak wouldn't last, but Doug played well enough throughout the spring of 1914 that he caught the eye of Sir Philip Noble, a wealthy landowner and industrialist. Noble enjoyed putting together exhibition matches for the entertainment of his well-heeled friends. Like stakes races, the challenge matches were a chance for lords and land barons to wager and drink while watching golfers ply their trade.

For this particular match, Noble decided to stake the North's newest star, Edgar, against England's premier golfing legend: Harry Vardon.

Edgar was so nervous that he didn't sleep the night before the match. He paced the parlor and practiced his swing in the dark as he had done as a boy. The Movement had yielded exceptional results against Newcastle's best, but Vardon? The previous summer, Vardon and Ted Ray had barnstormed America, taking on and beating all comers in a run-up to the United States Open where Vardon was the prohibitive favorite. The fact that Vardon and Ray were upset in a playoff by a local boy named Francis Ouimet was news throughout the world. Still, even at age forty-four, Vardon was considered the greatest golfer on the planet, and was favored to win an unprecedented sixth Open Championship later in the summer.

With all that history (not to mention Vardon's imposing physical presence) bearing down on him, no one was surprised when Edgar paced around the first tee like a barnyard chicken before the match began. Once announced, Vardon hit a perfect tee shot. Edgar could barely see his ball. His first tee shot soared right. As they walked down the fairway, Vardon realized that Edgar was a wreck. The poor guy's hands shook so badly he could barely grip the club. Vardon was accustomed to intimidating his opponents—he usually didn't mind, and in fact used intimidation to his advantage—but Doug was such a jolly sort, it was hard to watch him struggle.

As the two men headed for the first green, Vardon put his big arm around Edgar's shoulders and said, "Why don't you hum a tune or whistle, old boy; get your mind off this damned thing."

Edgar spent the rest of the morning whistling "How Sweet the Tuneful Bells," and his game improved tremendously. He made a couple of birdies in a row on the outward nine and remained steady until Vardon birdied the seventeenth hole to win the morning portion of the match three-and-one. They finished the eighteenth in pars, and those in attendance figured that Vardon shot an impressive round of 71, while Doug shot 74, holding his own with the greatest player in the world.

A strong wind kicked up in the afternoon, as did Doug's whistle. He couldn't sing, or at least that was what Meg had told him in unambiguous terms when he'd joined in a chorus or two at the pub, but whistling seemed to calm his nerves. "Music, When Soft Voices Die" was the tune for the afternoon contest, which was stroke play. Doug shot 78, a stout score in tough conditions, but not good enough: Vardon shot 74 and closed out the match.

Two months later Doug played four solid rounds at Prestwick and finished fourteenth in the Open Championship. Vardon shot back-to-back rounds of 78 on the final day to win an unprecedented sixth Open Championship, a record that remains unmatched.

Doug continued to get better, so much so that he begged the board of Northumberland (who controlled his purse strings) to send him to the French Open, the biggest tournament on the Continent at the time. "I will win it," he told them. "I will win it."

The committee voted to advance him ten pounds for the trip across the Channel, even though his proclamations about winning the thing seemed a little far-fetched. The French Open was one of the major tournaments of the day. The Open Championship was still on a pedestal all its own, but the U.S. Open had come into prominence as a major tournament, not the stature of the U.S. Amateur, obviously, since professionals were allowed in an open field, but with the amateur Ouimet's win in

1913, the U.S. Open had gained an element of prestige. Canada's Open was also rising in the ranks as a major event. But on Continental Europe, no golf tournament eclipsed the French. The ease with which the best golfers in the world could travel to Paris, plus the chance to partake in French food, drink, and friendship, made it a huge draw. For pros, the fifty-pound winner's check was a great motivator as well, although any discussion of a purse was downplayed. The tournament had all the components of greatness: a strong field, great golf course, and the enthusiastic support of the locals. Even though the term "major championship" did not carry the connotations it would in later years, the French was, by all rights, a major, one Edgar felt confident he could win.

To do so he would have to beat James Braid, J. H. Taylor, Ted Ray, local Frenchman Arnaud Massy, and the heavily favored Vardon. Not only was Harry still a favorite in every event he played, the big man vacationed regularly at Le Touquet and knew the championship course like the back of his hand. Good thing. With several holes cut through a forest of fir trees and the rest nestled on sand hills near the sea, some seventeen miles from Boulogne, Le Touquet was as demanding as any course in France. The caddies called the rough *"les épines."* Players who found themselves in it used more colorful language. The course also sported numerous forced carries that, when the wind blew, could be called unfair. Asking a man to fly a golf ball two hundred yards in a gale was tantamount to asking a human to scale Mount Everest: it was theoretically possible, although no one had done it. Still, if anyone could conquer this beast, it was Vardon.

In the early hours of the opening round, it appeared as though the favorite would come through. Even wind and squall could not slow Vardon. With three holes remaining in his opening round it looked like he would post a score in the 60s, a remarkable achievement that would probably put the tournament out of reach before it even began. But on the final couple of holes Vardon's putting lost its fluidity and he missed several short par putts.

Fans were left scratching their heads. What had happened? How could the greatest golfer in the world throw away shots so carelessly? Few people knew about Vardon's tremors at the time. Tuberculosis was, for many, a death sentence, and not a topic of conversation in polite company. It was the Western World's leading cause of death, an indiscriminate killer affecting kings and commoners equally. The medical treatment was the same for all: rest, isolation, fresh air, clean water, and a bland diet. If a man's constitution was strong enough and the disease was caught early, there was a decent chance of recovery. If not, shiny hillside domiciles like the Mundesley Sanatorium on the North Sea, where Vardon spent much of 1903 and 1904, were little more than freshly painted places to die. Harry made it out alive, but not without scars. His hands shook so violently that he had to put them in his pockets to hide his affliction. When the tremors came on, as they did without rhyme or reason for the rest of his life, Vardon could still swing a club, but the deft short shots, especially with the putter, became all but impossible. He did his best to conceal the condition—no sense letting fans or fellow competitors see his weakness— but the short misses were impossible to ignore and even harder to explain.

His opening round at Le Touquet, a decade after walking out of Mundesley with a clean bill of health, was just such an occasion. After short misses on seventeen and eighteen, he walked off the course with his hands in the pockets. Still, he'd posted a first-round 71, the lowest score of the morning and a statement to everyone that the Open Champion was, as always, the man to beat.

James Braid, who, along with Vardon and J. H. Taylor, was a member of the Great Triumvirate, had a spectacular ball-striking round, but also struggled with the putter. He posted a 75, three shots off Vardon's lead; very much in the hunt. Then Ted Ray, the burley Jerseyman who had toured America with Vardon the year before, shot 74 to join the early contenders. All eyes turned to Taylor, the expectation being that he and Vardon might fight it out just as they had done at the Open Championship at Prestwick. The buzz intensified when Taylor shot 72 and finished the day only one shot behind Vardon.

Then a score went up that surprised everyone. J. Douglas Edgar shot 71 to tie Vardon for the lead. Many of the French shrugged. Whoever this Edgar was, he would be no match for the Great Triumvirate.

Even those who knew Doug felt certain he would crumble under the weighty pressure of the lead. It was a fine effort, one English fan acknowledged by saying things like *What a surprise! Good for him!* But no one expected Edgar to be more than day-one window-dressing on the Vardon and Taylor show.

The second round (played that same afternoon) brought on a flurry of putting woes. Vardon and a crop of amateurs shot 77s due to atrocious putting. Doug played an hour behind Vardon, and while he didn't putt as well as he had in the morning, everyone, including many French golf novices who had come out to get a little fresh air and sunshine, saw a jolly man whistling his way around the course while hitting towering tee shots that seemed incongruous to his compact swing. Edgar finished the afternoon with a 74. His two-round total was 145, which placed him tied for the lead with Taylor.

Even so, the question at the start of day two was: could Vardon catch Taylor? Both men were in "fine and fighting form" as one English paper called it, but Taylor had an almost unblemished record when leading going into the final day of competition. Vardon, on the other hand, was known for coming from behind, as he had done in three of his six Open Championships, twice coming back to beat Taylor. He had also bested Taylor by two shots in the 1900 U.S. Open, while Taylor had returned the favor in that same year's Open Championship at St. Andrews, beating runner-up Vardon by a whopping eight shots.

The French were ecstatic at the prospect of another heavyweight showdown. No one expected the emergence of a handsome and gregarious Geordie, a glad-handing chap the French papers had dubbed "The Whistling Champion."

As famed golf writer Bernard Darwin wrote at the time: "Everybody had confidently expected a win for Taylor. He was not the man, so we all thought, to be dispossessed by an unknown young gentleman who had made bold to hold him for two rounds. But the young gentleman played so well that nobody could hold him."

Edgar put on an exhibition unlike anything the French had ever seen. He fired a 70 in the third round and never made a long putt, because he had very few putts of any substantive length. Almost every drive found the middle of the fairway and every approach looked as though it was going in the hole. The one tee shot that went slightly awry came at the difficult par five twelfth, known as "Sahara" for its long forced carry over sand dunes from the tee. Edgar carried the dunes without any trouble, but pulled the shot under the branches of a fir tree. From there he punched out, and then hit a low, boring iron shot into the teeth of the wind. The ball never left the pin, landing just short and stopping within four feet of the hole. He rolled in the putt for a birdie after missing his only fairway of the day.

Taylor struggled with the putter and shot 75 in the morning. Vardon also shot 75, while Ted Ray fired a 74.

When the final morning score went up on the board, a murmur went out through the gallery. With only one round to go, Douglas Edgar led by five.

As spectacular as Edgar's play was, he still wasn't the biggest final-round draw. Many fans flocked to see the showdown between Ted Ray and Frenchman Maurice Dangé. Their competition had nothing to do with the tournament—Edgar was well ahead of both men—but with the length of their tee shots. With the body of a footballer, Ray's massive drives often sent gasps throughout the gallery. He would take on all comers when it came to hitting the ball hard, and he had won more than a pocketful of quid betting that he could drive a golf ball through a wooden board. Dangé, a stump of a man who stood five-feet, nine-inches tall, but looked much shorter because of his breadth, was known as one of the most prodigious hitters in the game, a man who went after the golf ball with such violent force that men who saw him winced and women shuddered. The display they put on in this, their first head-to-head pairing, was, according to those in attendance, the most impressive driving display in the history of the game. If the contest had been graded, it would have ended in a draw. Ray launched his ball much higher than Dangé, and drove far past the Frenchman on downwind holes. Dangé had the advantage into the wind where his low, hard shots looked like they had been fired from a rifle. Neither man's score amounted to much, but the show was first-rate.

Those who were not interested in long-drive exhibitions (or golf in general) found plenty of other scenery, specifically in the form of the female caddies, a Le Touquet specialty. Tall, young, and sparkling, girls from age sixteen to twenty-two made up the majority of the caddy corps, and they were quite a sight. Bernard Darwin found himself taken by one tall "gipsy" girl with the brightest blue stockings he had ever seen, and "vivid legs [that] could be seen far off twinkling pleasantly over the ground." Just whose bag the girl carried, Darwin couldn't recall. But the spectacle was, in his words, "delightfully picturesque."

Meanwhile, Edgar, who had hired one of the club's few male caddies, shot a closing round of 73 to win his first major tournament by six shots over Vardon. Ray finished third, seven shots back, and Taylor came in fourth, eight behind.

The next day, *The Times* reported that

A new champion has appeared on the horizon in James Douglas Edgar, professional to the Northumberland Club. On the Le Touquet course yesterday he won the French Open Championship from one of the strongest fields on record with an aggregate of 288 for seventy-two holes, truly a remarkable performance when one takes into consideration the searching qualities of the course.

While the minds of many of the critics were exercised as to whether Harry Vardon would follow up his victory in the Open Championship, or whether George Duncan would repeat his success of last year, a comparatively unknown man stepped in and confronted all the prophets.

Darwin was even more effusive in his praise. "It was a really wonderful performance on Edgar's part for nobody has insinuated that the Vardons, Braids and Taylors did not play their game," he wrote.

No, they played very well, but Edgar played better. He played four rounds, two of them on a windy and difficult day, in an average of seventy-two strokes each. He led the field from the first round to the last and never showed the faintest signs of "cracking" when finding himself in the alarming position of being ahead with a ravenous pack of champions at his heels. He drove a long straight ball with a powerful rather short swing kept thoroughly well under control. His iron play was up to the highest standards, and he crowned his good work up to the green by free, confident and effective putting when he got there. Nearly everybody was missing a putt now and then but Edgar missed practically none. One or two of his enthusiastic admirers came into the clubhouse after every round and declared that he had had the worst luck on the greens and that if he had been reasonably fortunate, he would have been round in the 60s. This was I think to overstate the case: the real fact was that he was playing his approach putts so well that he left himself wonderfully little holing out to do, and he was so dead straight that the chance of a long putt was a remote one.

It really looks as if a star of the first magnitude had suddenly appeared in the person of Edgar. It is too early yet to be sure, but there is this to be said for his chances: many of our young professionals can play some wonderful golf, but when one looks at them compared with our burley, sturdy elder champions, one sees that they have not the physical powers to put them quote in the first rank. Now, Edgar seems to have conquered a certain nervousness or anxiety that used to keep him back, and he may well go very far indeed. His golf during the next year will be very interesting to watch.

At noon the day after Edgar's French Open victory, a special closed-door meeting of the Northumberland Committee was held at Milburn House. According to the minutes: "The secretary explained that the meeting had been called to collection if anything should be done in recognition of Douglas Edgar, the club professional, winning the French Championship of 1914, and further, that after consulting most of the members of this Committee, he had already posted a notice in the clubhouse to the effect that a fund was being raised for the purpose of a testimonial to Edgar.

"Resolved, this action and it having approval and that a copy of said notice be sent to all members of the club. Resolved also that a presentation be made from the club in the form of some plate as a memento to Edgar at a cost not to exceed fifteen pounds, fifteen shillings, and zero pence."

Mr. J. Smith Clark, the club secretary, had already shepherded those motions through the committee when he received a distressing cable from Edgar. It seemed their newly crowned champion had been far too exuberant in celebrating his victory. Not only had Edgar blown through all the cash he'd taken over for travel expenses, he had spent the entire fifty-pound winning prize buying drinks and food for every friend he could find, including a few of the lovely caddies.

In a quiet amendment, the committee agreed to wire Edgar an additional ten pounds, an advance against future earnings, to get him back home.

As always, Doug promised to make it up to them. He might have been an irresponsible gallivanter, but he was unfailingly earnest in his apologies and amends. This time, he felt certain that an exhibition match between himself, George Duncan, who would go on to win the Open Championship in 1920, and Mike Moran, a five-time winner of the Irish Professional Championship, was the perfect way to make up for his laggard behavior. The match would be at Seaton in the North, away from

Northumberland and in a spot where the odds would be in his opponents' favor. Doug told the members to bet heavily on him, and they did.

When the thirty-six-hole match was over, Doug had beaten Duncan
by six shots and Moran by seven. Just like that, all was forgiven.

The last round Doug would play in 1914 came a week after his
Duncan-Moran match. It was a hastily assembled game between Edgar
and two local pros, men who had once beaten him regularly. But, in typical fashion, Doug became so engrossed by the day's racing form that he
forgot about the match until a few minutes before his tee time. He rushed
out of his golf shop with nothing but a mid-iron, and grabbed the tram
down to City of Newcastle Golf Club at Three Mile Bridge. When he got
there one of his opponents, who was already on the tee with a caddy and
a full complement of clubs, said, *"Hey, what's this then, man! Where's ya
cloobs, Doug?"*

Edgar waved the question away and said, *"I divin't need mair then
one cloob to beat the like o' yous two."*

His pals laughed with him, but they also got their backs up at being
the brunt of such a joke. Adding insult to the matter, Doug beat his two
old cohorts' best-ball, closing out the match after only twelve holes. Then
he didn't play back to the clubhouse with them. He shook hands with the
men he had just trounced, and caught the next tram home in time to call
in for the race results.

Had he been able to know the future, he might have ended the year on
a loftier note, but Doug could see nothing but bright lights in the days
ahead. September was going to be a big month. A representative of the
Dunlop Rubber Company, makers of the golf ball Doug played, had
approached him in France with an extraordinary offer. The company
wanted to sponsor a first-class tour of the United States where Doug
would play exhibition matches against players like National Open champion Walter Hagen, and National Amateur and former Open champ Francis Ouimet. Tears had filled Doug's eyes when he'd heard the offer. This
was the sort of opportunity afforded only to the greatest players in the
game: players like Vardon. Then it dawned on Doug that he might just be
one of those men himself. That was when he realized he had finally made
it. He, J. Douglas Edgar, at long last, belonged in the company of champions.

He figured the rest of 1914 and all of 1915 would be a breakthrough
period. He could barely imagine the riches once he displayed his Move-

ment in America. The students at Northumberland had taken to his methodology, but there was still a great resistance. Tradition held powerful sway over most of his countrymen, even when their own self-interests suffered. Then, of course, there were the shackles of being a Geordie, a fact that would always work against him at home. But America! Now, there was a place where his innovations would be justly rewarded.

Unfortunately, Kaiser Wilhelm had other ideas. On the 3rd of August, Germany invaded Belgium. Bound by a centuries-old treaty, the British demanded German withdrawal. When the kaiser refused, Britain declared war.

Edgar joined the army immediately. Like most of his countrymen, he thought the conflict would be over before Christmas.

CHAPTER 8

From left: Ted Ray, Doug Edgar,
five-time Australian Open champion Ivo Whitton,
and the great Harry Vardon.

People have a way of referring to this or that one as having color when talking of people who figure in the public gaze in different lines of sport. Usually they mean that the man in question has peculiarities that set him apart from the ordinary run of mortals. Some critics hold that there is no color in golf or golfers. They are wrong. Golfers, at least some of them, are highly colorful. There is J. Douglas Edgar, English-born professional at Druid Hills Golf Club of Atlanta, for instance. I contend that Edgar is a very colorful athlete.

—O. B. Keeler,
1920

Comer had never seen the whitewash of a murder, and he wasn't sure he was seeing one now, but he did not like the tone and direction the Edgar investigation was taking. For starters, Tommy Wilson, who found a sympathetic ear in Comer Howell, had been questioned again on Tuesday afternoon for a couple of hours. This time detectives focused on Edgar's drinking habits, and his propensity for taking practice swings in the street. *"He did tha' quite often,"* Darkie told them. *"He'd always done it, but usually in light of day when he could see his reflection in one o' the windas."*

The narrative was shaped. Now it was just a matter of fitting the evidence to the story line. Edgar had been a drinker; no one disputed that fact. As frowned upon, and, indeed, illegal as spirits were in 1921, the man was far from alone in his love of a stiff nip. No data existed, but if Comer had been forced to guess, he would have ventured that more men partook after the ratification of the Eighteenth Amendment than ever wetted their lips in the free-and-easy days before Prohibition. Those assumptions would be borne out as correct. Five percent of all the moonshine produced in America between the two world wars would end up coming from the hills and hollows of North Georgia where it was brewed in backwoods stills near tiny towns like Dawsonville and Dahlonega, and transported in souped-up Fords that would outrun anything Georgia law enforcement put on the road. For now, though, figuring out who did and did not imbibe was pure guesswork. All Comer knew for sure was that, as a drinking man, Edgar's sin put him in fine and not particularly rare company.

What rankled him most was the fact that by raising Edgar's drinking, detectives were, through inference, blaming the victim. Edgar had spent his final day playing golf and then cards. Surely a man such as he would sneak in a swallow or two before midnight, or so the insinuation went. Couple that with Edgar's propensity to linger in the street, watching himself swing an imaginary golf club in glass windows, and it was a straightforward and not very taxing leap to a traffic accident.

Comer had another theory, one he wanted to discuss with Lowe, but the good detective was nowhere to be found. According to the desk sergeant at Atlanta police headquarters, Lowe was following up on the dozens of calls in connection with the case. Witnesses were rushing forward like born-agains at a tent revival. These were not people who had actually seen the accident, mind you, but those who had spotted this or that "wild car" or "crazy driver" on the day in question. The sergeant who answered the telephone told Comer that Lowe "was still searching for that renegade hit-and-run car," which simply added fuel to what was becoming a citywide obsession. Two column holes on the front page of that afternoon's *Journal* had been filled with a cartoon of a man labeled "B. Careful," driving the "No Accident Week" convertible with life-preserver tires from the "Safety First" tire and rubber company. A few pages later, the "Cartoonettes of the Day" featured a giant arm labeled "LAW" reaching out to grab a devil-like character in a racing car with "Speed Fiend" painted on the side. The caption read: "He Must Be Stopped!"

Chief of Police Beavers and Judge George E. Johnson of Traffic Recorder's Court had already met with the Junior Chamber of Commerce and promised to do more. From the chuckles circulating through the *Constitution* newsroom, His Honor and the Chief had put on quite a show. In the presence of the Junior Chamber delegates (and a few hastily called reporters) Johnson had convicted four negroes for reckless driving, fining each of them twenty-five dollars and revoking their licenses for thirty days. In another case, he'd fined a man fifty dollars for taking his employer's car without permission and running it into a tree.

Much to the chagrin of the chief and the judge, Junior Chamber committeeman John LeCraw then called the reporters into a scrum and said, "We have discovered some interesting figures. During the past seven months, only 1,275 arrests have been made for violations of traffic ordinances, and this with a force of 325 policemen. It is an average of about six arrests a day, which, we believe, is small."

According to witnesses, Beavers and Johnson turned red as Macon clay. LeCraw, sensing he held his audience, continued: "The recent high number of accidents—that which killed J. Douglas Edgar, the international golf player, for example—as well as a number of other serious accidents, has awakened the Junior Chamber to the fact that the situation requires more than just education of the public."

Beavers had forced a smile and hustled the committee downstairs to the evening watch for four o'clock roll call, while Judge Johnson did what he could to repair the damage, telling reporters that poor Beavers needed even more money and officers if the citizens expected him to keep their streets safe. As for Johnson himself, well, as with any law-bound jurist, he could hear only the cases brought before him by the police.

Laughter at that story almost drowned out the afternoon clacking of Royal typewriters as another deadline loomed. Meanwhile, any alternative theory in the Edgar case seemed to have been dismissed out of hand.

Howard Beckett had made a compelling argument that this was a deliberate murder, one somehow linked to Edgar's lack of sexual discipline and general love of a good time. Beckett's evidence was as vague as Lowe's phantom Death Car, but at least the pro had thrown out a couple of names, none of which Comer recognized. Beckett had been worked up about some florist, a "Jap flower man with a pretty Jap wife." Beckett had almost spit the words. Comer was taken aback, but didn't say anything. A Jap! Now, that would be a scandal! Atlanta had its fair share of Japs—a mysterious and insular lot with strange customs and their own closed society. Most of the Orientals had come to town with the railroads, migrating east from California as a cheap alternative to uppity negro labor. They stayed to themselves—many didn't even learn English—and they were always looked upon with an air of suspicion, especially since most rejected Christianity. Japs, as far as Comer could tell, paid no mind to the laws of gambling and drink; and as for sex, there were stories of Jap men having a wife and two, three, sometimes four concubines living in the same house. But as long as their debauchery didn't leech into white Atlanta, local officials seemed content to leave them to their pagan ways. The Japs even had their own law enforcement, a shady group of community protectors known as Yakuza, rumored to have descended from ancient shogun folk heroes called the machi-yakko, protectors of the poor and disenfranchised. Comer had heard that the Yakuza did a little more than protect their fellow Japs. Supposedly, they ran businesses like gambling houses, gin joints, and a bordello or two, but other than rumors, Comer didn't know much about them. He hoped he wouldn't have to learn. Wine, women, and song were all damning offenses in Atlanta, but if Edgar had been involved in miscegenation: well, that was something even Bishop Henry Mikell, who guided the Howells' spiritual journey every Sunday at St. Philip's Episcopal, would have trouble absolving.

Like all Southern gentlemen, Comer felt repulsed by the idea of probing into a man's personal proclivities. Married, single, widowed, or even, God forbid, divorced, men had certain expectations of privacy that extended beyond their natural lives. To sully one's name with unsubstantiated accusations was an unforgivable offense, one that would cast dishonor not on the supposed adulterer but on whoever dared pry into such matters. Comer had physically recoiled when Beckett broached the subject of sex, but he forced himself to jot more notes into his pad. "Adulterous affairs?" along with the words "Who?" and "Why?" were among his scattered thoughts.

After Beckett left, Comer went back through his files and reread what he'd assembled on Edgar, only this time he looked at the details in a different light. Passages like the one Morgan Blake had written in the *Journal* on April 15, 1919, the day Edgar arrived at Druid Hills, had a more telling angle. "The first impression that one gathers from Mr. J. Douglas Edgar, new golf professional at Druid Hills, is that he is more lively than the normal Scot."

When Comer initially read that line he had laughed so hard his desk shook. Not only was the word "livelier" lost in the wilderness of Blake's rambling, elementary prose, the pompous imbecile actually thought Newcastle was in Scotland. The late-night desk reporters at the *Constitution* had made a similar error in their first piece after Edgar's death, but no highly touted bylined columnist with plenty of resources at his disposal would make that kind of mistake at a Howell-run paper—at least not more than once. Now, Comer looked past Blake's tortured English and focused on the inference in his piece. What, exactly, had Blake meant by "more lively"? And what did the women who had been interviewed in a follow-up note mean when they had called Edgar "the most fascinating man ever to hit this town"?

Keeler had called him "whimsical, intelligent and always interesting," terms not often used to describe an athlete of any kind, much less a golfer.

Then there were Edgar's own words. "Golf is truly a Goddess, and must be wooed accordingly, with due meekness and humility, but at the same time with boldness and determination," Edgar had written in 1920. "Truly, there is something inexplicable about this Goddess whose devotees she alternately fills with ecstasy and despair. No game, perhaps, is so simple, but no game surely is so difficult, so exacting, so tantalizing and so elusive."

That sort of language reminded Comer of college, reading D. H. Lawrence in his room with a stash of cigarettes. It was not the kind of soliloquy one associated with sport, certainly not golf. In light of Howard

Beckett's revelations, Comer extrapolated that Edgar was, indeed, a man who enjoyed the lustful pleasures of life and who appeared unshackled by the constraints of decorum. It was also easy to envision the genteel ladies of Atlanta swooning over such a man.

"He had a way of knowing people," Beckett had said. "It never took him long. He could figure you out, and teach you in a way that was individualized." Then Beckett rattled off a list of people who had learned from Edgar, among them Atlanta's two most famous golfers: Bob Jones and Alexa Stirling. According to Beckett: "Bob never took lessons from Edgar—he has never really taken lessons from anyone, at least not since Stewart Maiden showed him how to grip a club—but Edgar taught him through example, through conversation. They played together quite a bit, talked even more. Miss Stirling was different, though. She learned as much as she could. She's quite the student, that one."

Miss Alexa Stirling was Atlanta's leading golf ambassador, a twenty-three-year-old international sports superstar (if such a label could be ascribed to a woman) and a firecracker of a girl. Spunky, smart, talented, vivacious, Alexa was a renaissance woman not unlike Edith Wilson, the woman who had all but run the executive branch of the United States government when her husband, Woodrow, became incapacitated. She was no rabble-rouser like Margaret Sanger or agitator like some of the more strident suffragists: Alexa was a woman who played classical violin, who had been home-schooled at the feet of her mother, herself a trained operatic soprano, and who engaged in spirited discussions with her father's professional associates (Dr. Alexander Stirling was a Scottish-born and Edinburgh-educated eye, ear, nose, and throat specialist). The young Miss Stirling could, in one moment, articulate an opinion on the systemic flaws in the Treaty of Versailles, and in the next, repair the engine of a Model T. She was an avid hunter, a fisherman who crafted an impressive collection of flies, and a woodworker who built chairs, tables, and beds. She was also the greatest female golfer in the world in 1921.

The middle of three daughters, Alexa spent most of her childhood outdoors. When her parents, in an attempt to escape the coal-fired industrial smokestacks and wood-burning residential kitchens polluting the Atlanta air, moved the family into one of the brick bungalows adjacent to the Atlanta Athletic Club at East Lake, a fifteen-minute streetcar ride from downtown, Alexa took up golf with several other children in the neighborhood. One boy, a sickly runt four years her junior, was Bobby Jones.

The area was perfect for kids. East Lake had a beach, a boathouse, a gazebo, lawn bowling, and a couple of badminton courts, in addition to a stately Tudor clubhouse and one of the best Donald Ross golf courses in the country. Children like Alexa and "Little Bob" could roam the neighborhood, play in the woods, fish in the lake, and, if the mood so struck them, swat a few golf balls around. The two of them turned to the East Lake pro, a Scot named Stewart Maiden, for guidance on golf. Bob never took formal lessons, but according to Maiden, Alexa became a "special student," one who absorbed information like a thick cotton towel. Maiden had a soft spot for the girl, her wavy red hair tied in a ponytail and her smiling face littered with freckles. With his typical Scottish gruffness, he would say on more than one occasion: *"If she'd only leave thon damned fiddle bide awhile she'd make a braw player."*

In the summer of 1908, Alexa, along with a frail and sickly Jones and two more children, Perry Adair (who would later become a student of Edgar's, win two Southern Amateurs, and be a teammate of Jones's at Georgia Tech) and Frank Meador, played in a thrown-together six-hole tournament on the high holes along East Lake's back nine. The prize was a small silver cup that Frank's mother had bought. She owned the boardinghouse where Jones's father had rented a couple of rooms, and wanted to give the children some activity that didn't involve catching snakes or otherwise getting into mischief.

At the conclusion of play, scandal erupted. Everyone knew that Alexa had shot the lowest score, but Frank, who was the oldest and thus in charge of keeping score, couldn't let the girl win, so he finagled the scorecard to give Little Bob a one-shot victory. "I'll always believe that Alexa won that cup," Jones would write years later. "I took it to bed with me that night. . . . I've got a hundred and twenty cups and vases and thirty medals, but there is one little cup that never fails of being well polished. And I never slept with another one."

Alexa, on the other hand, learned a hard lesson, one she would never forget: life isn't fair, especially when a girl beats the boys.

She also learned, over time, what a frightful fit some men can pitch when they feel threatened by a woman. During one of her many rounds with Bob (most of which she won when they were kids) Jones's soon-to-be-famous temper reared its serpentine head. After hitting one especially bad shot, Bob released a stream of vulgarities. Unfortunately, Dr. Stirling wandered onto the course to find his daughter in the middle of the eruption. The good doctor, who was the British consul to Atlanta at the time, struck an intense and imposing pose. With a bushy handlebar mustache, tall, stiff white collar, and homburg hat perched on his head, he looked ten feet tall as he marched over and put a finger in Bobby's doughy chest. "Young man," he shouted, "haven't you learned better than to use that kind of language around a lady?"

Dr. Stirling put his arm around his daughter and escorted her off the course. "She'll not play with you again until you learn some proper manners," he said.

"Good," Jones shot back. "A lot of good it does me playing with girls anyway. If I'm going to be a golfer, I've got to play with the men."

Alexa and Bob didn't play together for two years.

Even after they resumed their regular games, Alexa found herself admonishing Bob for his tantrums. His language got better, but he still threw clubs as part of his impetuous little snits. By 1915, at age thirteen, Jones had calmed his temper enough to win the East Lake and Druid Hills club championships. And Alexa, on the verge of womanhood, had established herself as one of the best lady golfers in the world. That summer she won the Southern Amateur and was beaten on the twenty-second hole of the semifinals of the U.S. Women's Amateur by Florence Vanderbeck.

A year later, and a month shy of her nineteenth birthday, Alexa defeated Mildred Caverly at Belmont Springs Country Club in Massachusetts to win the United States Amateur Championship, becoming, as the banner headlines in the Atlanta papers screamed, the first Southerner ever to win a major championship. She was also, at eighteen, America's youngest major champion.

Her parents and sisters tried to send her a note of congratulations, but Western Union refused to deliver the message. Alexa's nickname at home had started out as Lexie, but had, over time, morphed into Sexie, or sometimes, simply, Sex. So, when Dr. and Mrs. Stirling sent a transmission that read, "Hurray for Sex!" the telegram company deemed it too indecent to relay. That story made the rounds in Atlanta's social set for months, and was retold for years.

Comer remembered it all very well. He had been an impressionable boy back then, right at the age where a girl like Alexa Stirling was an older woman, the kind who tortured the dreams of a wide-eyed fifteen-year-old.

Looking back on it made him smile. The Atlanta Athletic Club had thrown a huge party for Alexa in the main dining room at East Lake, a white-tie-and-tails affair, one his father and mother had dutifully attended, and one Comer would have given anything to see. He still remembered the invitation, a four-by-four card of rich cream stock and Gothic Tudor print, secured in its cotton envelope with a red wax seal:

THE ATLANTA ATHLETIC CLUB
REQUESTS YOUR PRESENCE
AT A
DINNER DANCE
TO BE GIVEN AT
EAST LAKE COUNTRY CLUB
IN HONOR OF
MISS ALEXA STIRLING,
WOMEN'S NATIONAL GOLF CHAMPION,
WEDNESDAY EVENING,
OCTOBER TWENTY-FIFTH,
EIGHT O'CLOCK.
FORMAL.

Pictures of the evening made all the papers. It was the social event of the fall with 305 guests, a veritable Who's Who of the South, dining and dancing at East Lake. The club created a miniature scale replica of the East Lake course and clubhouse as the centerpiece of the main table. Alexa, in a white dress with frilled collar and a pageboy haircut, surrounded by mustachioed men in black coats, white ties, and matching boutonnieres, looked more like the flower girl at a wedding than the guest of honor. In the photos, she seemed overwhelmed by it all.

Comer had brooded for days about missing that party. But there would be more galas, more chances to celebrate Miss Stirling's successes. During the Great War, she and Bob barnstormed the East Coast with Perry Adair and the 1915 Women's Western Amateur champ, Elaine Rosenthal. They were known as "The Dixie Whiz Kids," and they raised $150,000 for the Red Cross. Alexa also enlisted and became an ambulance driver and auto mechanic for the Army Motor Corps. She reached the rank of lieutenant before the end of hostilities.

In 1919, a mature twenty-one-year-old Alexa won the U.S. Amateur for a second straight time, since no tournament was conducted during the war. That same year she met and started taking lessons from Douglas Edgar, the new pro at Druid Hills where she held an honorary membership. Stewart Maiden had vacated Atlanta for St. Louis immediately after the war. The tinkering, engineer-oriented portion of Alexa's mind found Edgar's theories of the golf swing fascinating and unquestionably sound. And the artist in her found his Movement exhilarating.

Throughout 1919 and into the early 1920s, the period of time in which Edgar had an influence on her game, Alexa Stirling became the longest pound-for-pound hitter of the golf ball in the world. At 110 pounds, her tee shots averaged 220 yards, some often bounding well past the 250-yard mark, an unheard-of feat for the gentler vessel.

O. B. Keeler wrote of her: "It has been the comment through the galleries, which have included many professionals and veteran golfers, that no such prodigious hitting ever has been done by a woman golfer in America."

In 1920 she traveled to the Mayfield Country Club outside Cleveland, Ohio, where she took on 113 other competitors and defeated them all to win her third consecutive U.S. Women's Amateur title, an accomplishment no woman had obtained since Beatrix Hoyt won the first three championships ever played from 1896 through 1898. A month later, Alexa put an exclamation point on her season by winning the Canadian Amateur title. She finished 1920 as the greatest and most famous female golfer on the planet.

According to the *New York Times*, "There is positively no American woman golfer close enough to the champion to be called a dangerous rival. She plays as near a perfect game on the links as any woman golfer who ever addressed the ball. She has that debonair nature, that championship quality over the course which is typical only of a great master of the game."

Right now, if Comer's sources inside the paper were correct, Miss Stirling was in a New York hotel room, distraught and inconsolable over the news of Douglas Edgar's tragic and untimely death.

She was staying in New York a few extra days after returning from an extended trip to England and Scotland. According to what Comer could piece together, Alexa had gone over with great fanfare to play in the Women's French Amateur, and the Women's British Amateur, which had been contested at the Turnberry Hotel and Club on Scotland's west coast. Built as a resort for railroad executives, the golf course at Turnberry had been converted into a wartime airfield while the hotel had served as a hospital. Since the war, the resort, and indeed, the entire region, hadn't quite found its footing. Alexa had been stunned by the grim conditions: women begging on the sides of the road, children hungry and gaunt with no shoes or coats. This sort of destitution so close to where her father had grown up, and in the hometown of Scotland's most famous poet, Robert Burns, had placed her on the verge of tears. She hadn't played well in either event, but the European press loved her.

Now, back in America, she was staying in New York for at least a month, and probably wouldn't return to Atlanta until sometime in October. "I haven't had time to make any definite plans," she told sportswriter Angus Perkerson before Edgar's death. "I only landed yesterday, but as things stand, I don't think I'll get back to Atlanta before the fall."

She planned to stay in the summer home of Mrs. Joseph Winnie, a family friend, near Port Washington on Long Island, and play a little golf at Nashua. "It's only a short way from here," she said. "Jimmie Maiden, brother of Stewart Maiden who gave me my first golf lesson, is there."

The *New York Evening World* had heralded her return by stating:

It would be well if more American sportsmen and sportswomen followed the example of Miss Stirling, the American woman golf champion, who arrived on board the Carmania. Miss Stirling returned without the British and the French golf titles, but, what is more admirable, without any excuse or alibis.

What Miss Stirling has to say of England is wholly in the way of thanks for the kindness she received there.

"I was gone five months," she said, "and there wasn't a moment or experience that wasn't pleasant. Everyone I met in Scotland and in England treated me splendidly. I think when we go to England to take part in the sports there we should remember that we are in another man's country and should adapt ourselves to his ways. The English are reserved, they don't open up at first, but after you've gotten to know them, you find them the kindest of people.

"In England, everyone plays some game or other. Whether a man is rich or whether he is poor, whether he is busy or whether he isn't, he always finds time there to play. In Scotland I found a surprising number of public golf courses, and in Edinburgh, particularly, it seemed every person I met had a golf club in his hand.

"I believe the best play in London is 'A Bill of Divorcement.' It deals with how divorce will be in 1932, but 'Dunsany's' is the cleverest. It shows what a bearing the little things can have on life.

"The London Bobbies, the police, you know, are absolutely fascinating. They are all more or less giants, and the most kind and polite giants you can imagine. The next most wonderful things are the servants. London servants are absolutely perfect. They do everything just as you want it done, walk as though they had on rubber heels, and never talk.

"In London, there are always cigarettes if one wants them. What I mean is that women there smoke as a matter of fact as men do here. It isn't considered a bit daring or even off. They look on it as we would on powdering our nose."

One line in that story stood out to Comer. He went back and read it again. " 'I was gone five months,' she said, 'and there wasn't a moment or experience that wasn't pleasant.' "

Five months. Alexa had been in England and Scotland since early March.

He tore through his notes. Tommy Wilson had said something earlier in the day that had struck Comer as odd. He thumbed through the pages until he found the page where he had written in shorthand, "Edgar sailed to Southampton England on the Aquitania on December 14, 1920, and returned to America from Liverpool on the Celtic, July 18, 1921. Eight months away?"

Comer had found it extraordinary that a man would be away from his professional duties for eight months, only to fall back into town as if he'd never left. Now, he realized, four and a half of those months coincided with Alexa's trip. If she had spent time in Edinburgh, as her quotes in the New York paper indicated, she had been an hour's train ride from Newcastle. Given the fact that they were student and teacher, it would have been peculiar if Alexa and Edgar hadn't seen each other during Alexa's much heralded five-month British tour.

It meant nothing. It certainly proved nothing. It just opened the door to more questions in what seemed to Comer like a never-ending stream.

Before leaving for the day, he tried Detective Lowe one more time.

No, Comer was informed, the detective had not reported in, and, since he would be testifying before the coroner's jury tomorrow, he wouldn't be at his desk until the day after. "I'll see him there," Comer said. He, too, had a busy day before the coroner's jury tomorrow.

He gathered his things, but before leaving the newsroom, he stopped by the desk of Cliff Wheatley, one of the reporters Comer trusted most. "Have you ever heard of a murder where the victim was stabbed in the upper thigh near the groin?" Comer asked.

Wheatley nodded before he'd finished pounding the keys of his Royal. "That's a woman's wound," he said as he leaned back in his chair and folded his hands behind his head.

Comer waited in silence, signaling Wheatley to explain.

"Stabbing a man in the groin isn't just killing him," Wheatley said. "It's telling him that he's been familiar or jilted the wrong woman. Either way, a wound like that: almost always a woman involved."

He thanked Wheatley and headed for his car, his head pounding. This seemed like the longest day of his life, and he still didn't have many answers. But he had enough to seriously question the random hit-and-run theory. Edgar's death probably had more to do with his affinity for the ladies than traffic carelessness or speed fiends. His facts were just as sketchy as those offered by the police, but Comer's theory was at least as viable. The biggest unanswered question, now, was: what did Comer plan to do?

CHAPTER 9

Doug Edgar on the first tee at Northumberland
Golf Club watching boxing champion
Bombardier Billy Wells.

Oh valiant hearts who to your glory came
Through dust of conflict and through battle flame;
Tranquil you lie, your knightly virtue proved,
Your memory hallowed in the land you loved

—Sir John Stanhope Arkwright,
"O Valiant Hearts"

Doug was ambivalent about fighting, but like most men of his generation, he assumed that in wartime, picking up a rifle and falling into formation was what one did. Getting a deferment never occurred to him. So it was with mixed emotions that he learned his gimpy hip made him ineligible for front-line service. He could still don the uniform for King and Country, but it would be in munitions and the Medical Corps. He could also, he discovered, play in morale-boosting and fund-raising golf exhibitions around the globe.

The army didn't mind him being the pro at Northumberland, either, so long as his duties at the club didn't interfere with his military commitments. Part-time, he was still a better teacher than most of the pros in the region. During the early years of the world war a club member named Tom Head retained Doug for lessons. Head, a dapper, highbrow fellow in his mid-twenties, managed a machining plant vital to the war effort, so he was excused from the army. With plenty of time and money, Head wanted Edgar to make him the best player in his peer group. Doug did better than that. In two years, he converted Head from an eighteen handicap into a scratch and then a plus-two golfer. Not only did young Tom become the best player at his club, he was one of the best amateurs in Newcastle.

Doug also organized games on his own. In early 1915, he exacted a little revenge on Harry Vardon by assembling a four-ball match pitting Vardon and Ivo Whitton (at the time, a two-time Australian Open champion who would go on to become the only Australian amateur to win his country's open five times) against Edgar and Ted Ray. The thirty-six-hole match was held at Northumberland in some of the stormiest conditions of the year. But if the boys on the front could suffer in the trenches, these men of sport could at least put on a show for the war effort. The Lord Mayor's fund was increased by fifty-seven pounds from the match. Edgar's value as a result of the match jumped even more, especially after he and Ray beat Vardon and Whitton two-and-one.

For the better part of a year, the army paraded Doug around the world like a rolling art exhibit. He put on displays and gave golf lessons to top British commanders as far away as Cairo. At home he played with a stream of celebrities to raise money for the cause. One game with British heavyweight boxing champion Bombardier Billy Wells attracted hundreds of spectators. But he didn't coast through the conflict. Edgar saw the horrors of modern warfare during his time in the Medical Corps. The service wasn't long, and he was never in danger from enemy fire, but watching men drown as their lungs dissolved from mustard gas had a lasting effect on him. Eighteen months into the war, Doug was back home suffering from what Meg and the family called "melancholy." Others would simply refer to it as "unsound health."

That was exactly how the committee at Northumberland described it in May of 1916. According to the minutes of their meeting, "Reported that J. D. Edgar, owing to unsound health, has been relieved from service and is now working on munitions. Instructions were given to the Secretary to enquire into Edgar's earnings and if he thinks it is advisable, the allowance now being made in Edgar's account to cease."

They started paying him again in October of that same year, noting that "Edgar, professional, is now out of munitions work and devoting himself only to his duties as professional to this club, and it is agreed that his wages should be twelve shillings and six pence per week. The secretary is also empowered to increase the wage to fifteen shillings per week if he considers it advisable."

The secretary didn't note it at the time, but Edgar's drinking was beginning to concern some members. It wasn't the quantity or frequency of his consumption at issue (those had always been top-notch) but how alcohol affected him that was raising some eyebrows. In the prewar days, Doug had been a happy reveler, the life of every party he attended. Now, his moods swung between extremes. He could still be the happiest man in the pub, but there were times when his gaiety went too far and he became overly familiar with anyone and everyone around him. Other times he could be the dour loner sitting in the corner nursing one pint after another.

Some of the younger members found Doug's behavior untoward, but he had plenty of defenders. His students considered him a genius. They excused his newfound eccentricities as the exotic workings of a brilliant mind. Older men who had battled the Boers in South Africa were his staunchest supporters. They knew the source of Doug's moodiness. In their day it had been called "soldier's heart," and it could lead to things far worse than drinking. For now at least, they were willing to forgive Doug a few foibles.

Putting Edgar on unpaid leave during his time in the service was a mistake as well. On March 15, 1917, Doug wrote a letter to the committee pleading for help with his finances. And why not? The club had been doling out his allowance and paying his bills for years. It was natural for him to go back to his benefactors when things got tight. According to the minutes of the next committee meeting, "It is resolved that the sum of ten pounds, ten shillings and zero pence is duly noted as a present to Edgar to assist in meeting expenses incurred through illness."

Doug wrote a cheerful letter of thanks for the gift, just the kind of breezy, backslapping note that had been winning friends to his side for years. He went back to teaching and playing, and did well enough to earn another raise in 1918, despite tough economic times. War had taken its toll. Not only were young men dying in droves, non-war-related production was at a generational low and consumer spending had ground to a virtual halt. For the first time in the twentieth century, English children teetered on the verge of starvation. The Edgars were lucky. At a meeting at Milburn House on Thursday, January 24, 1918, the committee reported that "The question of wages paid to J. D. Edgar as professional and as acting caddy master was considered, and it was approved that Edgar's wages be now increased by five shillings per week, making thirty shillings, and that the secretary be empowered to further increase this by two shillings and six pence per week if he classes it necessary." Doug's salary had more than doubled in fourteen months! This offset the loss of income he experienced from a decrease in clubmaking contracts, but most Englishmen simply dealt with lower wages during wartime. The Edgars, it seemed, had achieved a privileged status in the region.

Tommy Wilson wasn't so lucky. Like Doug, the teenage Wilson signed up for service the second hostilities broke out. But unlike his mentor, Darkie was a prime candidate for the front. Young, sturdy, and a good shot, Tommy was given a Lee Enfield .303 and a bayonet, and dropped into the trenches of the Western Front. In December of 1917, he was shelled by enemy forces for days. Huddled against the frozen wall of a narrow ditch, Darkie wanted to die so he wouldn't have to see any more blood or hear any more screams. That prayer went unanswered, although it was a close call. One mortar round landed a few feet to his right, but two of his battalion comrades absorbed the blast. Darkie was thrown almost twenty feet.

When he regained consciousness he was deaf and covered with the organs and entrails of the men who had been at his side.

It took two weeks for him to regain his hearing, but he never fully recovered. For the rest of his days, he avoided fireworks or any exhibitions involving crashes or booms. Even the circus made him anxious. A lover of sports, he would never again be comfortable at large events, and it was many years before he would go to a baseball or football game in America. Cheers from large crowds too closely resembled the cries of dying men.

A half century later, he said little about his army days. He would only tell his children, "It's like a dream I can't forget."

Golf had become an afterthought for most Europeans. The Open Championship had been discontinued during hostilities, and many of Britain's courses were converted into training grounds or convalescent areas. Like others in the business, Doug's golf shrank to the point where he could arrange only local matches during the waning months of the war. This added to his unpredictable moodiness. He felt as though the best years of his life were escaping him. Like a racehorse being confined to the stable during its prime, Doug knew that every passing month was a lost opportunity to find the fame he had sought for so long. Vardon, Taylor, and Braid had peaked during peacetime. They hadn't been relegated to teaching pompous generals and hapless amateurs for four years (Doug conveniently forgot about Vardon's battles with TB). In his mind, he could have made a fortune in those lost years. He felt that with his talent and personality, there was no question that he would have become the most famous sportsman in the world.

The drinking continued. With it came a hardening of Doug's childhood hostility toward the British class structure. He considered it a fatal Anglican flaw that who you came from remained more important than who you were. Merit should be earned not inherited. Doug wasn't in a position to deal a death blow to his country's hierarchical mind-set, but he could engage in civil disobedience by joining the members of Northumberland for a drink in their clubhouse. Why shouldn't he have a pint or two with the boys if they invited him? No one else at Northumberland had won the French Open. No one else had beaten Vardon, Taylor, Braid, and Ray.

When Doug followed a group into the clubhouse bar one afternoon and bought the first round, he crossed a line even his staunchest support-ers could not defend. The veterans had been patient, but Doug had been home for more than a year: time for their man-child pro to pull himself to-gether and get on with it. Heroes were coming back by the hundreds. Doug's service, no matter how honorable, seemed ancient and ancillary by comparison. Assuming the privileges of membership was an unforgiv-able breach, especially from a golf pro, one with whom the club had been eminently generous.

The secretary had stiff words for Doug that afternoon. Days later, on December 18, 1918, the Northumberland committee reported that "The professional, J. D. Edgar sent in his resignation and same was accepted, to date from 1 February, 1919."

It was time to move on. Golf pros were having trouble making ends meet throughout Europe. Many clubs had failed to reopen after the end of hostilities, and with the economy getting worse, recreational pursuits were a dwindling fancy.

So on March 17, 1919, Edgar signed a "Declaration of an Alien About to Enter the United States," where he affirmed that he was an En-glishman born in Heaton, and that both his father and mother were citi-zens of Great Britain and of the White Race. He also declared his intention to depart from the port of Liverpool on March 25, 1919, bound for New York on the steamship *Scotian*. He would ply his trade in Amer-ica as a "golf expert."

He didn't have a job lined up. In fact, the address he listed in the United States was 425 Fifth Avenue, New York, a commercial building that housed *Golf Illustrated* magazine. None of that seemed to matter to him. Golf professionals were fleeing Britain like rats from a burning ship, and America offered the brightest future for players like Doug. He would carve his niche in the New World, just as he had wanted to do prior to the war. The family would soon follow. But for the early months of 1919, Doug would have to rely on his charm and wits to make his way, just as he had done as a boy hustling tips in the Town Moor. It was an exciting ad-venture, one he couldn't wait to undertake.

PART TWO

The Greatest of Us All

CHAPTER 10

The elegant clubhouse at
Druid Hills Golf Club, Atlanta, 1919.

He couldn't get his beer. I think that finishing lack had a good
deal to do with the nostalgic symptoms that unmistakably
marked his face and touched his demeanor for his first weeks at
the Druid Hills Club in Atlanta.

—O. B. KEELER

Edgar wasn't much of a sailor. Despite living his entire life within sight of the North Sea, gulls screeching overhead and the pungent aroma of rotting seaweed wafting through the morning air, his stomach rebelled whenever he ventured onto the water. The voyage to the New World was no exception. By the time the *Scotian* docked in New York Harbor, Edgar had been begging God to take him for the better part of a week. Since the Almighty had failed to comply, Edgar arrived in lower Manhattan looking like a starved refugee, every ingested morsel having been retched over the steamship's rails. Gaunt, pale, and slumping, he shuffled gingerly down the gangplank and began his new life in America.

Once he regained his shore legs, he set out in search of a hearty meal and a pint, but was crestfallen to learn that Americans took their new Prohibition laws seriously. There would be no beer. Ever. He'd read about the sumptuary movement, but hadn't paid much attention, and didn't for a second think the Yanks meant it. How could rational people outlaw drinking? What would become of the pubs? In addition to his concern for the plight of American barkeeps, Doug also failed to realize how important alcohol was to him personally, a fact pounded home with each throb of his temple. Unemployed, undernourished, and unable to find comfort in a malt and barley beverage, Edgar wept for two full days before looking for work.

Luckily, employment came easy. Country clubs were springing up like summer weeds in America, and there weren't enough quality pros to fill all the jobs. Golf was in its four hundredth year in Britain, but the game didn't jump the Atlantic until 1888 with the founding of the St. Andrews Club in Yonkers, New York, America's first golf club. Twenty-five years later, at the end of 1913, there were 7,000 golf clubs in the United States, each averaging 200 members, plus another 600,000 golfers not affiliated with a club. Any golf pro worth his salt could find work.

John McKay, president of *Golf Illustrated* magazine, the oldest and most respected American golf publication, fancied himself a power broker in that process, which was true in the sense that whenever one of the nation's best clubs needed a pro, McKay was one of the first people contacted. Letters and telegrams littered his desk, many from pros seeking employment, and many others from club presidents seeking a discreet recommendation on this or that candidate. By the time Edgar presented himself at McKay's Fifth Avenue office, the publishing scion had already lined up an interview. He'd gotten a letter from a prominent Atlanta real estate tycoon named George Adair stating that the Druid Hills Golf Club needed a pro. Its first professional, Willie Mann, a scruffy-looking Scot with a wide nose, boxed ears, and bad teeth, had retired after eight years due to poor respiratory health. Mann had been a fine player, pairing with Stewart Maiden to take on Vardon and Ray when the latter two barn-stormed America prior to the 1913 U.S. Open. But by the end of the world war, Mann could barely take a breath. Arid desert air was the best remedy, so Mann caught a train for Arizona at the beginning of 1919.

McKay invited Adair to New York, but the forty-six-year-old Atlantan struggled with health problems of his own (he would be dead of heart failure in another two years), so he sent his brother, Frank Adair, to interview Edgar. When Adair met Edgar, the pro poured on the charm despite his queasy stomach. They hit it off, and Adair knew he had his man. A deal was struck on the spot and Edgar hopped the first train for Georgia.

Once in town, he told the board he was *"Trilled te be yer new golf expert,"* and that he would be setting up residence immediately. His assistant, young Thomas "Darkie" Wilson, would be following close behind, sometime in June. Doug planned to travel back to England in September to fetch his wife and darling children. In the meantime, he would attend to his duties: teaching, playing, clubmaking, and engaging in cordialities with his members.

He would find himself engaging more cordially with some than with others.

In many ways Atlanta was a lot like Newcastle. Natives took pride in their town and heritage, and they enjoyed sticking a finger in the eye of those who looked down on them. A Southerner was judged by his accent, just like a Geordie, and an insult to a man's city or state was an invitation to a fistfight, not unlike many of the territorial brawls Edgar had seen in pubs throughout England. Both populations had an eclectic charm, with every social element thrown together in a simmering progressive stew. Both cities had farms on their outskirts, and while Newcastle had its shipping tycoons and coal executives, Atlanta had railroad and real estate men. The Georgia city had steel mills and auto plants and pencil factories, just as Newcastle had blacksmiths and dock hands to go with its teachers and musicians. The Geordies had Newcastle Brewery, a beer and ale maker that quenched plenty of thirsts in the North of England, while Atlanta had its own soda drink, Coca-Cola, a "Wonderful Nerve and Brain Tonic," owned by the city's mayor, Asa Candler, who also happened to be one of Doug's new members at Druid Hills.

Mr. Candler was one of the original founders of Druid Hills, and, by extension, the man indirectly responsible for Doug's move to the South. A successful chemist and manufacturer of patent medicines in the 1880s, Candler didn't invent Coca-Cola: he bought it from fellow druggist John Pemberton. Despite persistent rumors, the drink did not contain cocaine (Candler was a devout Methodist and staunch teetotaler), but the ingredients were a closely guarded secret, which only added to its popularity. Purchasing Pemberton's recipe made Candler so wealthy that he diversified into other fields, organizing the Central Bank and Trust Company (later Trust Company, and then SunTrust Bank), and building the largest elevator building in Atlanta, the seventeen-story Candler Building, which housed both his bank and soft drink offices.

He also spent a half million dollars on 1,300 acres in the northeast quadrant of the city for a residential and recreational development. He called the new neighborhood Druid Hills. With botanical gardens, spacious parks, and quiet wooded streets, the area was designed as an enclave for the well heeled, *the* new address for the New South. Architect Neel Reid moved there (into a home he designed), as did architects Walter Downing, who built a Renaissance Revival Foursquare on three lots, Neal Robinson, who built "Robin's Nest," a Prairie School structure in the Frank Lloyd Wright style, and Lloyd Reacher, who constructed a traditional Spanish Colonial villa. Joseph Rhodes of Rhodes Furniture, banker James Robinson, and Dr. Dunbar Roy, whose father had been the physician in charge of the Andersonville Prison Camp in the closing months of the Civil War, all moved in as well. George and Forrest Adair, P. S. Arkwright, W. H. Brittain, Arnold Broyles: these names meant nothing to someone like Edgar, but they, and others who took up residence in Druid Hills, were Atlanta's ruling elite, and Edgar's new members. Candler also set aside a large section of his development for a Methodist institute of higher learning, relocating tiny Emory College to the site and renaming it Emory University. The school would become his greatest love, and the recipient of the bulk of his estate.

Three blocks south of the university and three miles from the business center of the city, Candler, at the urging of his real estate partner George Adair, set aside a beautiful rolling swath of land for an eighteen-hole golf club. He hired British pro and noted architect Herbert Barker to design the Druid Hills Golf Club, which, upon completion, was described by Robert P. Jones (Bob's father) as "one of the most beautiful courses in the South, and the most picturesque in Atlanta." Barker, who designed Arcola Country Club in New Jersey, Roebuck Country Club in Birmingham, Alabama, and the course at the Grove Park Inn in Asheville, North Carolina, before returning to his native England to serve in the army during the world war (he would die from war wounds in 1924), considered Druid Hills his best work.

Just before the course opened, a report in the *Atlanta Journal* called it "one of the best in the country." The reporter said that, "before deciding upon the many intricate and pleasing features, Barker studied golf courses the country over, and the Druid Hills course comprises the very best features of the best known courses in the world. There are short and long holes with many natural hazards throughout the course."

Edgar had to have been stunned when he first laid eyes on the place, not because of its "many natural hazards," but because of its uncanny resemblance to Northumberland Golf Club. The topography and tree inventory were almost identical. From the large oak near the first tee to the bubbling brooks that meandered through the property, the Druid Hills course could have passed as the younger sister to Northumberland. Except for Northumberland's racetrack, manor house, and, of course, pub, the courses could have been mistaken for each other.

The weather was a little different, especially in April, as Doug found out when he got off the train and visited his new club for the first time. It had rained during his time in New York, so he'd felt at home. When he got to Georgia, however, the temperature hit a mild eighty degrees, and Doug thought he was going to die. Not only did the midday sun feel like steam from a boiling kettle, the air was filled with a yellow-green dust—dogwood, pine, and maple pollen—that left his eyes watering and his nose on fire.

"When I first made acquaintance of Edgar, I found myself regarding him as a rather pathetic figure," Keeler wrote a year after meeting his new pro. "It was his first visit to the States. His family had remained behind in England. He had not been well on the boat, and the climate—even the suave Atlanta climate of early spring—was strange and ungracious to him."

Edgar's pitiable demeanor softened quickly, and Keeler saw the charm and charisma that had been Doug's stock-in-trade for so many years. "J. Douglas was not a happy little Briton at all, but he was interesting even so," the columnist wrote. "As a golfer, or as a man, J. Douglas Edgar is our whimsical, intelligent and always interesting character; and he'll tell you things about golf or half-things, that cause you to wonder which of you is nutty; and then some golfer, lately come into his own, or approaching thereto, will tell you solemnly that you can give Edgar all the credit for the 76 he shot the other day—that chap has forgot more golf than the rest of them ever will know, says the blossoming neophyte."

It didn't take long for players of all skill levels to say similar things about Doug. Asa Candler had taken to golf late, but attacked the game with the same gusto as everything else in his life. After becoming mayor, he had found golf to be a great escape, the perfect remedy for the turmoil of public life. Whether it was dealing with the devastating aftermath of the Great Atlanta Fire of 1917, an inferno that started in one of Candler's own warehouses and spread through the city destroying two thousand homes and three hundred acres before being extinguished, or seeing Atlantans off to war in the spring of 1918, Asa could unburden himself on the golf course, sneaking out to Druid Hills and slipping the shackles of responsibility for a few hours. Edgar proved to be the perfect teacher and partner for those rituals.

"I believe he has analyzed the game as thoroughly as anyone who plays golf," Candler said. "He can give you a reason for every detail of his play—grip, stance, swing. He is not only a natural golf player, but a golf student. That, I believe, made it possible for him to succeed as he has.

"His method of teaching you is to have you take the stance and adopt the swing that is natural to you. He studies you as an individual, and he doesn't try to force cut-and-dried rules on you. For one thing, he has a keen sense of personality. He found, for instance, that I have done a good deal of rifle shooting, and in teaching me, he goes at golf from a marksman's viewpoint, and makes it easier. In a word, he is a golf student as well as a player."

Keeler called him a "psychic golfer," a reference to an unheard-of way of learning at the time, one that would later become known as "positive visualization." In 1919, it sounded like voodoo.

We had got to number seven on the Druid Hills course; an elbow drive-and-pitch that turns to the left with a little stream edging the fairway to nip a nook, and crossing the fairway just before the green, forming the elbow. Here, J. Douglas paid a trifle more attention to his tee shot and played a deliberate tall-end pull around the elbow, his ball coming to rest exactly in the middle of the space formed by the stream, out of sight from the tee, and with not a dozen yards to spare in front or to the left.

Naturally, I commented on the shot at some length. I asked if he had changed his stance and swing much. "Not at all," he said, promptly. "Neither stance nor grip nor swing: I thought a pull and swung as usual."

Well, I saw what happened, and I have seen him do it on other occasions at the same hole, but it rather has me under, this "thinking a shot." I told Edgar I frequently had thought diabolical things when confronting a big water jump or a well-trapped green. "Yes, and you topped one, too, didn't you?" he asked. This was so nearly accurate that I did not argue the point.

"Next time think your shot well over the water or on the green," he suggested. I confess that I do not recall if I have done this, and if it worked. As I said before, J. Douglas does say some odd things.

It might have sounded like golf witchcraft at the time, but seventy years later the lesson Edgar gave Keeler that afternoon would be conventional golf wisdom, repeated thousands if not millions of times by every teacher in the world.

"Everything in golf is the way you feel," Doug wrote.

You've got to feel that your stance is right before you can hit the ball. For the club professional to tell you that you must stand this way or that way is all nonsense. You must adopt the stance and grip that are natural to you. Then your swing must be so adjusted that will be right.

The other day I had a new pupil who had never held a club in his hands before. I had him to swing about forty minutes. Then I teed up a ball and told him to swing, but not to think of the ball at all. He got a distance of nearly eighty yards. Then I teed up another ball and told him to try to hit it. He swung eleven times and missed it every time.

You know how perfect your practice swing is when there's no ball there to think about. You'll swing just as well when the ball's there if you'll think about your swing and not about hitting the ball.

These were all radical concepts, decades away from being considered mainstream.

His playing style was years ahead as well. "He plays with an open stance, with the ball well in front of him, and his hands well out from his body," wrote Druid Hills member Richard Hickey, one of the better golfers at the club. "His long game, I should say, is the best part of his game. He gets great distance from the tee and keeps them straight. He likes a wooden club and plays his spoon a good deal. A good many times he'll play for the green with a spoon, giving a cut to the ball in order to make it slice and stick. With his irons he plays the ball off his right foot, taking plenty of turf, and getting both direction and distance."

Another member, Forrest Adair—one of the real estate Adairs, whose family tree spread wide throughout Atlanta—said, "When he's going good it's rather monotonous to watch him, his playing is so faultless."

He put that game on display early in his tenure at Druid Hills. On April 26, 1919, three weeks after taking his first steps on American soil, Edgar teamed up with Perry Adair, George Adair's son and one of the Dixie Whiz Kids, in an alternate shot (or foursome) match against Bob Jones and Willie Ogg. Ogg, of North Berwick, Scotland, had been one of the best players in the world during the reign of Old Tom Morris and his son Tommy. Like many of his countrymen, he left Britain after the war. Ogg took Stewart Maiden's place as the pro at East Lake after Maiden went to St. Louis Country Club.

The match was nip-and-tuck, although it was a little unfair. Ogg and Jones had played together enough for each to know the strengths and weaknesses of the other's game, a critical element of alternate-shot where, as the name implies, a two-man team plays only one ball, alternating shots so that each player plays every other shot. Fresh off the boat, Edgar barely knew Perry's name, much less his game. Still, the match went down to the wire with Jones and Ogg winning one-up when Bob sank a putt on the final green.

It was one of the few times Jones would beat Edgar that year, or the year after. In June they would play another public match, this one a best-ball between the pros, Ogg and Edgar, against the Whiz Kids, Jones and Adair, at Druid Hills. It was a thumping. Ogg and Edgar beat the amateurs four-up, shooting 32 on the front nine and 33 on the back. Other than that, the matches between Jones and Edgar were private, and plentiful. Years later, Jones would say, "We played thirty-six holes together every Monday at East Lake. He was a marvelous teacher, and while he was never my 'instructor,' I learned, of course, from observation. He was an attractive player to watch, not flamboyant on the course. He was no Walter Hagen in that respect, but I think he would have done very well playing today. He would have been great, but I think this would have depended on his competitive drive. He was, I'd say, an inspirational player. He played in spurts. When his game was good, it was brilliant; when it wasn't it could be miserable, and most always it depended on his temperament."

His temperament would lead to erratic behavior off the course as well. When he took the train to New York in June to pick up Tommy Wilson, who came over after finishing his service in the army, Edgar was in a down state. He met Wilson in the lobby of the Hotel McAlpin, and instead of asking about his own family or the trip, Doug said, *"Oh God, it's good to see you, man! Howay, let's gan straight up to me room an' you can have a look at the way I'm swingin' the cloob. It seems every bloody iron shot's gannin left o' the green."* They rushed to Edgar's room where Wilson watched a few swings and determined that Edgar was closing his left shoulder to the target line, and then compensating during the swing to produce a pull to the left.

"Tha's it!" Edgar shouted; his mood suddenly exuberant. He then threw down the club and embraced his assistant, welcoming him to America.

Druid Hills members got to know both Merry Doug and Moody Doug, and found both intriguing. The Candlers and Adairs loved him, as did Lowry Arnold, a well-known attorney in town whose brother and law partner, Reuben, gained national attention when he defended Leo Frank. So did Lester Shivers, who would end up being the last golf partner Doug had. The Stirlings thought very highly of him. And why wouldn't they? He had taken their daughter, Alexa, under his wing, and coached her in a style that was perfect for this stage of her life. She would successfully defend her U.S. Amateur title in 1919 and play some of the best golf of her career under Edgar's watchful eye. It was hard to see how anyone wouldn't be fond of him.

As had been the case throughout most of his life, Edgar had no trouble making friends and building allies. But with the mood swings came a painful sense of emptiness, one that could be filled only through close human contact. He needed social intimacy more than ever. With Meg and the children so far away, he would stay at work longer to interact with the members and staff. New friends would invite him over for dinner and bridge, invitations he almost always accepted, and he would engage with as many of his members outside of work as possible. Keeler took him to his first baseball game—the Atlanta Crackers hosting the Memphis Chickasaws in Southern Association play. Doug asked a thousand questions during the game, until, finally, Keeler said, "Why don't you write a column for the paper about your first baseball experience?"

"A'd be happy te, if I knew what the bloody hell was going on," he said.

"Just write your impressions; what you've seen and what you think," Keeler said.

Edgar did just that, writing what Keeler would later describe as "a corking good story using cricket terms; and he liked the game first rate."

He liked other new things in Atlanta, as well, especially the ladies. It started out innocently enough. He was expected to engage the women of the city as well as the men. It was part of his job as a golf ambassador and representative of Druid Hills. He had always been friendly with both genders, and never seen harm in it. But it didn't take long for him to succumb to the excitement of fresh female companionship in a foreign country. Doug did his best to keep his indiscretions quiet—there was the honor of the ladies to be considered, after all—but like many straying men before and since, his cloak of invisibility soon faded, and he found himself in over his head. The affection that pushed him to the brink was a stunning dark-haired beauty, young and exotic, with a demure voice and skin like a porcelain statue. He wasn't sure what he felt about her, but the chemistry was unmistakable. She was exciting and dangerous and he couldn't stop thinking about her. She was also married, making things even more complicated.

No one spoke of Edgar's dalliance, not even in whispers. Such things were simply not discussed. Besides, he would be gone for several weeks in the summer, representing Druid Hills in the United States Open, the Western Open, and the Canadian Open, with other tournaments and matches along the way. If there had been any inappropriateness, surely the man's absence would cool any lingering fires.

What no one could have known at the time was just how famous the new pro from Druid Hills was about to become.

CHAPTER 11

Atlanta street car garage, 1921.

When I left Douglas he felt as well as I have ever seen him in my life. He was as happy as could be and had spent a great part of the evening telling about you and the children joining him, and that he had been looking for an apartment that would be nice and comfortable for you somewhere near Druid Hills. Hundreds of people are grieving deeply over the loss of this fine man in the prime of his life. He truly was a friend. He had taken a great interest in me and my golf, and only recently under his tutorship, I was able to be the runner-up in the championship at Druid Hills after having played only one year and eight months.

—Lester L. Shivers,
Letter to Margaret Edgar
August 13, 1921

A wooden cross would be erected on West Peachtree Street later that Wednesday, a gaudy three-foot monument with the word "BE" prominently printed on the crown and "CAREFUL!" covering every inch of the horizontal beam. Not to be wasteful, the Junior Chamber of Commerce, which was responsible for the cross, covered the remaining wood with yet another message: "A Life Was Lost Here as a Result of Carelessness!"

J. C. Robinson, secretary of the Junior Chamber and son of banker James Robinson, and Roy LeCraw, chairman of the traffic safety campaign, grabbed a photographer from the *Constitution* to shoot the ceremony as the cross went into the ground. They also draped a wreath over it, carefully, so as not to cover any of the letters. At that very moment, Paul Warwick was hunched over his Royal, churning out copy to run beneath the photo on the front page. It would be a poetic call to arms, filled with righteous indignation and lofty moralizing:

> Somewhere, not five thousand miles from Five Points and its noise of traffic, is a miserable man. His eyes should, and by every right ought to be sunken, and should gleam with that anxious regard which marks the man who has tossed in wakeful sleep; the man who knows the torments of a relentless gnawing conscious.
>
> This is the man, if such the person was, who drove the car which sent J. Douglas Edgar into eternity Monday night. This is the man who felt the impact, saw what he had done, then fled precipitately to leave the internationally famous golfer and beloved citizen to die in a pool of his own blood. Indications point to the fact that there was such a man.
>
> The Junior Chamber of Commerce has instituted a plan which will make it justly hard for that man to forget what his carelessness cost—if he ever dares drive near the fateful spot of that death at the juncture of West Peachtree and Fifth. Wherever a death occurs from an accident, the junior chamber will erect a wooden cross emblazoned with the words, "BE CAREFUL," The first of these will mark the spot of West Peachtree, the second will mark the spot at Jones Crossing where J. B. Tanner was killed.
>
> Carelessness is the mother of accidents, and the chamber has determined that in Atlanta, she is too prolific. Erase the reason and rejoice in the absence of effect, is their shibboleth: Hence, the reminders,

which will be seen in Atlanta today for the first time. Every fatal accident will have its place of occurrence marked by such a shaft. They will serve as realistic warning to the man who lets his desire for the thrill of speed override his better judgment. They will be a caution to the pedestrian who takes needless chances in crossing a thoroughfare. They will perpetuate the effect of fatal accidents on a city's care in a more substantial and more lasting manner than will the headlines which clamor for a day or so, and are then silent.

On the first of these signposts of death will be placed a wreath to the memory of J. Douglas Edgar, the sportsman who met his death at the hands of a man who was not even enough of a sportsman to aid the man he had maimed.

The junior chamber believes that the shafts will have their effect, and that belief seems logical.

Warwick had been far less eloquent when he had stumbled out of Comer's car and inched his way toward Edgar's bleeding body. In fact, the reporter had looked like a trembling goat. There had been no wailing or cursing the "miserable man" who had run Edgar down; no bemoaning carelessness as the birthing agent of all accidents; and no shibboleths about erasing reason. Like the others who had been first on the scene that night, Warwick had done little and said less. They had crept up to Edgar's body like schoolboys, and then run around the neighborhood searching for a telephone like madmen.

The only person who had postulated the hit-and-run theory that night was Comer, something he regretted more and more with each passing second. Now, it appeared as though Comer was the only person in town who did not think Edgar was killed by a speeding automobile. The trend toward consensus was understandable, and in some ways compelling. Everyone wanted it to be an accident. The police chief wanted more officers on the streets, and with traffic safety on the minds and tongues of every citizen in town, a high-profile traffic death provided the perfect pretext for such a request. Politicians and business leaders wanted citizens to behave more responsibly, especially when it came to piloting the popular Model T through Atlanta streets. Turning Edgar into a symbol of the consequences of carelessness drove that point home. Then, of course, there were the citizens themselves who were eager to believe whatever the police and politicians told them, in part because of the intrinsic trust Georgians placed in local uniformed officers, but also because to believe otherwise would mean that Edgar's death had been something else, something far more sinister and malicious than a hit-and-run driver.

Comer had his own theory, one he had allowed to rumble through his mind for the past twenty-four hours in the hopes that he would find fault in it and pack it away. But he couldn't sink his hypothesis. Every aspect of it seemed more plausible than the one gaining steam at police headquarters and City Hall. The way Comer saw it, Edgar had angered the wrong man—a jealous husband or suitor, a gambler, a bootlegger, a slighted vendor, or just someone whose honor Edgar had managed to insult; the possibilities seemed limitless. Perhaps the person or persons had been aggrieved prior to Edgar's eight-month hiatus in England. That was a long time for a wound to fester. Then the famous golfing star returned, riding into Atlanta like Caesar through the gates of Rome. He would no doubt make headlines again. Georgians loved their sportsmen, and Edgar was considered among the greatest golfers in the world, perhaps *the* greatest. There would be more victories, more celebrations, more honors bestowed upon this adopted son of the New South. The thought of it would no doubt infuriate someone with a long-held grudge.

It would have been easy to find out where Edgar was, and what he was doing on Monday. Plenty of people would be happy to reveal the whereabouts of one of Atlanta's more prominent celebrity sporting figures. They would even throw in a tale or two about the time they themselves had played with the great man. It would also have been easy to recruit some friends, especially if the grievance was serious enough and the aggrieved party knew the right people.

So, Comer thought, the three men on the corner, the ones spotted by the streetcar conductor, Irvin Fisher, between eleven forty and midnight, the ones who appeared to be going nowhere, had, in fact, been waiting for Edgar. There might have been a fourth man waiting in the car, the one Fisher saw parked around the corner at Fifth Street. That was logical. A quick getaway most often required a driver. The men retreated out of sight, either around the corner or into the darkness of their car, when Lester Shivers pulled up and deposited Edgar on the opposite side of West Peachtree.

Edgar could have walked straight in, but that wasn't his nature. He most likely stopped near the curb. The streetlights reflecting off the parlor windows created a giant mirror where he could see himself swing. He wasn't drunk—Mrs. Shivers wouldn't have tolerated it, nor would Lester have had any part of illegal alcohol with his daughter there for dinner—and a sober man would have seen or heard a car, no matter what speed it was traveling. Comer drove the most advanced automobile on the road, and his Type 59 sounded like a mini-locomotive when he ran it full out. On an empty street at midnight, sneaking up on a pedestrian in a speeding automobile would have been all but impossible.

In Comer's theory, Edgar stood near the curb swinging an imaginary club for a few seconds, just long enough for the three men to jump him. He must have struggled. The hat was thrown several yards away, and the shoe, fully laced and tied, came off and was tossed into the shrubbery. Then a knife or stiletto was thrust in an upward stabbing motion. It hit the intended artery. Edgar never had a chance.

Comer discounted most of the ear-witness accounts, except that of Miss L. S. Warren, who seemed quite credible. What had she said again? *"I heard some sort of ruckus, I don't know what all, just a commotion that startled me awake,"* and a motorcar that was *"running rapidly, and from the sound it seemed to be a high-powered car."* A coordinated assault and stabbing would stir up quite a commotion, enough to awaken an elderly lady across the street. And a getaway car would run rapidly, since getting away was, after all, the point.

The nature of Edgar's wound, the lack of bruising anywhere else on his body, the absence of skid marks or tattered clothing or broken bones, the location of the hat and shoe, along with Miss Warren's account of a high-powered car and conductor Fisher's vanishing mystery men on the corner of West Peachtree and Fifth, all pointed away from a hit-and-run. As much as Comer didn't want it to be true, his theory of a premeditated attack seemed a lot more plausible.

To apparently be the only person thinking this way put Comer in a terrible spot. It was shameful enough to have one of the world's greatest golfers killed in his town; for it to become known that the killing had, in fact, been a premeditated murder would thrust Atlanta into the middle of another scandalous story, and stain the city he and his fellow citizens worked so hard to protect.

· · ·

Comer hated to think about past turmoil. It should have been ancient history, and was for most: but not for the Howells. For them, some of the city's sins remained deeply and sorely personal.

He had been only five years old when his father ran for governor, so the only things Comer recalled were parades and rallies with balloons and hand-churned ice cream. As he got older, he realized that to call the campaign contentious was understating the matter by a wide margin. Clark Howell loathed Hoke Smith, and didn't mind if everyone knew it. Clark's bushy mustache would curl up as if some malodorous vapor had crept into the room at the very mention of Hoke's name. Hoke appeared to feel the same way about his opponent, going out of his way to insinuate that Clark Howell was unfit to serve for this or that reason. The worst insinuation was that Clark wasn't the man his father had been. The other charge, made in hushed tones in diners and barbershops, accused Clark Howell of being a nigger lover, soft on segregation and ambivalent on the question of suppressing the negro vote.

The problem with those allegations was that there was just enough truth in both to make them hard to refute. Clark was a devoted son, and like most men of his generation he held his father in reverential esteem. As successful as Clark was, he would, as a good son, readily admit that he wasn't the man his father had been. E. P. Howell had ridden alongside Stonewall Jackson and battled Billy Sherman; he had hired Henry Grady and built the state capitol; he had been the best father a man could have; a man Clark Howell would never, in his own mind, match. As for the negro question, Comer knew that his father harbored no animosity toward Atlanta's dark-skinned citizenry. Clark had always believed that white men should care for and encourage their negroes. He believed the negro should read and work, and move up as much as he was able. Mingling should, of course, be discouraged, but as long as they understood the boundaries—and most of the ones the Howells knew did—then Clark had no problem with them.

Hoke Smith had twisted Clark's position and used it as a club against him. By the summer of the 1906 campaign, voters would have thought that Clark Howell supported mixed-breed marriage and negroes using a white man's commode. It was a shameless display of dirty politics, but one that would stick to Clark like tar to a hide. He tried to fight back, turning the tables and accusing Smith of being the one that was soft on negro suffrage, but the charge continued to plague Howell. In a last-ditch effort,

Howell pulled out all the stops during a debate in Columbus, just a week before the August election. He decided to throw Hoke Smith's argument back in his face by being more anti-negro than any candidate since Reconstruction.

"First, I shall deal with the reason behind the candidacy of Mr. Smith for the office of governor," Clark said.

Who doubts the real reason that animates his campaign? Who can doubt it who reads the countless triages of abuse and vituperation he has heaped upon the heads of democratic administrations in Georgia? Who can doubt it? Oh Democrats! We learn from Holy Writ that the cock crew thrice before our Lord was betrayed. The warning voice availed not, and the traitor's kiss became the kiss of death, for so it was ordained. Does the dim veil of destiny portend your party's downfall?

The Disfranchisement bill is a regular dyed-in-the-wool, four-by-six, head-over-heels flop with no strings tied to it. And that's why Hoke is, today, advocating an educational qualification that will put in the ballot box in Georgia 93,000 educated negro votes, and keep out the votes of many an old fashioned Democratic hero who was too busy shedding his blood in defense of Georgia to learn "readin', 'ritin', and 'rithmetic."

Hoke says that the division of the white vote is so close that the vote of the negro is the balance of power that will sway the state. And how does he propose to relieve the state from the impending danger of negro domination? By striking down the white democratic, and putting in its place a system which by his own admission would pack the ballot boxes of Georgia with 93,000 largely unqualified negro votes, every one of which would kill or nullify the ballot of some white Democratic voter, who under the present system, vies with white Democrats alone in the selection of the officers who administer the affairs of state.

What is this so-called negro disfranchisement bill so violently opposed by Mr. Smith as a Democrat, and so ardently embraced by him now? Have you read the bill? I have it here, and I tell you that nowhere in all its weary length is even the word negro mentioned!

Concede the honesty of the bill and its supporters, and admit that the measure means all that it says; what does it propose to do? To take away the negro ballot? God bless you, no! Unless the bill is a shameless subterfuge, the mongrel offspring of clap-trap and hypocrisy, its purpose is patent on its face.

If enacted into law, and honestly administered, it would disfranchise every unfortunate white man in Georgia whose opportunities and necessities had prevented him from obtaining an average education. It would say to the old confederate soldier who, as a boy, handled the knapsack and the bayonet instead of the dinner pail and the blue back spelling book, "You were good enough for us to send to the front to defend with your blood the sacred principles for which we fought; now you've got to obey the law or go to jail, but you've got no more voice in assessment of those taxes or in the making of those laws than the barking dog that wakes the stillness of the night!"

They propose, therefore, not only to punish the poor illiterate white man for his poverty by taking away his right to vote, but they actually offer the forfeit ballot as a prize to every negro in Georgia who will get out of the cotton patch and into the negro college.

Make the ballot the prize of education and every negro child in Georgia will trot right straight from the cabin to college. Every cotton boll in Georgia could rot on the stalk before they would pick it, and every blade of corn in Georgia would smother in the grass before they would lay down the grammar and the Greek, and pick up the shovel and the hoe!

You have heard the old saying that "Whenever the nigger learns his haec, hoc, he forgets all about his gee-haw-buck." Already, from the very agitation of this question, our farmers are suffering from scarcity of labor, and the governor of North Carolina, who is quoted as so earnestly advocating disfranchisement in Georgia, is calling for Chinese labor to till the fields of that state.

Already every hill around Atlanta is crowned with vast negro colleges, whose combined endowment from the northern philanthropy far exceeds the total endowment of every white college in Georgia, and which turn out, every year, more graduates than all the white colleges in Georgia combined. Already, throughout the entire state, countless thousands of negro children are getting bow-legged with the burden of carrying their books to school. Already thousands of negro women content themselves with pot liquor and wallow in wretched squalor in order that their children may be qualified to kill the white man's ballot when the day prophesied by Hoke Smith shall arrive when "organized democracy in Georgia can no longer be maintained by the white vote."

No, gentlemen, I am where Hoke Smith stood before he was a candidate, and traded in his conviction. I am opposed to the agitation of the question here in Georgia, where peace prevails, where the people are content, and where white supremacy and democratic rule are no longer theories, but assured conditions.

One month later, on Saturday afternoon, September 22, 1906, after transcripts of the debate were printed in several papers, and stories of uppity negroes harassing white women also found their way into print, thousands of white men and boys stormed the streets of downtown Atlanta armed with clubs, shovels, and guns. The mob stormed negro businesses and residences along Decatur Street, Pryor Street, and Central Avenue. They broke windows, beating and abusing negroes and negresses regardless of age or station. Three negro barbers were killed in their shop and another three were beaten to death after being pulled from a streetcar.

By midnight, the state militia arrived and the city was shut down. Rioting continued, even after some negroes armed themselves and turned away invading mobs. Gunfire could be heard throughout the night and on into Sunday. On Monday, September 24, a group of negro leaders met at Clark College and Gammon Theological Seminary, two of the negro colleges Howell had spoken of in the debate. The negroes were heavily armed and appeared to be setting up fortifications at the college. Police, fearing a counterattack, launched an offensive against the college, sending three companies of militia into the area. A police officer was killed and 250 negroes were arrested.

When the smoke lifted, twenty-five negroes and two whites were dead (although one white death was an elderly woman who suffered a heart attack upon seeing the mob outside her house). Hundreds of homes and businesses were damaged or destroyed.

The world was appalled. Headlines around the globe proclaimed the barbarism of the American South. The French publication *Le Petit* was only one of the international journals to excoriate the city. The story, entitled "Lynching in the United States: The Massacre of Negroes in Atlanta," questioned whether Georgia whites had, through years of inner breeding, become a violent subhuman species.

W. E. B. DuBois wrote a poem after the riot entitled "A Litany of Atlanta":

> O Silent God, Thou whose voice afar in the mist and mystery hath left
> our ears an-hungered in these fearful days—
> *Hear us, good Lord! . . .*
>
> We are not better than our fellows, Lord, we are but weak and
> human men. When our devils do deviltry, curse Thou the doer and the
> deed: curse them as we curse them, do to them all and more than ever
> they have done to innocence and weakness, to womanhood and home.
> *Have mercy upon us, miserable sinners! . . .*

Whither? North is greed and South is blood; within, the coward,
and without, the liar. Whither? To Death?
Amen! Welcome dark sleep!

Like most civilized Southerners, the Howells were grief-stricken by the
carnage of the riots. And Clark Howell would live with the guilt of his
words from the Columbus debate for the rest of his life.

Comer knew his father hadn't meant to incite violence. It was politics. Outrageous statements were part of the game. The point his father
had been making was a good one: a literacy test at the polls would disfranchise white Georgians as well as negroes. But the tone of the argument,
the racism, had bled out, quite literally, into the streets. Clark Howell had
not only allowed it, but fanned the flames. Against his nature and contrary
to his true beliefs, he had chosen a political tactic that would haunt him
forever.

As a family, the Howells were more racially tolerant than most of their
neighbors and friends, including those who lived outside the South. A
prime example was the recent public stand Clark had taken on Orientals at
a time when the entire nation seemed determined to send the yellow man
packing. Japanese immigration began in earnest in the late nineteenth century, mainly in California where Japs were seen as a cheap alternative to ex-
isting Chinese labor. In the early days, the Japs took agricultural jobs,
backbreaking work that had once belonged to slaves, but, like the China-
men before them, it didn't take the Japs long to set up their own prosper-
ous communities. By the dawn of the twentieth century most major cities
had Jap neighborhoods with the little fellows owning taverns, inns, board-
inghouses, and shops. They even formed cooperatives to provide financ-
ing and political support. By 1920, Jap farmers controlled 450,000 acres
of California farmland and 10 percent of the state's crop revenue.

That success came at a price, though. As was the case with almost
every economic downturn, immigrants became scapegoats, and in this
one, the Japs were easy targets. Yes, the Irish were treated as second-class
citizens, but at least they were white. In the post–world war depression,
Orientals faced open hostility. Samuel Gompers, president of the American Federation of Labor (AFL), barred them from membership and en-
couraged every state legislature to pass a Japanese Exclusion Act, stating
that white Americans needed protection from "the brown toilers of the
mikado's realm."

Atlanta was considered one of the more tolerant cities in the South on that front, but that wasn't saying much. As the *New York Times* reported in 1920, "The Japanese need not turn for sympathy to our Southern States. There the anti-Japanese note rings loud and sure. 'I am in favor of exclusion of all Orientals,' says Duncan U. Fletcher, United States Senator from Florida, and Joseph Hergeshiemer, the novelist, puts himself on record thus: 'I dislike intensely the Japanese: they seem to me a race of marvelously efficient automatons moving about with their brutal precision, a cold, dangerous, secretiveness into which our sloppy sentimentality has never been able to filter. And since it is my special weakness to only write about and associate with people and things I can, more or less, grasp and like, this wonderful little people is not for me.' "

It wasn't just Southerners who vented such vitriol. Robert Stevenson, editor of the *Westbury Republican* in Westbury, Connecticut, said, "I am convinced that we in New England, just because California is so far away, have been blind to the real peril of allowing Japanese to pour in without restriction. East is West and West is East, and they cannot be made to meet."

Even more emphatic were the writings of Robert Moses, the "master builder" of New York City, Long Island, and Westchester County. According to Moses, "The negro in the South led to the Civil War and nearly wrecked the nation, and is not assimilated yet. Orientals on the Pacific Coast in large numbers would be even harder to absorb and would, in addition, involve us in grave foreign complications. It would be the height of folly not to stop such immigration. The question is not one of the superiority or inferiority and could be stated in such a form as to make this plain to the Japanese government. The point is that Orientals are fundamentally different in their economic, social, and political outlook. Such differences are of less importance in autocratic countries. But democracies can govern themselves successfully only when they are composed of like-minded men with harmonious ideals and congenial political institutions."

One of the few voices of reason came from Atlanta. "Here in the South, our view is that the Japanese peril is a scarecrow, that there is little foundation for the view that a Japanese peril exists," Clark Howell wrote for the *New York Times.* Comer's father was appalled by the xenophobia of his fellow editors and intellectuals. He had seen, and been a party to, the disastrous effects generated by this kind of straw man hatred. He wanted no part of it this time around.

Most of Atlanta's elite followed Howell's lead. As long as Japs stayed in their place and didn't cause trouble, Atlantans had little problem with them.

The right thing never came easy. Standing astride a rising tide took courage as well as strength. His stand on behalf of Atlanta's Japs was an attempt to atone for the guilt Clark Howell felt after the disastrous gubernatorial debate massacre when he had gone against his own beliefs for the sake of political expediency. He would spend the rest of his days trying to make up for that mistake.

On the other side, Comer had seen a later Georgia governor, a man named John Slaton, stand up to a lynch mob. The governor had gone against a tidal wave of public opinion and commuted the death sentence of Leo Frank, a decision that forced Slaton to slip out of the governor's mansion in the dead of night just steps ahead of vigilantes. Comer had been a teenager by then, impressionable and keenly interested in the drama playing out on the city's streets. Part of his interest had to do with the fact that his family knew almost all the people involved in the Frank trial—Frank himself was the son of the former postmaster general of the United States—but Comer was enthralled by the matter because the victim, a beautiful girl named Mary Phagan, was his own age.

Phagan, a worker at the local pencil factory where Frank was the bespectacled, effete manager, would forever be a smiling, fair-skinned thirteen-year-old with bows in her wavy, dark hair. On April 27, 1913, little Mary was found dead in the dark basement of the factory where she and Frank worked. After a number of failed arrests and more fits and starts than a cold engine, the police arrested Frank based on coerced testimony from another thirteen-year-old friend of Phagan's, who said he had seen Frank flirt with the girl, and the Franks' housekeeper, who was also a local madam at one of Atlanta's seedier bordellos. Both witnesses later recanted when they were away from police interrogators, claiming to have been threatened.

Frank was summarily convicted, despite having detailed alibis for every second in which the crime could have taken place. He was sentenced to death—a sentence that was heralded by such agitators as Thomas Watson, a supporter of Hoke Smith and ardent segregationist who believed that Jewry was an evil second only to negro suffrage. Frank was a rich Jew. Mary Phagan was a poor white Protestant working to support her widowed mother and siblings. Once the locomotive of guilt reached full steam, no amount of contradictory evidence could assuage public opinion.

Frank's innocence was so evident to outsiders that his trial and conviction prompted American Jews to form the Anti-Defamation League in 1913. But such moves only hardened the resolve of Georgians, led by Thomas Watson, to uphold the purity of the white Protestant bloodlines in the South. Watson, along with former governor Joseph Brown, a couple of lawyers, the son of a U.S. senator, and Bolan Brumby, who owned a rocking chair factory just north of Atlanta in the town of Marietta, formed the Knights of Mary Phagan, a Klan-like group intent on seeing their version of justice done.

The whole nation was captivated by the plight of Leo Frank. His trial and sentence received more sensational coverage than any story in American history at that time. Twenty-two months after the jury's verdict, with the gallows looming, Governor Slaton, after reviewing more than ten thousand documents, commuted the sentence to life in prison. He was convinced that a court would eventually find Frank innocent and set him free. Watson called for the governor to be lynched, and for a while it looked as though that might happen. A mob with a rope gathered outside the governor's residence until the Georgia National Guard, under the command of Asa Candler, showed them the error of their ways.

Frank wasn't so lucky. In a highly coordinated kidnapping (with plenty of inside help), Frank was taken from his jail cell on August 17, 1915, and lynched on the property of one of the conspirators, a local sheriff named William Fray. His hanging body was photographed with a crowd of onlookers posing in the shot. Postcards were made and sold. Many were mailed throughout the South.

He was buried in Flushing Meadows, New York. Afterward, half of Georgia's Jews packed up and left the state.

There weren't many heroes in the Leo Frank story. Thomas Watson used the trial and all the surrounding publicity to solidify his base and gin up resentment for Northern industrialists, Jews, Catholics, and anyone who wished to educate or integrate the negroes. Out of his movement, a new Ku Klux Klan was born in a grand ceremony atop Georgia's Stone Mountain in the fall of 1915. But John Slaton, lawyer and governor, put his life at risk, not for a friend or even a man he liked (by all accounts,

Frank wasn't a very likable fellow), but because someone had to stand for righteousness and justice in Atlanta.

At the time, Governor Slaton had said, "The performance of my duty under the Constitution is a matter of my conscience. The responsibility rests where the power is reposed. [Trial] Judge [Leonard S.] Roan, with that awful sense of responsibility, which probably came over him as he thought of that Judge before whom he would shortly appear, calls to me from another world to request that I do that which he should have done. I can endure misconstruction, abuse, and condemnation, but I cannot stand the constant companionship of an accusing conscience, which would remind me in every thought that I, as a Governor of Georgia, failed to do what I thought to be right. There is a territory beyond reasonable doubt and absolute certainty for which the law provides, allowing life imprisonment instead of execution. This case has been marked by doubt. . . . [This decision] means that I must live in obscurity the rest of my days, but I would rather be plowing a field than to feel that I had blood on my hands."

Douglas Edgar wasn't a negro or a Jew, but what sort of white man was he, really? A philanderer? A drinker? A gambler? A player of games? He was all of those things to be sure. Who would stand witness for a man like that as public opinion swung toward an easy verdict? Edgar had been an extraordinary golfer, a teacher and friend of the best Atlanta had to offer, which dimmed the pox on his character somewhat, but in death he had become a valuable political tool, a vehicle for advancing an agenda. To go against the idea of the hit-and-run death—to even suggest an alternative theory—was to go against everything the city was striving to do. Plus, to insinuate that Edgar's killing was anything more than a horrible calamity would require admitting that another prominent outsider had been brutally and intentionally murdered in Atlanta. Once anyone made that dramatic leap, the next question was: what motive could be found for killing Edgar? With those answers would come the names of every woman who had ever taken a lesson, had a conversation, or spoken admiringly of Edgar—some well known and respected, many innocent and unfairly accused. It would be another scandal that *The Georgian*, a gossipy rag of a newspaper owned by that Hearst fellow, would plaster all over the country; every lurid detail, no matter how inaccurate or inane, given prominent front-page space with extra editions running daily.

Who would do the right thing?

Asa Candler would track Edgar's killer to the ends of the earth, or so it seemed. The former mayor and Coca-Cola founder loved his pro, and by all accounts, openly mourned him. Candler had, no doubt, been instrumental in the $5,000 reward Druid Hills was offering to anyone with information leading to an arrest. The club was also closed in memoriam, an unheard-of occurrence on a Wednesday. But Mr. Candler was a man of fact, not theories. For him to go against the prevailing wisdom of the police and politicians, he would need concrete and irrefutable evidence, more evidence, certainly, than Comer could provide.

Then there was O. B. Keeler. One of Edgar's best friends in the city, Keeler wouldn't hesitate to do the right thing, but in what forum? Keeler knew only what the police told him. He hadn't been there. He hadn't seen Edgar's blood, hadn't felt the sticky air, or sensed the eerie quiet of that vacant street. And he hadn't been the first person to shout, "A man has been hit by a car!" thus starting this avalanche. Keeler didn't know what Comer knew.

None of them did.

If right was to be done, there was only one person who could do it. Comer was due at the Patterson funeral home at nine o'clock, where he would be called as a witness to testify in front of the coroner's jury. If that jury declared Douglas Edgar a victim of a hit-and-run, then no alternate theories would ever be explored. If anyone was going to stand against the tide, it would have to be at that hearing. And, Comer knew, he was the only person who could make that stand.

He wasn't Governor John Slaton. He wasn't even Clark Howell. He was a twenty-year-old cub reporter, the editor's son, who just happened to have been at the wrong place at the wrong time. He was also the only person in Atlanta in a position to do the right thing for Douglas Edgar, and for the truth.

CHAPTER 12

The lovely Alexa Stirling,
America's greatest female amateur golfer.

To get on the right road to one's ultimate destination: does that
not conjure up the secret success in life? Surely it is better to
travel in a donkey cart on the right road than whiz along in a
Rolls-Royce at sixty miles per hour on the wrong.

—J. DOUGLAS EDGAR

Doug was expected to play in the major events of 1919. Members at Druid Hills wanted to see how their man stacked up, and Doug was anxious to show them. Pros rarely played tournament golf for the prize money, since no one could feed and house a family on the purses. But a good showing in a major event put a professional in good stead with his members, and upped his exhibition and challenge match fees. Walter Hagen had his members at Rochester Country Club brimming with pride after he won the 1914 U.S. Open, and his appearance fees went up accordingly. Jock Hutchison, born in St. Andrews but a naturalized U.S. citizen, gave an air of old-world traditionalism to the relatively new Glen View Club in Chicago. His members adored him and compensated him well. The members of Sunset Country Club in St. Louis reportedly rewarded their pro, "Long" Jim Barnes (so called because of his lanky six-foot, four-inch frame), with an astronomical stipend of $15,000 after he won the PGA Championship. Even a mercurial pro like Johnny McDermott could make good wages based on the fact that he would always be the first American to win back-to-back U.S. Open titles, something his members at Atlantic City Country Club would boast about forever. Amateurs still grabbed most of the headlines, but pros provided bragging rights to the clubs that employed them. A high finish in a tournament or two and a pro could be assured of employment for many years to come.

Doug wasn't worried about a job. His French Open title still carried enough cachet to keep him fed, and his radical teaching methods were finding an audience, though small, in Atlanta. The members at Druid Hills hoped he would contend in the big events, but his main job in the summer of 1919 was to chaperone the city's teen sensation, Bob Jones. Edgar had already proclaimed Jones to be one of the best amateurs he'd ever seen. He also told everyone who would listen that he planned to take Jones to the British Open Championship in 1920 (the postwar Britons weren't quite ready to resume golf in 1919). "I'm not only going to enter myself, I want Bob Jones and Perry Adair to go with me," Doug said. "I believe Bob would lead the field of amateurs. There's more power to his game than any amateur I've ever seen. If he had any trouble at all, it's a slight lack of control with his wooden clubs, but he has a perfect swing."

Doug also wanted to make a name for himself as a player in the States. He would sorely love to return home for the 1920 British Open as a heralded champion. The U.S. Open was his first shot at that fame and glory. He hoped to make it a good one. The tournament was played at Brae Burn Country Club in West Newton, Massachusetts, a bedroom community outside of Boston and a club where another good friend of Doug's, a Frenchman named Louis Tellier, was the pro. Tellier had been a key player in the drama of the 1913 U.S. Open, contending until the final round, when the amateur Francis Ouimet beat Vardon and Ray in a playoff. With the American Open being played at his home course, experts picked Tellier as one of the favorites.

As had been the case throughout most of his career, Doug was a pretournament afterthought—that was until some of the reporters in Boston saw him play a few practice rounds. After spending a few days in New York playing exhibitions and impressing many of the most influential reporters in sports, Doug took the train to Boston where he played three pre-tournament rounds at Brae Burn and never shot worse than 70. Two of his rounds were deep into the 60s: unheard-of scores on a U.S. Open course. It didn't take long for the assembled scribes to dub Douglas Edgar as a pro to watch.

Unfortunately, five years out of major competition had rusted Doug's tournament readiness. The prewar nerves that he'd gotten under control with a whistle and a hum came roaring back in West Newton. He didn't sleep a wink prior to the opening round. Before sunrise, he got out of bed, caught the first car to Brae Burn, and walked every inch of the course before breakfast, a bad decision given that his hip wasn't getting any younger. He ordered a large breakfast, but was unable to eat a bite of it, and was so nervous by the time he got to the first tee that he could barely tee up his ball.

By sunset, Edgar was nine shots out of the lead. After the second day (for the first time the USGA extended its open to three days instead of two, with competitors playing eighteen holes each of the first two days and thirty-six holes the last), Edgar's dreams of making his mark in the U.S. Open were over. He was a dozen shots behind the leader, and so out of sorts that he considered withdrawing from the tournament and catching the next boat back to Newcastle.

Adding a sour note to the sorry state of affairs was the fact that Mike "King" Brady seemed to be running away with the thing, having shot back-to-back rounds of 74. Louis Tellier and Walter Hagen were three shots back, but Brady appeared to be in full command of his game and the tournament, shooting scores that Doug had beaten with ease prior to donning the yoke of competition.

Brady extended his lead to five shots in the third round with an impressive round of 73. Hagen shot 75 to stay within striking distance, but Tellier's putting fell to pieces and he limped away with an 82, putting the local pro twelve shots back with only one round to play. Jock Hutchison hung around in third place, nine shots back. Everyone assumed Brady would cruise to victory in the afternoon eighteen. He had worn the lead like comfortable shoes from the start, and showed no signs of cracking, even though the crowds were among the largest ever seen at an American golf event. Men in dark suits and boaters accompanied ladies in bonnets and dresses, many hoisting parasols skyward to protect their delicate complexions from the summer New England sun.

Then a strange thing happened. Whether it was the weight of the situation, or the mental and physical fatigue of a thirty-six-hole final day, Brady lost his momentum and his ability to drive the ball in the fairway. While Brae Burn was not particularly long, accuracy was paramount, especially in major championship conditions. Missing fairways from the tee made it almost impossible to get the ball onto the green. Approaches from the rough that did find the green finished so far from the hole that getting down in two putts proved too much, even for the best players in the world.

Brady missed one fairway after another. His walk slowed. His smile faded, and his lead continued to evaporate. When he reached the eighteenth green, he had to get down in two putts for an 80, not a disastrous score, but not the way he had hoped to capture his first major title. He had no idea that Walter Hagen was in the middle of an incredible run. Hagen played the final six holes with five fours and a three. When his final putt fell, Hagen had posted a score of 75, good enough to bolt him into a tie for the lead.

Brady and the swashbuckler were knotted at the top. Both men had finished seventy-two holes with scores of 301, seventeen over par. They would square off in a playoff the following day.

Thousands of Bostonians turned out for the playoff. It was the first time the U.S. Open had been in their town since the Ouimet win, and even though nothing as dramatic as a skinny amateur beating the best pro in the world seemed likely, Brady was a Massachusetts boy, and the locals didn't want to miss one of their own winning another title. The golf was good, but not spectacular. There were a couple of rules questions involving stymies and other vagaries differentiating match and stroke play, but they didn't play critical roles in the outcome other than to confuse the spectators. Hagen shot 77 to beat Brady by one shot, and capture his second U.S. Open title.

By now, Hagen was the most famous professional golfer in America, in no small part due to the man's flamboyant self-promotion. He showed off the $500 winner's check from Brae Burn to every crowd he could find.

Meanwhile, Doug Edgar finished a miserable nineteen shots off the pace, shooting 320 for seventy-two holes. Sullen and slump-shouldered, Doug caught the first train for Chicago. He would play in the Western Open (not very well) and then head up to Canada for the Canadian Open at Hamilton Golf and Country Club in Ancaster, Ontario. He couldn't get there fast enough.

The Open Championship of Canada lagged behind the major tournaments of the United States in terms of size and prestige, a fact that did not sit well with the Canadians. Golf in Canada had mirrored the States, with Victoria Golf Club ratifying its charter as the nation's first course in 1893, and Hamilton Golf and Country Club opening a year later on property adjoining the local jockey club. Canadian courses were just as challenging and pristine as those in the States (although a new course in California called Pebble Beach Links was said to be untouchable in terms of locale and layout). As far as the locals were concerned, there was no reason the Canadian Open could not be every bit as grand a major championship as the U.S. Open. Many Canadians hoped 1919 would be the year they caught up with their southern neighbor.

Not only was the field for this Open twice the size of previous years, Canadians had wisely scheduled the International Matches, an amateur event pitting a team of Canada's best against a similar squad of young Americans, the week before the Open on the same golf course. Because of this, Chick Evans, reigning U.S. Amateur Champion, and Bob Jones both entered the Canadian Open for the first time, as did former amateur champ W. C Fownes (a future USGA president whose father, H. C. Fownes, founded Oakmont Country Club near the family's home in Pittsburgh). They were joined by a stellar group of pros. Long Jim Barnes, fresh off a win at the Western Open, made the trip to Ontario, as did Wilfred Reid, a native of Nottinghamshire who made his mark in America as both a player and a course architect and was rumored to hold twenty course records. Leo Diegel, a Detroit pro who would go on to win thirty professional tournaments, including the PGA Championship, also made his Canadian Open debut in 1919.

With no Open being played in Great Britain or France, Canada stepped in and filled the "major championship" void, putting together a solid field of competitors on the country's best golf course.

The buzz going into the week surrounded the amateurs, especially Bob Jones and Chick Evans. Many writers penned wistful fantasies about how wonderful it would be if the game's two young stars made a run at such a prestigious title. The fact that no player had ever broken 70 in two tournament rounds on North American soil did not jump to the front of anyone's mind. Certainly nobody expected Douglas Edgar to be the first. Again, he was an afterthought, an "oh, by the way, the former French Open winner is here" end to a sentence. No one gave Doug much of a chance, especially after how he'd played in West Newton.

Plus, no one could find him before the tournament started. While other pros were getting in as many practice rounds as possible, Doug remained out of sight. Nobody knew where he was or what he was doing. It turned out he was in the pubs, partaking of the nectar he so sorely missed in America. As he later confessed to O. B. Keeler, *"A divin't mind tellin' ya, when Ah got up to Canada where Ah could get mesel' a pint o beer—or something a bit stronger—and it made me feel right, you know. No, you can't know, so Ah'll tell ya. At home, before a round Ah'd have a pint of stout to quiet me nerves. When Ah came to America, Ah was fightin' me nerves from the first tee, and that's no way to play golf when championship's at stake.*

The tournament at Hamilton started on Tuesday, so on the Sunday Ah had a bit of a party with a mate of mine. It turned out that it was enough of a do that Ah didn't feel at all like getting up in the mornin', so Ah stayed nice and comfortable in bed till noon. When I got up, me mate—Ah knew him back in England—drove me to the course.

Well, Ah didn't gan for a round like the others. What Ah did was hire a caddy, took me clubs and a dozen balls and went out to a quiet spot on the women's course. So, there was just me and the caddy, and Ah hit a few prac-

tice shots. With what? Oh, it was a jigger Ah think, but that doesn't matter. And then the feelin' came to me in me wrists—it was a feelin' that Ah was right—and Ah went back to the clubhouse, put me clubs away, and that was all me practice."

Bob Jones remembered it much the same way with a few added details. "We never saw him until the day of the tournament," Jones recalled. *"Willie Ogg became somewhat concerned, and traveled back to the house where we were staying to see about Edgar's well-being. When Edgar finally came out to the course, as I recall, his preparation was to hit six shots from the practice tee. Then he came away saying, 'I'm ready. I'm ready.' He had that sort of moody game. When he was 'right' he was unbeatable.*

He used to characterize it by saying, 'When my hands feel thin, I'm ready to play.' By this, I suppose, he meant that he had the feel of the clubs. And when he did, he could make the ball talk. He loved to play draws and fades.

There was one particular hole at Hamilton with the fairway bordered on the right by a fence. Over the fence was out of bounds. Edgar would play his tee shot out over that fence with a draw that brought it back into the fairway. The crowds just loved it."

That sort of precision was a must. While the course wasn't a monster—it measured 6,350 yards—it was one of the hardest tests in North America. As *The American Golfer* noted, "To the chap who finds himself the least bit off, there are penalties galore from ditches, water hazards and scraggly traps."

Doug showed up on Tuesday morning with his hands "feeling thin" and his game as sharp as ever. His driver, which he had crafted himself, was ahead of its time by a good seventy years, with an oversized head and whippy shaft. At seventeen ounces, the clubhead looked like a giant stone on the end of a hickory stick, a precursor to the large clubheads that would be common three generations into the future. Clubs came in all shapes and sizes, with such silly contraptions as an aluminum-headed driver and spoon earning Reginald Brougham a patent in 1893. William Ballingall also got a patent for an iron with a half-inch-wide flange on its sole. These were just a few of the exotic instruments found in pros' bags. A British pro named Francis Brewster invented an entire set of center-shafted clubs with clubheads that looked more like croquet mallets than golf clubs (he would also use aluminum heads in later models), and a Philadelphia pro named Henry Febiger had some limited success when he bore two holes in the head of a driver and filled the holes with lead balls. At impact the balls would shift forward, and according to Febiger "an additional impact or blow is imparted to the ball." Still, clubs like the sand wedge were decades away from being seen, as were any rules or standards regarding the number of clubs a player could carry. Some pros showed up at Hamilton with thirty clubs in their bags. Chick Evans played with only seven. As for Edgar, Canadian golfers were at first curious about the average-sized man with the giant driver, but they forgot about the dimensions of the club when they saw Doug's compact swing and the towering shots it produced.

"His mashie shots are also extremely high with plentiful backspin," *The American Golfer* reported. "He has no inherent weaknesses."

His opening round was a respectable 72 in a strong, cool breeze—one bogey and two birdies on the front nine, and a three-putt bogey on the final green. At the conclusion of the morning round, a buzz circulated through the gallery, not because of Edgar's solid performance, but because the first-round leader was none other than the young Bob Jones, who came in with a 71. Locals were also heartened by the performance of Nicoll Thomson, the pro from Hamilton, who shot 73.

After lunch, the wind picked up and the scores went higher. Two thirds of the eighty-eight-player field shot higher scores in the second round than in the first. The noteworthy exceptions were Jim Barnes, who followed his lackluster 78 with an afternoon round of 71, and defending Canadian Open champion Karl Keffer, who shot 76 in the morning and 73 in the afternoon.

The other player to better his morning score was Edgar, who had seven consecutive fours on the front nine, going out in 36. The only blemishes on the back nine were back-to-back fives at fourteen and fifteen, which were offset by a marvelous three at the 345-yard tenth and a four at the 500-yard seventeenth. Edgar finished the afternoon with a 71 and a six-shot lead over Barnes and Jones.

The whistling started on Wednesday morning—"I'm Forever Blowing Bubbles" and "The World Is Waiting for the Sunrise" were his favorite refrains. With each bar, the shots got better and the scores continued to improve. As Edgar would later recount, *"Things were just ganin' from better to better with each round. But Ah was always thinkin' to mesel' it'd be an awful mistake to take two putts on a green, or to leave mesel' one of more than a yard on an approach. For a while, when Ah'd make a par, you could hear people in the crowd whisperin' 'Has he blown it at last?' "*

His outward nine of the morning began to take form on the fifth hole. He made a four on the fifth, and from that moment forward, his scores were: three, four, three, four, three, three, four, three, four, four, four, four, and four, a display that stunned the crowds and had everyone wondering if they were witnessing history.

His back nine was spectacular, beginning when he almost drove the green on the 345-yard tenth, a towering tee shot that rode the wind and sent shock waves throughout the gallery. An easy pitch and putt for birdie set him on his way. He made another three at the 430-yard eleventh after hitting a mashie-iron approach to within six feet of the hole.

At seventeen, he thrilled the gallery again, as well as the reporter for a local paper. According to an account in the *Hamilton Spectator,* "The English professional and former French champion who represented the Druid Hills Golf Club of Atlanta, played one of the most sensational games ever witnessed on American or Canadian links. The seventeenth hole, one of 500 yards, saw one of the most remarkable plays seen in the tournament. Edgar's 275-yard drive pulled into the rough, and the ball chanced to drop plumb on a lost ball which caused it to bound farther in the rough. Undismayed by the bad luck, the Englishman made a mighty 225-yard drive which landed dead on the green. A bad putt neutralized that wonderful play, but Edgar romped home with a birdie four."

His third-round score of 69 tied the course record and gave Edgar a nine-shot lead over the local pro, Thomson, and the defending champ, Keffer. Barnes was ten shots off the pace and Jones stood eleven back with eighteen holes to play.

As *The American Golfer* put it, "There was every reason in the world for a breakdown in the afternoon as far as Edgar's golf was concerned. He had a safe lead, assuredly safe with a half a stroke a hole advantage over his nearest competitor; there never was any need for him to do aught but play safe as occasion required, and there seemed no need for nerving oneself up to a supreme effort."

Edgar didn't appear to be playing it safe in the after-lunch round, but a couple of casual shots cost him some early bogeys, the first coming at the first hole, a 410-yard par four. When his putt for four failed to fall, a murmur went out through the now massive gallery. The memory of Mike Brady blowing a lead in the final round of the U.S. Open was still fresh on everyone's mind. No one in attendance at Hamilton had ever seen Douglas Edgar before. Some of the more ardent golf fans had read about his French Open win, but nobody knew about his radical swing theories. All they saw was a man who took the club back a short distance compared with the other pros, who kept his hips so still on the takeaway that he looked like he was swinging flat-footed, and who hit an incredibly long and high ball for such a slight fellow. He could still lose this lead, or so they thought.

An impressive three at the 450-yard second hole more than made up for his bogey at the start, but then he made another five at the 380-yard third. Such a seesaw performance in the early going was perceived by some as an opening for the rest of the field. If Jones or Keffer or Thomson could get on a roll, anything could happen. Doug must have sensed this as well, because from the third tee throughout the rest of the afternoon he played the most inspired golf of his life, and some of the best that had ever been played by anyone in history.

Two massive shots on the five-hundred-yard third left him with a fifteen-foot putt for eagle three, which he promptly sank. He made a four on the next hole, and then rattled off two more birdies.

It started when he hit a mid-iron on the two-hundred-yard par three sixth that looked like it might go in the hole. The ball stopped three feet short of the hole on a direct line from the tee. That sent a rousing cheer through the gallery. When Edgar rolled in the putt for a two, several women squealed with delight. Then he birdied the par four seventh with another approach that looked like it had a chance of finding the hole for eagle. When he missed a birdie putt on nine and tapped in for par, there were groans, because the gallery had grown accustomed to Doug making every putt.

Still, he walked from the ninth green to the tenth tee having smashed the front-nine record with two bogeys on his card. His score of 32 on the outward half would stand as a record for more than a decade.

He kept the great play going on the back nine, starting out with two consecutive fours, a great three, followed by a par on the 205-yard par three thirteenth, and a birdie on the 375-yard fourteenth. He played the remaining holes in an average of fours, for a closing round of 66, the most impressive golf that had ever been played in North America.

The crowd roared its approval when Edgar tapped in. Those in attendance knew that they had stood witness to history, and they showed their appreciation with a level of cheering never before heard at a sporting event in Canada. A headline in the next issue of *Canadian Golfer* magazine would say it all: "Records Run Riot: Open Championship of Canada is won by J. Douglas Edgar in the Most Sensational golf ever seen in the Dominion."

The accompanying article would give an overview of Doug's feat. "There is no question at all about the 66 being the record for the Hamilton course," it read. "It was easily the best round ever. There is also no question, whatsoever, that in no previous Open or Amateur Championship either in Great Britain or on this continent have two rounds of under 70 been recorded by one competitor in the same day."

His total score of 278 was also a record for a major event, one that would hold up for seventeen years until broken by Byron Nelson, who played with far more advanced equipment.

But the most impressive record, the one that showed Hamilton Golf and Country Club as no pushover, was the margin of Edgar's victory. He won the 1919 Canadian Open by sixteen shots over his student Bob Jones, Western Open winner Long Jim Barnes, and the defending champion Karl Keffer. It was Jones's best finish to date in any national open, and the largest margin of defeat he had ever suffered.

As impressive as Edgar's win was at the time, it only grew in stature as the years passed. Comparing the performance to other major tournaments, Edgar's score would have won all but nine of the first one hundred U.S. Opens and would have tied the winning total in three others. Only twenty-three British Open Champions topped his winning score, the first coming in 1958, almost forty years after Edgar's win.

While his scoring record stood strong against the test of history, Edgar's record margin of victory would hold up even better. In 2009, ninety years after the fact, J. Douglas Edgar still held the record for the largest margin of victory in a top-flight event, making it the oldest unbroken record in American professional golf. No one topped it: not Jones, not Ben Hogan, Sam Snead, Byron Nelson, Arnold Palmer, Jack Nicklaus, or Greg Norman. Tiger Woods came close in 2000 with a fifteen-shot victory in the U.S. Open at Pebble Beach, but even he had not bested Edgar's winning margin.

In 1947, Ray Haywood wrote that

As a shotmaker, Edgar had no equal, yesterday or today. He played tricks with the ball during the Canadian tournament. On dogleg holes he either sliced or hooked so the ball wound round the turn with a strong run toward the green.

The natives still speak in hushed voices of that final round 66 at Hamilton. On the three-hundred-yard twelfth hole, Edgar, a small man, wound up with his wooden-shafted driver—a caddy would be ashamed to use such a club today—and drove the green. He missed a long putt for an eagle two. It was the only putt of any consequence he missed that day. His iron play to the greens was so sharp that on practically all the greens his putts were inside twelve feet. He sank many of them.

Numerous players, both American and foreign, appear to have legitimate claims on the title of greatest. They include Walter Travis, who took up the game at thirty-five and won the British Amateur at forty-two—an incident that gave the American businessman cause for hope that he too could have a day of athletic glory, stomach or not—Sandy Herd, Gene Sarazen, Long Jim Barnes, Tommy Armour, Chick Evans, Jerry Travers, Johnny McDermott, Francis Ouimet, Lawson Little, and Samuel Jackson Snead.

In each decade, some man is regarded as the superior of his contemporaries. With the passage of time, this eminence is dimmed by the performance of younger men. In golf, once Allan Robertson was the greatest. Then came Young Tommy Morris, Vardon, Jones, and Nelson, to skip lightly over the years. Each, admittedly, was, or is, as the case may be, a great golfer. Even now, the greatest player of the coming decade is registered in some high school. When he reaches maturity, he too will have his disciples.

However, until it is time to use the unknown as a comparative yardstick, Douglas Edgar (this is strictly one man's opinion, you understand) must be considered the world's greatest golfer.

It wasn't just one man's opinion. As word of Edgar's extraordinary accomplishment spread, more and more people nodded and said things like, "I knew it. He was always top-notch." He was also, whether he wanted it or not, an ambassador for the city he had lived in for four months. In his gossip column entitled "Boy Howdy!" Leslie Rawlings wrote in the *Atlanta Constitution*: "If there is one thing the city of Atlanta does, it is take honors in the sport world. Wednesday, J. Douglas Edgar, of the Druid Hills Golf Club, won the Canadian Open golf championship and put this city on the map in more than an emphatic way. Just stop and figure up the many tournaments and meets won by Atlanta sportsmen during a season, and don't forget the baseball and football races are yet to be run, and you will see where the 'New York of the South' is going to stand before long, athletically speaking."

A Druid Hills member named John Bothamly, an eyewitness to Edgar's play in Canada, was one of the first to arrive back in Atlanta and give testimony to what he'd seen. "We haven't realized here in Atlanta what a wonderful golfer he is, but the truth is, he is one of the best in the world," Bothamly said, shaking his head as if he still couldn't believe his eyes. "He went there with his ire up; he took a little nip of scotch—just a nip—started at top speed, and kept it up all the way."

Four thousand miles away, another man of some stature realized the significance of what had happened at Hamilton. As Harry Vardon prepared for another whirlwind tour of the United States in 1920, he was asked about Edgar's extraordinary display in Canada. With a wry smile, Harry took the pipe from his mouth and examined its contents, a standard ploy he used when wanting to gain everyone's undivided attention. "Edgar?" Vardon said. "Well, I will tell you: I believe this is a man who will one day be the greatest of us all."

CHAPTER 13

Southern night at the intersection of
Peachtree and West Peachtree.

Whereas, an apparent nationwide attempt through public statements in the press and conduct of lawless citizens and traitors within our ranks, there appears to be a concerted effort to discredit the Knights of the Ku Klux Klan in the eyes of the public, I, the Imperial Wizard of the Knights of the Ku Klux Klan, do hereby officially proclaim: the Knights of the Ku Klux Klan does not encourage, or foster lawlessness, racial prejudice or religious intolerance. The Knights of the Ku Klux Klan is a law-abiding, legally Chartered, standard fraternal Order, designed to teach and inculcate the purist ideals of American citizenship with malice towards none and justice to every citizen. If we are being lied about by those who are unworthy and who are not pure Americans at heart, the time will come when all their falsehoods will react on them and the Knights of the Ku Klux Klan will come into its own and take its place in the hearts of real Americans.

—WILLIAM JOSEPH SIMMONS,
IMPERIAL WIZARD OF THE KNIGHTS OF THE KU KLUX KLAN,
full-page ad in the *Atlanta Journal*
August 11, 1921

The queasiness that he thought had passed returned with a vengeance as Comer entered H. M. Patterson and Sons Undertaking. The smell might have had something to do with it. Formaldehyde had replaced arsenic as the primary embalming fluid, and even with all the windows open in the summer, residual fumes lingered, especially in the back, which was where Comer and the others were to meet. The parlors in the front would have been better. They were nicely furnished with upholstered chairs and large windows for cross-ventilation—just the kind of place for civilized people to conduct an inquiry—but those rooms were kept open for families sitting up with their dead. As important as the Edgar case was, the commerce of death had to continue.

Edgar himself lay in state in one of the front rooms. Members of Atlanta's club society had been parading by for two days to say goodbye to their great golf champion. The guestbook read like a Who's Who of Atlanta. Others who paid their respects didn't sign their names. Negroes were allowed to view white remains in the heat of the afternoon when no respectable citizen of means would be there and no relative would have the energy to complain. Edgar had no relatives in Atlanta, but most of the caddy corps at Druid Hills and East Lake showed up, along with more than a few lovely ladies from the city's inns.

Comer didn't go forward to see the body. He'd already seen Edgar and would pay his respects in other ways. Several members of the coroner's jury were already in the back room when Comer arrived. They stood in quiet discomfort not twenty feet from the four-foot-high marble rectangular table where bodies were prepared for viewing and burial. While the practice of embalming went back to ancient Egypt, the art had been lost to most Westerners until the time of the American Civil War when many survivors wanted their slain brethren shipped home rather than buried on the battlefield. Now, the bodies of Comer's fellow Atlantans were chilled in an icebox like deer meat until Mr. Patterson or one of his sons could get around to draining their blood and filling the waxy carcasses with enough formaldehyde to delay rotting for a week, sometimes longer depending on how much kin a fellow had coming in to bury him.

Every living soul in the room looked like he wanted to be some-where—anywhere—else.

The foreman of the coroner's jury was Charles Girardeau, a respected businessman with thinning hair and a thick mustache. He was joined by Mr. Clifford E. Dollar, Mr. John F. Stern, Mr. Thomas C. McLaurin, Mr. William F. Reeves, and Mr. Robert B. Gaines, all upstanding men com-pelled by law to serve in this grave arena. The job of the coroner's jury was to hear testimony from interested parties and assist the coroner in deter-mining the cause of death. If they concluded that a homicide had been committed, they could, through the coroner, draft an arrest warrant for the suspected murderer. If they deemed a death to have been an accident or act of God, no further investigative action would be taken. It was an awesome responsibility, one the empaneled jurors assumed with sober constitution.

None of the jurors were doctors, but, then, neither was the coroner, a man in his thirties with an ample midsection named Paul Donahue. Like almost all coroners in Georgia, Donahue was an elected official, duly sworn to act on behalf of the good and honorable citizens of the state. The position of coroner dated back to medieval England when organizing the dead was an arduous and often overwhelming task. It had evolved (in Georgia, at least) to something akin to a co-sheriff and circuit judge. The coroner had subpoena powers; he could execute arrest warrants, and serve process; he had the power to compel testimony and could hold any-one who refused to answer his questions in contempt. Since his primary job was to determine a cause of death, he usually allied himself with doc-tors, pathologists, and undertakers who were trained in the science of human expiration. The coroner didn't even need a college degree. His only legal requirements were a high school diploma, no felony convic-tions, and he had to be registered to vote.

The fate of the Douglas Edgar investigation rested in the hands of just such a man. Like a district attorney in front of a grand jury, Donahue would call the witnesses and ask the questions. And like any good public official, he understood theatrics. Wearing a high-collared suit, he made sure all the jurors and witnesses were present before making his grand en-trance, at which point he called the hearing to order and asked everyone to take their seats.

Jurors nestled themselves in hard-back wooden chairs near the front of the room while witnesses sat in folding chairs normally reserved for graveside services and tent revivals.

"Bringing the session to order, the question before this coroner's jury is the manner and cause of death in the case of James Douglas Edgar, one citizen of Newcastle, England, who resided on three-eighty-five West Peachtree Street and was employed by the Druid Hills Golf Club as professional golfer," Donahue said. "Mr. Edgar was officially pronounced deceased at twelve fifty-one on August ninth of this, the year of our Lord, nineteen hundred twenty-one. The first witness in this matter is Doctor George H. Noble, Jr., hereby called."

Dr. Noble was a handsome man, tall and square-jawed with a sturdy carriage that drew the eye. He wore a sacque suit with the large knot of a tie perched at the base of his strong neck. When called forward, he placed his ever-present black doctor's bag on the chair he had vacated: the Alpha intellect marking his territory.

After swearing in the witness, Donahue presented Noble with Edgar's death certificate. "Do you recognize this document, Dr. Noble?"

"Yes."

"Could you identify it for us?"

"It is the certificate of death for J. Douglas Edgar, the one I—"

"And is that your signature on the death certificate, Doctor?"

It appeared as though Noble had been trying to say just that before being interrupted. Donahue must have known it, too. He seemed to be sending a message about who was in charge of this proceeding. Witnesses were to answer the questions asked of them—nothing more, nothing less.

"It is," Noble said.

For the next hour, Donahue walked Noble through his actions in the early-morning hours of August 9. Noble had been the first physician to examine Edgar, and had realized immediately that the man had died from massive blood loss caused by a puncture of the femoral artery.

"The cut was on the interior of the leg approximately six inches above the left knee," Noble said. "It was about one half inch in length and approximately three inches deep. It entered the leg at a slight upward angle puncturing the femoral artery and causing the patient to hemorrhage. He died of blood loss in a very short amount of time."

"Do you have any idea what could have caused such an injury?" Donahue asked.

Comer was surprised by the question, and from the look on Donahue's face, the coroner wanted to snatch the words out of the air and start over.

Too late. Dr. Noble said, "That is a most curious and odd circumstance. The cut in the trousers leg, by whatever the instrument which made this deep and fatal wound, was very small, almost smaller than the wound itself. It must have been driven in with great force and extracted quickly. While I cannot say for certain, it appears to have been a slender object such as a stiletto."

Donahue's back stiffened and his nose crinkled. His inexperience in Socratic examination had allowed Noble to plant the first seeds of doubt about the hit-and-run theory. This was obviously unacceptable, as the coroner assumed a stronger posture and ratcheted up the tone of his questioning for the next several minutes.

"Was there not also massive bruising on the legs of the deceased?" he asked.

"There was bruising on the ankles," Noble said. "The extent is difficult to judge given the blood loss."

Strike two, Comer thought. The bumper of a car would have left massive bruising and fractures of both legs at the knees, not the ankles. A group of men grabbing and manhandling Edgar, however, could have caused such bruises.

Almost three hours into Dr. Noble's testimony, Donahue finally got to the question he wanted. "In your opinion, Dr. Noble, could these injuries have resulted from the impact of an automobile running at high speed?" he asked.

Comer wondered how the coroner's question could have been more leading. The wound *could* have been caused by a Martian ray gun out of an H. G. Wells novel. It was most likely caused, as Dr. Noble indicated, by a long, slim strip of steel, or a stiletto. To imply that this was a hit-and-run, cut-and-dried, no need for anything more than confirmation, said it all. Donahue had bought into the collective thinking of the political power wielders in town. A traffic accident was needed to advance a cause and promote an agenda, so, by granny, a traffic accident was what the coroner, a fellow elected official, would give them.

Dr. Noble tried to answer the question in a way that left some room for interpretation. After a long pause he said, "I . . . think so." It was as definitive as the doctor would get. Through the nature of the questioning, he must have understood what Donahue was doing, and he wasn't going to make too big a fuss. Plus, he'd been on the stand all morning. If the jurors didn't get it by lunch, there wasn't much Noble could do. Sure, the wound could have been caused by a speeding car, if that car had an inch-wide blade sticking out at a perfect angle to catch a man in a vital artery, and if the man were so nimble that he could pull away without tearing half his leg off, and if, at that same moment, a gust of wind had blown the man's cap ten yards away, and if said man had, for some inexplicable reason, left one fully laced and tied shoe in the bushes near the front door of his boardinghouse.

With Dr. Noble's testimony going much longer than anyone had imagined, Donahue adjourned the proceedings until the afternoon when more witnesses would be called.

As he walked out the undertaker's back door and filled his lungs with fresh summer air, Comer asked himself again why he had to be Edgar's lone champion. The man was an undisciplined philanderer. It had become apparent that, as much as his friends loved him, Edgar had lived for the moment. Money was nothing more to him than a means of getting to the next day, and he spent whatever he had whenever he had it. The good times were always very good, and the bad times were . . . well, the man bled to death alone in a street. It was ironic that Comer would be the one to take up the cause of this man. The power structure of an overachieving adolescent city was pushing for a politically expedient outcome, and an overachieving minor figure in a powerful Atlanta family was the only man standing athwart this onrushing train.

Why are you doing it, Comer?

Because it was the right thing to do would have been the easiest answer, but that was incomplete. This felt like a compulsion. He had no choice. Every fiber of his body screamed for him to stand for logic and reason, to be the one skeptic willing to break with the collectivist mind set. He wasn't doing this for Edgar; he was doing it for himself, and for his city. He was doing it to purge himself of some of the go-along and get-along guilt of past sins. No matter what consequences were wrought, Comer committed himself to bathe in the truth as he knew it.

Lloyd Wilhoit was the first person called after lunch. The city editor looked like a wrinkled prune. He would be a no-nonsense witness, clear with his facts but devoid of speculation. Journalists dealt in grounded truths. That was what Comer had heard since he was in short pants and frills, and Wilhoit, a man who looked like he'd been born in trousers, embodied that code. No matter how hard he tried, the coroner would not get the editor to offer an opinion on anything other than the weather.

From the tone of the questions, Donahue must have known he was dealing with a biting old bloodhound who could take a nip out of his hand at any moment. After a number of "please state your name and occupation" type of questions to establish a rhythm, Wilhoit finally gave a passable explanation for why he and Paul Warwick were in Comer Howell's car on Monday. Then he got to the heart of his testimony.

"We were traveling northbound on West Peachtree a few minutes before midnight when we saw a man lying in the street on the right side of West Peachtree with his feet facing the curb," he said.

"Who saw the man first?" the coroner asked.

"I did."

"And what did you do?"

"I called to Mr. Howell, who was driving the motorcar, that there was a man in the street, and that he should stop immediately."

"And then?"

"We all got out of the car and found Mr. Edgar lying facedown in a growing pool of blood. He was not conscious, but he was breathing. This was a few minutes after midnight. We were the first to reach the body, so we each set out in search of a telephone to call for an ambulance."

The mention of the blood sent Comer's stomach into tailspins. He had almost forgotten, or at least pushed it to the back of his conscience. He still hadn't gotten a restful sleep—God only knew when that would come—so he watched yellow finches in a birch tree and let his mind wander as Wilhoit continued his perfunctory recitation of things Comer already knew.

Wilhoit was excused. The manner of Edgar's death had been established. The cause of the trauma was still an open question.

The heat of the afternoon brought Lester Shivers to the chair. His face looked pained as he agreed to tell the truth as he knew it to this jury.

"What was your relationship with Mr. Edgar?" Donahue asked.

Shivers winced before saying, "He was a very dear friend in addition to being my golf instructor and occasional playing partner."

"Is it true that you spent most of the day on Monday with Mr. Edgar?"

"That is true. We played golf together at Brookhaven on Monday afternoon, and around seven o'clock I invited Mr. Edgar to my home at 75 Springdale Road for supper, and he accepted. He had not been to my home since returning to America, and my wife and I very much looked forward to him joining us. My daughter, Caroline, dined with us as well. After supper the four of us engaged in a game of bridge. Caroline had to leave us and return downtown around nine o'clock, so we played a three-handed game until shortly after ten o'clock when my wife also retired. Mr. Edgar and I conversed for another hour or so."

"What did you discuss?"

"Many things. His plans for the rest of the golf season, as well as his health, and his affairs. He spent a great part of the evening speaking of his wife and children, most especially his daughter. He quite looked forward to them joining him next month. He said he had been looking for an apartment that would be nice and comfortable for them somewhere near Druid Hills."

That answered one of Comer's questions. During their earlier conversation Shivers had said "I believe [Edgar] had things worked out." It had jumped out at Comer as a curious thing to say, so much so that he had made a note of it. Now, he thought he knew what it meant. Whatever problems Edgar might have had on the family front appeared to have been reconciled. If there had been dalliances or other problems at home, the months Edgar had spent in England must have salved the wounds.

"Then what happened?" the coroner asked.

"He spoke of taking a streetcar back to the home he and Mr. Tommy Wilson shared on West Peachtree. Of course, I insisted on driving him home in my motorcar, which I did. We reached the corner across from Mr. Edgar's boarding house—385 West Peachtree—and he got out, standing on the curb a few minutes while we talked. Then I drove on West Peachtree to Fourth Street and thence to Peachtree and on home."

"Did you see any other persons?"

"No, I did not."

"Did you see or hear any other motorcar?"

"I did not see or hear any other car in the vicinity."

"Finally, Mr. Shivers—and thank you for taking the time to be here today to testify in his matter—how would you characterize Mr. Edgar that evening? How did he appear?"

Comer almost fell out of his chair. *Why not just say it? Was the man drunk?*

Shivers stiffened at the question. He knew the rumors and insinuations that were being made. He raised his chin slightly and answered, "Normal. He was perfectly normal in every way."

Lester Shivers nodded to his friends, including Comer, before he left. Then Miss L. S. Warren was called. She had been fanning herself for hours, but like a punched-out fighter, her arms had finally given way. By the time she took the chair nearest the jurors, her white face glistened with moisture beneath her bonnet while the pace of the fanning had slowed.

"Miss Warren, how did you know the deceased?" Donahue asked.

"I did not know him well at all," she said. "I had been his neighbor for only a few short weeks, since he returned to Atlanta from England I believe. He was renting a room in the neighboring boarder house with the other younger fellow, Mr. Wilson. They seemed like fine gentlemen. I did not know until after Mr. Edgar had lived there for a week or more that he was a world famous golfing champion. I don't play much golf myself at my age, you see."

"Yes, ma'am," the coroner interrupted. "Moving forward, can you describe the events of Monday night for us?"

"Certainly," she said, the fanning hand picking up steam again. "I was awakened in the night, around midnight, by a loud noise near the house."

"Would you characterize the noise as a crash?" Donahue asked.

If Comer had known the coroner would be leading the witnesses like this he would have brought a bridle and bit from the tack room in the family carriage house.

"I imagine you could," Miss Warren said. "It was followed by a groan, which I distinctly heard. I went to the window and saw a man lying in the street. I did not see it, but I also heard a motorcar. It seemed to be going out West Peachtree Street, and from the sound it made, it was a powerful car traveling rapidly."

"What did you do then?"

"I telephoned the police, and reported what I had seen and heard," she said.

Comer shook his head again at his own stupidity. While he and Wilhoit and Warren had been calling for every ambulance in town, the little old lady next door had remained collected enough to telephone the police, who could, of course, reach the necessary emergency medical personnel much easier than a private citizen. In the heat of the moment, their first decision had been a bad one. Not that it mattered much: Edgar was too far gone for anyone to save him. Still, these proceedings would be reported and transcribed, the testimony living for many, many years to come. Anyone interested in looking would know that the first men on the scene had run amok like field rabbits while the neighbor lady in her nightgown had taken charge.

Donahue thanked Miss Warren and dismissed her. It was getting late in the afternoon, and Comer feared he would not be called at all. If the jury thought they had heard enough to render a bill, there was nothing he could do. His heart sank when he heard Donahue call Tommy Wilson. This would likely be the last witness, which was something of a shock. The coroner hadn't even called Detective Lowe. Donahue had questioned only those witnesses he thought would bolster the hit-and-run story.

Comer hung his head knowing that Tommy Wilson fit into that category as well. And that was Comer's fault.

"We were livin' together until he foond a proper place fre the family, summat canny like, near the club," Tommy said.

The jurors stared at him like he had two heads. After two years in Atlanta, Tommy's Geordie accent had softened into a charming mix of northern England lyricism with a tint of Southern drawl. But when he got nervous he reverted to the language of his youth, which, while technically English, bore only a faint resemblance to the vernacular of the men in the wooden chairs.

Donahue pretended to understand Tommy perfectly. He asked the next question a little slower. Perhaps making the witness comfortable would also make him more intelligible.

"Can you tell us your experiences from Monday night?" the coroner said.

"Yeh, sure. Aboot twelve-thorteen o'clock on Tuesday mornin' Ah got oot o' bed te ger a drink o' water. As Ah woz getting back into bed Ah hord a motorcar drive up in front o' the hoose an' stop, an Ah imagine thet woz the car in which Mr. Edgar retorned. A few minutes later, Ah canna say jus' hoo lang, Ah heard a car comin' at high speed, judgin' by the exhaust. Then Ah hord the car stop. Then it started off again. Ah paid ne attention tiv it until a few minutes later when someone came into the hoose askin'

te use a telephone, an sayin' there woz a gadgie whee'd been struck by a car."

"I'm sorry, a what? Could you repeat that last part?" Donahue asked.

"There woz a man in the road struck by a car," Tommy said. *"So Ah jumped oot of bed an' ran doon te the road. Ah recognized Douglas at once."*

Tommy's voice cracked and he had to stop for a few moments. Donahue stood rod straight, his chin high. He did not make eye contact with the jurors. If nothing else, the man knew his theater. Ethel Clayton's latest moving picture, *Wealth*, was playing at the Howard this week, and Constance Talmadge and Harrison Ford were starring in *Wedding Bells*, which would open at the Metropolitan on Friday. None of those performances would best Paul Donahue's dramatic turn in the undertaker's room.

"Am I to understand that Mr. Edgar attempted to speak to you just before he passed?"

"Ah held his heed in me lap, an' leaned close, but he canna make the words. He woz tee far gone."

"And you have been in contact with Mrs. Edgar?"

Tommy nodded. Then he took a deep breath, and said, *"Ah cabled Mrs. Edgar at hyem in The Toon, an' got a cable back frem hor. It has been decided tha' Douglas should be buried here. The funeral service will be to-morrow, Thursday."*

With that, Tommy was excused.

Everyone was tired. A thunderstorm appeared to be brewing to the east, maybe near Stone Mountain, maybe closer. The men on the jury looked like they wanted to get home before it hit, which did not bode well for Comer. A rushed jury made hasty decisions.

The men huddled with Donahue in the rear of the room for a few minutes, and while the voices were hushed, the tone seemed intense. Comer saw the coroner's shoulders stiffen. More talking; and then a collective nodding of heads. One juror hooked his thumbs into the waist of his trousers and rocked on his toes as if satisfied.

The huddle broke, and Donahue raised his hands to get everyone's attention. "It has been decided that more testimony is required in order to render a proper decision in this matter," he said. "Those of you who have not yet been called should make yourself available here tomorrow morning at nine o'clock."

Comer let out a long *"whewww,"* only then realizing he had been holding his breath.

CHAPTER 14

The Edgars sailing to America.

About ten years ago, when I was in the same state as everybody else in America—hitting golf shots by luck while stupefied by bad theories—I happened to meet the man I consider to be not only the best golfer I ever saw, but the man who knew the most about the game as well. I refer to Douglas Edgar. In my opinion, he was undoubtedly a genius.

—Tommy Armour

There were only smiles after Doug's Canadian Open win. He was, once more, the jolly champion, quick to buy drinks (in Canada) and happy to be the center of the party. He didn't dwell on the win, though. He felt certain there would be plenty more to come. No need to become emotional about it. In fact, it wasn't until later that year when his star student, Miss Alexa Stirling, won the Canadian Women's Championship (also played at Hamilton Golf and Country Club) that Doug wept tears of pride and joy.

His own game, while one of the best in the world, didn't seem as important to him as advancing his swing theories and revolutionizing the game through his students. "He was a wonderful teacher, a natural really," Bob Jones would say later. "I think he leaned more toward instruction than playing, but he was equally brilliant at both."

Doug certainly enjoyed the perks of being a champion, and he didn't lack for ego, taking on all challengers and continuing to win most of his matches, but he talked only about his personal accomplishments when he was teaching. In September of 1919 he and Jones took Leo Diegel and Jim Barnes to nineteen holes in an exhibition match at East Lake prior to the Southern Open before Diegel made a long putt for birdie to win one-up. Even though Doug carried his young partner for most of the day, he had nothing but praise for "Little Bob" after the match. *"Bob's game woz off from the start, but he continued te work an' improve throughout the day until the end o' the match when he woz shootin' better than par golf,"* Edgar said. *"He stuck wi' it 'til the end."*

He also used his own game to illustrate lessons to his students. *"In Canada, Ah found tha' a draw would ride the wind on the par fives,"* he told O. B. Keeler. *"Most o' the players faded the ball again' the wind, 'cos of an out-of-bounds fence on the right-hand side, but if ye kna' ye can play a draw, ye have nee fear o' the out-of-bounds, 'cos ye kna' the ball's not gannin' there. Ah played it out over the out-of-bounds wi' a draw an' let the wind take it well past every else's shot. Tha' was a big advantage."*

He never missed a teachable moment, and when it came to his students, he could go on for hours about what they had done, how much they had improved, what scores he had been able to extract from the athletically challenged. Not long after his Canadian Open win, a wealthy

Northeastern industrialist named H. J. Topping, a fine player who summered in Pinehurst, sought out Edgar for a lesson. Topping fought a slice, a shot that would curve farther and farther to the right as the pressure mounted. No matter how hard he tried, the man's shots spiraled to the right, costing him distance and making it all but impossible for him to play holes that doglegged from right to left. Despite the best efforts of pros from around the world, Topping could not work the ball from right to left.

"The bad golf o' the present day is chiefly due te the fact tha' golfers gan te play golf with the wrong idea in their heads, namely, te try te clout the ball instead of concentrating on swinging the club," Doug said. *"This brings in all the golfin' faults sooch as pressin', slicin', socketin', pullin', smotherin', an' losin' balance.*

"Every golfer knows how beautiful the swing is when ye swing at a daisy as ye wait yer turn te play. Yet, once ye've the ball to clout instead o' a daisy, 'Phut!' the swing is ne more. Why? 'Cos the ball beats ye! This little ball proves stronger than ye, an' you're not able te swing the club at the ball, even though ye can do it every time at the daisy."

Topping listened intently, and followed Doug's instructions. It seemed so simple, the student was skeptical at first. How could the golf swing that had so befuddled him—the one that countless pros had made more complicated by turns—be reduced to such an effortless motion? Edgar wasn't telling him to do twenty-five things during the swing: if anything, the pro was eliminating a dozen movements he said were unnecessary. Fifteen minutes with Doug and Topping was hitting the ball straight. Another fifteen and he hit the first draws of his life.

The man was so ecstatic he retrieved his pouch and paid Doug the staggering sum of $275 on the spot. But that wasn't enough for Topping. He was so grateful that he promised to pay for Doug's next trip to the British Open. "Whenever you return, I will pay all your expenses," the man said.

Not all of his students were so generous, but the audience for Doug's theories was growing exponentially. So much of what he said made sense that many wondered why no one had said it before. "For many years certain principles of this game have been treated as sacred; to breathe against them was heresy," Doug wrote in 1920. "Whenever any famous player has literally disregarded and flouted these principles, he has been described as the exception that proves the rule, the genius who is a law unto himself, and on no account to be copied. It seems never to have struck people that the truth was to be found much nearer home, namely, that said principles were not only nonessential, but very misleading.

"Surely, golf may be allowed to move with the times as everything else does! Because certain principles were said to be right fifteen or twenty years ago, is that any reason why they should be slavishly adhered to today?"

Doug had learned from his own trial-and-error experience that the traditional theories of the game were not just pliable, many of them were simply wrong. His struggles had proved that creativity and simplification were paramount to good golf, and great golf instruction.

"Take, for example, the supremely orthodox and very much belabored maxim, 'Keep your head rigidly still with your eyes steadfastly fixed on the ball throughout,' " Doug wrote. "Watch the best players; surely their heads move a little on the backswing. . . . Or let us consider the other equally sacred maxim, 'Turn the left wrist on the backward swing until it is underneath the shaft at the top.' The left wrist turns a little on the backward swing, but do not strive to get it completely underneath the shaft at the top. The left wrist must turn sufficiently to allow it to be bent to a certain extent, but if it is completely underneath the shaft, power is lost, and, unless some adjusting is made later on, slicing will result."

If golf heretics were burned at the stake, Doug would have been doomed. Luckily, he presented these theories in a place, America, where the game was fresh and new, and at a time, the dawn of the 1920s, when challenging orthodoxy was applauded as avant-garde.

"My keenest delight and pleasure in this game has not been in playing but in teaching," he wrote. "Often I have become tired of much playing, but never of teaching—so many pupils with different physical powers and diverse temperaments, each with his own particular troubles to be met and overcome, have always been to me a great source of interest."

While his ideas about the swing would not become mainstream for several decades, his theories on the psychology of golf had an immediate impact.

"It is desperately difficult to prevent the ball from beating one at times, as I have too often found to my bitter cost at tournaments," he wrote.

It is up to you not to allow the ball to intimidate and beat you, nor to allow its personality to overpower you. The ball is only an incident that lies in the way of the swing. Eliminate it. Disregard it altogether if you can.

The merest tyro can hit at a golf ball, but it requires great self control for anybody not a natural golfer or a clubswinger to make the club do the right movement. Some golfers swing back correctly and are in an excellent position at the top of the swing, and then something goes amiss. Whether the ball hypnotizes them, or whether it is fear or lack of confidence that proves their undoing, it is hard sometimes to say; but the result is hopeless.

The difference between a game played with a stationary ball, such as golf, and a game played with a moving ball, such as cricket, lawn tennis, or even ping-pong, is that in the former your ball is your chief opponent, while in the latter you are playing against the brains of your opponent or opponents. Golf, therefore, can be taught, but it seems doubtful whether the other games can be. As a rule, the greatest players of the other games have either taught themselves, or more likely have had a natural aptitude or genius for them.

Either the ball will master your swing, or your swing will master the ball.

In the case of Doug's own game, his swing had become the master. He returned to England in the fall to retrieve Meg and the kids (a trip that had a far less disastrous effect on his system this time around), and was surprised by the superstar status he had obtained. He assumed that news of his win had reached *The Toon,* but he had no idea how celebrated he had become. Just as Atlanta took pride in victories from their own, the whole of Newcastle cheered the triumphant return of their international champion.

Doug took full advantage, scheduling a few big-money matches while he was home, and playing in a couple of exhibitions. His only loss came in a thirty-three-hole match at Northumberland against the best-ball of the city's two best amateurs, Peter Rainford and Syd Ball. The pair won the match three-and-two, but Doug still made off with a handsome appearance fee. During the remainder of the trip, he beat all comers, often topping the three best-balls of some of the region's most accomplished golfers.

At first Meg embraced her husband's fame. They had toiled in the darkness for so long it felt good to bask in his glow. However, staying home and enjoying Doug's accomplishments from four thousand miles away was much different from loading up the family and leaving the only country she had ever known. Even though she'd had eight months to prepare for the move to America, when the day came to board the boat, Meg was neither ready nor happy. Not only did she not share her husband's zestful adventurism, she was scared, a fact she shared only with her sister, Lilly, her closest sibling and confidante. Meg had no idea what to expect in Atlanta—new people, new culture, and a strange, new land—but she also feared what might happen with her husband.

He hadn't been home long, but Meg noticed changes, subtle things no one but a life partner would see or feel. Everyone understood that Doug's gusto, while a great attribute and the main reason he was experiencing such professional success now, was also his Achilles' heel. Alone for seven months in a foreign country, flush with new money and fame, a social animal like Doug Edgar would no doubt be a magnet for trouble. Meg hoped her fears were unfounded—an extension of her anxiety about leaving home—but in the back of her mind she knew she needed to keep a close eye on her husband, no matter what country they were in.

The trip was uneventful; the week at sea becoming old-hat for the now world-famous sportsman. The kids loved it, frolicking from bow to stern and turning the ship into a giant floating playground. Then they spent two days in New York where they stared open-mouthed at the Woolworth Building, an astonishing fifty-seven-story tower jutting above the surrounding cityscape, and a grand monument to what was possible in America.

Their new home in Atlanta, a white cottage with a front porch and a fence at 221 Williams Hill Road, oozed the kind of charm synonymous with the South. Still, Meg seemed wistful from the beginning. A letter to Lilly from eleven-year-old Rhoda dated January 25, 1920, provided a glimpse into what would become a worsening family dynamic.

> My Dear Aunt Lilly,
>
> How are you keeping now? I was pleased to read the letter you sent to mummy. It seemed to buck me up a little to learn all the news of old Gosforth. We got the post cards and Douglas and I are going to take one each to school to let the teacher see them, but the only thing the matter is that I am feeling homesick.

The day before yesterday we had an awful thunderstorm. Mummy was out in it. She was terrified. The thunder shook the ground and the lightning was flashing one after the other, and the rain; Oh! I thought that it was never going to stop. It was coming down and going up as far as it could go. This morning it was just as bad.

I like school very much now. How's everybody at the factory? I'm going to write you such a lot of letters, and they are going to be long as well. It is just bucking me up writing to you Aunt Lilly.

Goodbye with love from your loving,
Douglas and
Rhoda

In terms of climate, January in Atlanta, where the average daily high was fifty-two degrees, was a paradise compared with Newcastle, but Meg complained about the weather in every correspondence. Granted, the thunderstorms were a surprise. Rhoda would remember them the rest of her life, telling her own children that they sounded like mortar explosions at the front door with flashes in the night sky that terrorized them all.

As if that were not enough to set them on edge, the people in their neighborhood, while courtly, were a strange and foreign lot who spoke in long, slow rambles as if they had molasses stuck in their cheeks. They seemed friendly enough, although Meg thought them "gossipy" from the outset. The one incident that set her mind against Atlanta and Atlantans came early in their tenure as new residents. As Rhoda described it years later: "Mum and Douglas and I were walking on the sidewalk when an older black woman approached the other way. I stopped and stepped aside to let her pass, as I'd been taught. Then another woman, one of the proper ladies of Atlanta, lit into Mum and me, saying that a white girl was never to step aside for a negro. Mum didn't say anything at the time, but I could tell she was furious. I think that was the beginning of the end for her."

It also didn't help that Doug spent so much time at the club or on the road playing tournaments. When he was home, he seemed distant and distracted, as if he had other things or other people on his mind. It was difficult to begrudge him getting in as many competitive rounds as possible. He'd lost a lot of time during the war. Now, there was plenty of money in tournament golf, or so it seemed. One of the winter events in Los Angeles had paid out a purse of $10,000, a sum healthy enough to make the dusty cross-country train trip worth it for East Coast and Midwest pros.

Doug hadn't gone to California, but the *New York Times* reported in January that he would return to Deal to play in the 1920 British Open along with Walter Hagen, Jock Hutchison, and Jim Barnes, a fact that was surprising and unwelcome news to Meg. They had just arrived in America, and she was not amused to learn of her husband's British Open intentions—a monthlong trip that would be made without her—from the nation's largest newspaper. She chalked it up as another in a growing list of indignities.

Doug assured her that the paper had gotten it wrong, that he didn't have any plans concerning the Open, even though he had already informed the members at Druid Hills of his plans to play, going so far as to say he "hoped to take Bob Jones and Perry Adair with me, if they will go." Robert P. Jones, Bob's father, had said, "He will," at the time, a tidbit Doug left out of subsequent discussions with Meg.

It turned out he would not go to the Open that year. The Georgia Amateur Championship was the same week, and Doug had to prepare his charges for the state title. He did, however, leave his wife and kids alone to unpack their crates while he trekked off to Pinehurst for the North and South Open, one of the premier tournaments in the country. Fred McLeod, winner of the 1908 U.S. Open, won in the Carolina sand hills, but Doug had another good week, issuing notice to the best players in the game that his 1919 records were no fluke.

He stayed in Pinehurst a few extra days afterward to spend time with Mr. Topping and a few of his friends, another decision that did not sit well at home. Once he got back to Atlanta, Doug tamped down the home fires by staying near Druid Hills through the remainder of the spring, but by the first of July—in the midst of a sweltering heat wave unlike anything Meg had ever experienced, and one she thought might be the end of her— he prepared to embark on a whirlwind tournament schedule, most of it without the family. *The American Golfer* previewed the coming season with action shots of the stars expected to compete in a plethora of summer events: J. H. Taylor demonstrating his follow-through; Walter Hagen illustrating his wide stance; Princeton golf star Simpson Dean at the top of the backswing; and J. Douglas Edgar, "the Atlanta star and one of the most accurate approachers in golf," eyeing a pitch shot. At the center of the piece was Harry Vardon gripping a spoon, his massive hands enveloping the leather wrapping on the end of the hickory shaft.

Vardon and Ted Ray were spending the summer in America, the

duo's first transatlantic trip since their celebrated 1913 tour. The antici-
pated return of the Britons was all the rage among fans of the game. Vardon and Ray were certainly on Doug's radar. He had beaten them in
France before the war, and set a scoring record that neither man had come
close to touching. The only missing piece to the puzzle in his mind was a
head-to-head victory in America.

He got his chance in July.

Doug had traveled to New York to play in the Shawnee Open and the
Metropolitan Golf Association Open, called The Met, another big tournament that drew a stellar field. In the week separating the two events, he
played several practice rounds at Greenwich Country Club, site of the
Met Open. It was during one of those rounds that he got an invitation.

According to the *New York Times,*

In one of the groups of players and caddies which dotted the Greenwich Country Club course yesterday morning was J. Douglas Edgar.
This Englishman, who adopted America only a couple of years ago,
should have been in Atlanta where he is professional at the Druid Hills
Club. But he wasn't. He was on a junket up North. Early last week he
played in the Shawnee Open and clicked off a 70 for one round, a feat
not at all surprising for Edgar, since last year he won the Canadian
Open with a total of 279, the lowest ever made for seventy-two holes.

J. Douglas was trying to mind his own business yesterday. He had
decided to stay north until after the Metropolitan Open championship
this week and pay a visit to the Greenwich links where most of the Eastern pros will battle for Walter Hagen's title. In short, Edgar was inspecting the course and trying to keep as cool as possible. He knew Harry
Vardon and Ted Ray were on hand for an exhibition, but paid no attention to this, for Edgar had played with his fellow English countrymen
so much in recent years that the experience had long since ceased to ex-
cite him.

Edgar was playing the second hole when up came a panting, per-
spiring messenger with a strange kind of summons. "Will you pair up
with Tom Kerrigan and play Vardon and Ray?" he gasped. "Jim Barnes
was scheduled to play, but has not arrived." The truth was that Edgar
was a bit "peeved" at being asked to play a second fiddle, but probably
it was just as well, for Edgar and Kerrigan, this patched-up team, went
out and defeated Vardon and Ray by three and two, the first defeat
chalked up on the Britons' record on this tour.

It was Edgar who had most to do with the victory. He won the first
hole with a birdie three and continued to display golf which only a

champion can exhibit. At the turn, Edgar had equaled the Greenwich par of 35, which Vardon had needed 39, Ray 38, and Kerrigan 36. Edgar made scarcely a slip for the rest of the morning and finished the round with a 72 to Vardon's 78, Ray's 76, and Kerrigan's 73.

The superintendent estimated that twelve hundred people saw the match. Meg Edgar was one of them. Doug had sent for her between tournaments. They hadn't seen each other in almost a month, and the summer season was just getting into full swing. Meg would describe the events of her trip in a letter to Lilly written on the veranda at the Sun Dial Inn in Greenwich:

Dear Lilly,

You will be surprised to read of me being in Greenwich, about forty miles north of New York. Douglas was up here playing and I thought I would like a trip up. I'm sitting by the seashore writing this, looking into the Atlantic, and just so hot.

Well, Douglas and I are going to New York on Tuesday to do a little shopping. I want a white skirt and a new white sailor hat and new white shoes, since I did not know I was going to travel around. Then we will come back to Greenwich and Douglas plays a tournament here on Wednesday, so I will follow him round.

He played Vardon and Ray here on Saturday and beat them three up, and in doing so, there was great excitement. Given the fuss people made over me, I thought I had been playing.

Then we will travel back to New York again on Wednesday, and stay there awhile before I leave for that darned old Atlanta again. The children are fit and staying with my house sitter.

Your dearest,
Meg

It was the last trip Meg would make with her husband. At least she got to see some of his best golf. After beating Vardon and Ray he shot 71 in the opening around of the Met Open, putting him in fourth place with only Jim Barnes, Walter Hagen, and Willie MacFarlane ahead of him.

Scores went up in the second round, but Doug stayed steady, shooting 75 to inch a little closer to the lead. At the halfway mark, he was alone in third, five shots off Barnes's lead and three shots behind MacFarlane.

The Friday thirty-six-hole final was filled with drama, and Doug was right in the middle of all of it. Barnes had an awful putting round in the morning, shooting 78, while Hagen, the two-time defending champion looking to make it three Met titles in a row, shot a course-record 69 to gain a one-shot lead going into the afternoon. Doug stayed in third place, three shots off the lead thanks to a 73. It was as close as he could come. An afternoon 76 was good enough for sole possession of third place, but four shots out of the playoff between Barnes and Hagen; Hagen would go on to win his third consecutive Met Open the following day.

According to the *New York Times*, "Edgar, the Canadian champion, beat MacFarlane out for third place which carried a purse of one hundred dollars. His eagle on the thirteenth in the morning, when he deliberately hooked his second shot around a clump of trees and onto the green, and when he followed this with an eight-foot putt, was one of the most delicately achieved feats of the whole tourney. Despite a run of two, three, three, three on the start of the second half, Edgar shot 73 because of a seven and a five that followed, although par would have given him a course record of 68. His total for seventy-two holes was 296, and MacFarlane's 297."

One of the first people to congratulate Doug was his student H. J. Topping, a member at Greenwich Country Club, who not only qualified for the Metropolitan Open, but shot a respectable 310 to finish twenty-fourth in the field and second among the amateurs behind Yale star Jess Sweetser.

After the final round, another amateur approached Doug and asked if he could spare some time to help him. "I simply can't hit the ball straight enough," said Tommy Armour, who shot an 80 and a 76 on the final day to finish well back in the pack.

Doug put his arm around the skinny young Scot and said, "*'Course ye can, man! Anybody can clout it straight enough. Ye just have te be shown how te.*"

Armour spent the remainder of 1920 learning Edgar's way.

After the Met Open and a couple of dinners in New York, Meg left for "darned old Atlanta," her new white skirt, hat, and shoes tucked in her luggage. Doug kissed her goodbye and hopped a train for Chicago where he played in the Western Open at Olympia Fields. Then it was off to

Toledo, Ohio, where the USGA was hosting its Open Championship at the Inverness Club.

With Vardon, Ray, Hagen, Diegel, Hutchison, Barnes, McLeod, Jack Burke, Sr., Willie MacFarlane, and, of course, Edgar in the field along with noted amateurs Bob Jones, Chick Evans, and Tommy Armour, interest in the U.S. Open was as high as it had been since the war. According to *The American Golfer*:

> When the vanguard of the big field began to arrive a day or two before the qualifying rounds were started, they found that every arrangement had been completed. They found a very fine golf course in excellent condition—a course well trapped and well bunkered, without a blind hole or a touch of trickery; smooth, rolling greens that gave one a chance to go for the cup, and a fairway that completely wrecked the ancient alibi of the cuppy lie.
>
> They found also that from the Inverness Club officials and officials of the United States Golf Association that no single detail had been overlooked to handle the banner championship of American golf. Inverness had put on its gala attire for this occasion. Thousands had gathered from the first day, including both the beauty and chivalry of the Midwestern citadel, where, darting back and forth among the shifting crowds, alert photographers spent their time in snapping the golfers or photographing some section of the gallery where vari-colored feminine costumes caught and held the eye.

Doug welcomed the distractions. He played late in the opening round with Mike "King" Brady and had one of the best ball-striking days of his career, and one of the best ever witnessed in a major tournament. Doug shot 73, and when they came in, Brady told a group of reporters, "I have just stood witness to the greatest round of golf that has ever been played or that may ever be played. [Edgar] never had a putt outside ten feet, and he never made one. If his putter had been on, he would have won this tournament before it even began."

He was tied for third place with Bob McDonald after the opening round, trailing only Hutchison, who shot 69, and Diegel, who came in with 72.

No one is sure what happened next, but Doug later offered his version this way: *"Between the first an' second rounds a fella came to me an' sez he wanted te offer me a pro job in New York. Ah divin't kna' who he woz, but it sounded a canny job, and Ah'd be makin' three times what Ah woz earning in Atlanta. Well, it broke me concentration. Ah couldn't focus on me own game fre thinking about tha' job. Well, Ah played terrible in the second round, an 82, shootin' mesel' reet out of it. After tha', Ah couldn't find the gadgie again. Ah never heard another word about the job."*

Once again, he was close to breaking out, but failed to hold his game together for four rounds. He closed the final day with respectable rounds of 74 and 78 to finish twentieth, a dozen shots behind winner Ted Ray, who had made his return to America a triumph.

As Grantland Rice wrote of that Open:

> By the flip of a coin—the turn of a card—a wink from one of the gods of chance—a breath blown from destiny—and one man wears the laurel where four men wait in the shadows, beaten by a margin entirely too thin and vague to be pictured by mere words. It is taking no credit from Ted Ray to present the case from this viewpoint. The crown of American golf champion is his, fairly won and fairly earned by the mightiest hitting and finest putting ever seen in one of our championships.
>
> But it is at least adding a sprig or two to the olive wreaths deserved by Harry Vardon, Leo Diegel, Jock Hutchison, and Jack Burke to show by what an infinitely thin wedge victory can be separated from defeat.
>
> Only those who were banked around the last fairway at Inverness in the waning summer sunlight verging upon August dusk can understand the thrill of the continued climax as one by one each fighting survivor took his shot at the title, only to miss by a hair's breadth as big Ted Ray emerged triumphant to carry our championship cup on its second long journey to English shores, where the milk white cliffs of the little kingdom await its coming.

Doug didn't ponder his second-round collapse for long. He had finished high enough to earn another check, and played well enough to earn even greater respect from his peers. He also didn't have time to dwell on rounds gone by. Ray won the U.S. Open on August 13. Three days later, the PGA Championship got under way back in Chicago at Flossmoor Country Club. Doug hopped a train north for the two-hundred-mile ride to within sight of where he'd been only a week before (Olympia Fields, which hosted the Western Open, abuts Flossmoor Country Club). Better planners would have scheduled the Western and the PGA back-to-back. But, then, nobody asked the pros, and none of them were about to complain. They were entertaining crowds in the thousands and earning legions of fans with every swing. It was paradise, a life Doug never thought possible, and one he planned on living to the fullest for as long as it lasted.

Meanwhile, back in Atlanta, Meg's discontent grew by the day. On August 18, with her husband having a stellar season, she wrote to her sister:

Dear Lilly,

I know you will be thinking you are not going to hear from me again, but really there is no news to give you. It is much harder for me to write to you than it is for you to write to me, and you don't know anybody here. The place is so dead and quiet, the only little bit of excitement for me is a thunderstorm. We have them about every third day, and some storm, too.

It is so hot that in writing this the perspiration is just simply standing on me, and I only have on a petticoat and a thin dressing gown. Douglas is killing and pressing bugs on paper. Rhoda is reading the funny pieces out of the Sunday paper. Douglas is in Chicago playing off in a match he qualified for about three weeks ago. He has been away now about four weeks and won't be home until the second week of September. From Chicago, he goes on to play in the Canadian Championship.

The children are just so hot that I can't keep their clothes clean. Rhoda is in a pair of straps with buttons on for her knickers, and a thin dress, no shoes or stockings. Douglas almost lives in his overalls, no underwear or shoes or stockings. I wish you could see him when he is hot. You really would think he had jumped out of the bath.

I have Darkie every day. He is real good company. I can talk over a lot of things with him, of interest I think. I would have gone crazy if I had not had him to talk with while Douglas has been away.

Love from,
Meg

Four days later, she wrote another letter home.

This darned old trip over here has taught me such a lesson. People will think I'm crazy now when I get back, as I won't know anything anymore. No gossip anymore. Anyone coming to me with news will get the right answer. The people here, they are just awful for gossip. They sit all day on their front porches, rocking in their chairs, and talking about people. Really, just to sit and listen and then say "yes or no." If I said another word I probably would have said all kinds of things, so I'm just sick of them. I'm deaf and dumb to everybody.

The weather here is just awful. On Monday, we had very heavy rain and thunder and lightning from eight o'clock in the morning until about six o'clock on the Tuesday morning. It thundered the whole time. You certainly would be scared to death. I was a bit scared during the night, but I've got so used to it, I think of it now as the only bit of excitement (except the gossip). All the electric lights go out, and we are left in darkness except for the lightning. If you could only just see one storm: the thunder simply shakes the place, and does a lot of damage.

Darkie was out playing on Tuesday, and he saw a tree cut right down and the man he was playing with had his clubs taken right out of his hands. I was at the club at the time of the storm. Darkie came in shaking as he had had shell shock. I dare not show fright before he came in, as there was only a great big black nigger in the shop with me, and about six nigger caddies. I thought if they set about me, it would be all up on Wednesday.

I had to go to the club taking the Highland Avenue streetcar, then transfer to the Ponce de Leon car. While I was standing about fifteen minutes waiting, a terrific lightning and then thunderbolt came down. I got palpitations. I thought my end had come and I took one of those funny fits. I was in a right old fix. I had to go into the Druid Hills apartments and wait awhile until I pulled myself together. Then I proceeded to the club for an hour, and returned in the storm. I'm still alive through it all.

I don't think I can say any more. Heaps of love to everybody. Hope to see you all soon.

Love from,
Meg

P.S.: Douglas is going strong in the Pro Golfers match. Today is the last day. I think he will win as there are just two left in now, out of 264 entrants. He leaves later today to play in Ottawa Canada in the Canadian Championship. Then he will be home again in about three weeks' time. I'll let you know how he comes on in Chicago. Of 264 players, sixty-four qualified, then the winner plays the next winner and they run down to two for the final. So there are two left, he and a man called Hutchison.

The Pro Golf match Meg referred to was the Championship of the Professional Golfers' Association of America, more commonly known as the

PGA Championship. Indeed, Doug had not only survived the thirty-six-hole stroke play qualifier, which whittled the field from 264 qualifiers to 64 match play contestants, he had won five matches to get into the finals against Western Open winner and U.S. Open runner-up Jock Hutchison.

As *The American Golfer* put it, "The final test left Hutchison matched against Douglas Edgar, the psycho golfer from Druid Hills, Atlanta, and it was a contest worthy of the title which was at stake. Through the first eighteen holes, it was a give-and-take affair, with neither able to gain any considerable advantage."

Doug jumped out to an early lead with a par and a birdie on the first two holes, both good enough for wins. He remained out front for the first eleven holes, but Hutchison's putter got hot on the back nine. When they broke for lunch after the first eighteen, Hutch had a one-up lead.

Hutch kept the pressure on in the afternoon, winning the second hole with a three. The next three holes were halved before Doug cut into the lead with a fifteen-foot birdie putt at the fifth. Ten minutes later, though, Hutch made another long birdie putt on the par three seventh. Doug then three-putted the eighth to go three down, which is where the match stood when they made the turn with nine holes to play.

Doug then lost the tenth to go four down, but he won the eleventh to cut the margin to three. They halved twelve and thirteen with pars, and then Doug birdied the fourteenth to cut the deficit to two.

The par five fifteenth was a pivotal moment. If Hutch won the hole, he would have Doug dormie, three down with three holes to play. Every hole he halved at that point was like a win. Doug was running out of holes and options. Both men drove into the fairway. Hutch played first and chose to lay up short of the flowing stream that ran in front of the green.

Sensing an opening, Doug pulled his brassie. This was the moment of truth. If the ball made it over the water, he had a chance to cut the lead to one. If he missed the shot, the match would be all but over. All those years perfecting his movement came flooding back to him as he gripped the club and went through his quick pre-shot routine. The swing was as short as usual, but the ball shot off the club and sailed just to the right of the green. From there he chipped to two feet and made the putt for birdie.

Hutch's approach sailed over the flag, and he missed his putt for four. The Scot was one up on the Englishman with three holes to play.

The thirty-fourth hole was the knockout blow, though. After pulling his tee shot, Hutch went back and forth between his spoon and his mashie. The lie was iffy, so near a bunker that hitting the ball fat was a fifty-fifty proposition. After taking his stance with the mashie, Hutch backed away and went back to the wooden club. Then he hit the shot of the tournament—a screaming two-hundred-yard approach that cleared another bunker by an inch. The ball rolled to within ten feet.

Doug had hit a longer tee shot and had an iron into the green, but he misjudged the distance and hit it just onto the front edge, well short of the pin. Then Doug's putter, the one club in his bag that came and went with the wind, abandoned him. With the sixteenth green being wetter than the others on the course, he left his first putt ten feet short of the hole, so short in fact that he didn't lose his turn. When he missed the second putt, Hutch simply had to two-putt to put the match dormie with two holes to play. He did, and it was all but over.

Even though Doug birdied the thirty-fifth hole to force the match to go the distance, he couldn't win the final hole. A halve with pars gave Jock Hutchison a one-up victory, and his second win in three weeks.

Doug was dejected, but not depressed. Hutchison had hit a spectacular shot at the sixteenth, and Doug's putter had let him down. He wasn't happy, but he wasn't disconsolate. He didn't have time. The Canadian Open was five days off. He had to get to Ottawa to defend his title.

The greens at the Rivermead Club in Ottawa let everyone know that there would be no scoring records this week. Undulating, firm, and fast, the slopes of the greens made it almost impossible to get the ball close on an approach. If you were on the wrong side of the green, a three-putt was almost a foregone conclusion. It was critical that players shape their approach shots to complement the curvatures of the greens.

Doug loved it. Any course that required you to bend shots left and right and hit different trajectories played right into the strength of his game. As long as the putter behaved, he liked his chances.

He opened with a 76—not great, but 72 was the lowest score of the day—to put himself in third place. Then he followed it with a 75 to move to within two shots of the lead. That was when he found himself torn. The leader was the young amateur he had been mentoring for the better part of a month. Tommy Armour, the lanky Scot, had come to Doug with a loose swing and no real concept of what made the golf ball fly in a particular fashion. They had worked together in Connecticut, Illinois, and

Ohio with Edgar cramming the boy's head with enough information to earn him a golf Ph.D.

"Ye don't hit the ball on a straight line any more tha' ye'd hoy a ball wi' a straight arm," he told Armour. *"The club travels te the ball from an inside-out path on all canny good shots from all canny good players, even if they divin't kna' it. Now, if ye understand tha', ye've got an advantage, 'cos ye can start the club back on tha' same path, whipping it 'round the right hip ratha' than dibbling wi' taking it straight back an' up. From there ye're in a position where ye can swing freely, an' the club will come back te the ball the proper way."*

Armour learned quickly. The boy had talent and a future. Now he was leading the Canadian Open with two rounds to play.

If Doug didn't win, he would love to see Armour's name on the trophy. Doug tried to ignore Armour—to be a player and not a teacher for a few more days—and he continued to get better with each round. His third-round score was a 74, leaving him tied with a Canadian named Charles Murray, the pro at Royal Montreal Golf Club. Both men trailed Armour by three shots with only eighteen holes left.

In the afternoon, Doug didn't try to make birdies. He knew that the course required more defense than offense. He shaped shots below the holes, took his pars and moved on. A par on the final two holes gave him an early round of 73. He had bettered his scores by one shot with each successive round. With a total of 298, Doug enjoyed a proper Canadian drink as the leader in the clubhouse.

His score was soon matched, though. Murray also shot 73 in the afternoon to post 298.

Neither man thought their scores would hold up. After an even-par opening nine all Armour had to do was shoot 40 on the back nine to win the title. But the situation got to the kid. He took a six at the thirteenth, missed a short par putt at the fifteenth, and almost blew it entirely at the sixteenth when his second shot hit a tree and bounded into the deep rough. Armour was fortunate to salvage a five, but he was left with the daunting task of parring the last two holes to tie Edgar and Murray.

Doug found himself pulling for his pupil, even though it might cost him the championship. When Armour holed a three-foot par putt on the final green for a 76 and a 298 total of his own, Doug was the first person on the green to congratulate him.

The three men would play off for the title the following day, eighteen holes for the national championship of Canada.

Doug had an advantage in the playoff on several fronts. Not only did the course suit his game, he had just come from the PGA Championship final where his was the only group on the course. It is one thing to have several thousand people spread out over eighteen holes watching different players at different times; it's quite another to have every eye trained on you. Doug knew that feeling. Murray and Armour did not.

Murray's tee shots flew like scattering pheasants in the early holes of the playoff. He was fortunate to hit a couple of spectators in the first six holes or he might have lost his ball. Doug made birdies on three and seven, and took a three-shot lead over Murray and a four-shot advantage over Armour into the turn.

Doug faltered at the thirteenth, three-putting for bogey, and again at the sixteenth, where he failed to find the green and couldn't get up and down for par. That allowed Armour to take the lead for the first time all day.

Standing on the seventeenth tee with a one-stroke lead over Doug and a two-shot advantage over Murray, Armour's hand shook so badly he could barely put the ball on a tee.

"Divin't worry about all that, man!" Doug said to his student. *"Just whistle a tune te get yer mind off it. Ah kna' a few if ye need help."*

All three men laughed. But the nerves were too much. Armour hit two balls out of bounds from the seventeenth tee, the first hooking just enough to trickle out of bounds, and the second hitting a rock or a root and bounding out on the fly. His third ball found the fairway and he played the hole normally from there, finishing with a six (out of bounds carried no stroke-and-distance penalty at the time, only a forced replay from the original spot) to Doug's four.

With one hole to play, Doug had a one-shot lead over both his competitors. All three found the fairway on the final hole, but both Murray and Armour hit their approach shots into a bunker. Doug calmly found the green, effectively ending the tournament. He two-putted after Murray blasted out to ten feet and Armour hit his bunker shot slightly longer beyond the hole.

Douglas Edgar became the first man in history to successfully defend the Canadian Open title and the first man to successfully defend a major national championship since Johnny McDermott won back-to-back U.S. Open titles in 1911 and 1912.

None of that mattered to him after the final putt fell, though. As the crowd cheered, Doug shook Murray's hand quickly and then put his arm around Armour's shoulder, pulling the young man close as they walked off the back of the green. Spectators could see Doug talking to the young amateur, but no one could hear what he said. All they saw was Armour nodding his head, and Doug's hand patting the boy on the back.

He traveled straight from Ottawa to Atlanta, the returning champion, now the holder of three national open titles. Even though he was home, he didn't spend a lot of time mending fences on Williams Hill Road. Doug was a star; a handsome one at that. Those Atlantans who had paid little attention to their conquering golf hero before lined up to celebrate his triumphant homecoming. Photographers snapped him at every turn—Doug sitting on a pine bench petting a cat, his clubs propped next to him, trousers pressed just so; Doug addressing a shot, the clubhouse behind him, a hint of a smile on his face; Doug in a dapper cap and sweater standing next to Vardon and Ray, or fondling the watch he received for winning the French Open with a Labrador retriever sitting dutifully at his side. Cultured club members throughout the city claimed to have played with him or learned from him. Demands on his time exploded as lessons from Edgar became social accoutrements. Everyone had an Edgar quote, or a tip they had picked up from the great man himself.

Doug recognized the fleeting nature of fame, and he planned to capitalize on it while it lasted. He had already completed his book *The Gate to Golf,* and had developed the accompanying swing aid—the gate—to go with it. The contraption consisted of a slender curved piece of wood with a hinged arm that acted as a golf tee, along with two other small wooden blocks—chips, really—with sharp pegs to secure them in the ground. According to Doug's writings, "Has it, I wonder, ever struck the reader how much the greatest players of the present time, amateur or professional, differ in their style and method of playing, and yet seem to get there more or less consistently? They have different stances, different kinds of swing, different lengths of swing, different finishes and many have even different grips. What is the secret? Are there several ways of playing golf of the highest order? No! There is only one. Great golfers have individual peculiarities of style and method, but they have one attribute in common, and that attribute is the essential of good golf. Some people call it 'The Pearl of Great Price,' others 'The Golden Key to Golf,' or 'The Master's Secret.' I call it 'The Movement.' To explain what that movement is, whence it is derived, and how it may be achieved is the object of the mechanical contrivance which I have termed 'The Gate.' "

The gate was a swing-path guide. A player would secure the curved piece of wood in the ground so that it pointed toward his target, and then place his ball on the rotating arm. The curvature of the wood would force the player to swing the club on an inside-out path, no different from the thousands of guides that have come and gone over the decades, with one noteworthy exception: Doug's was the first.

He believed that this fundamental—delivering the club on the correct path—superseded everything else in the game. "How often does one read, 'Which is the master hand in golf?' " he wrote. "Does it matter very much? I hardly think so. Let the player decide for himself according to his style and peculiarities. Personally, I am of the opinion that it is best to use whichever hand the stroke or his mood seems to require. Some may prefer both hands to be so blending that they work as one.

"Golf is a more human and less mechanical game than some people imagine."

Doug was more human than mechanical as well. As such, he had a hard time transitioning from the hectic, high-class schedule of a traveling golf champion—dining out and hobnobbing with the best and most beautiful people in the finest cities in North America—to the home life waiting for him in the cottage on Williams Hill Road. The pace of his existence had quickened. He was in great demand, the focal point of every function he attended. Cheers and applause had become an opiate, one he felt depressed to be without once he returned home.

Thankfully, he wasn't out of the spotlight for long. The Vardon and Ray exhibition tour continued with all the full-throated enthusiasm of a traveling carnival, and Doug was part of it. Eight days after collecting his second Canadian Open title, he was off to Alabama to team with a local pro named Charlie Hall against Vardon and Ray at the Country Club of Birmingham. It was the first of three matches Doug would play against Vardon and Ray in three consecutive days.

The Birmingham match, held on September 7, went Doug's way to the surprise of many Alabamians. Even though Vardon and Ray did not seem to be the unstoppable forces they had been during their 1913 tour, they still won the vast majority of their matches. Vardon was still the only man in the world with six British Open titles, and Ray had just won the U.S. Open with Vardon finishing second. They stood as overwhelming favorites in every match they played. The citizens of Birmingham were stunned when the Canadian champion, a striking English fellow hailing from Atlanta, beat the two great champions and acted as though the feat were as easy as shelling peas. Then word spread of Vardon's "one day be the greatest of us all" comment concerning Edgar. Many wondered if that day might have already come.

Doug stayed for the celebration dinner, a ritual that was part of the show everywhere Vardon and Ray played, but he knew he had to travel soon. The next match was in Atlanta at the Brookhaven club. Doug's partner was Howard Beckett, the weakest partner possible for a match of this caliber, but, in addition to being a great friend, he was the host pro. It wouldn't do to say, "Sorry, Beck, we know you don't get much publicity as a player, but we're going to trade you in for the teenager Bob Jones." Besides, the sponsors of the Vardon and Ray tour had been very deliberative in selecting their opponents. Like managing a good boxer, the trick to any successful tour was picking a good fight, just not too good. Fans had to feel that the matches were competitive, and the competition first-rate, but Vardon and Ray were playing six, sometimes seven matches a week and traveling at night. Nobody wanted to see them embarrassed.

The locals in Atlanta didn't seem to question the value of the match. On September 8, the *Atlanta Constitution* breathlessly proclaimed that

> Vardon and Ray are here today for the feature golfing event of the season. This morning at ten o'clock, they will tee off with Douglas Edgar and Howard Beckett for a thirty-six-hole match over the Capital City Club course at Brookhaven. Ted Ray is the greatest driver and most spectacular putter on earth.
>
> Harry Vardon is the greatest figure in the golfing world today. Vardon announced today that he is making his last trip to America and thus his last trip to Atlanta. He is the grand old man of the golfing world and prefers to stay on his side of the pond.
>
> Edgar is the present Canadian champion, winning the title for the second consecutive time a few weeks ago. On his first victory, he turned in the greatest card for seventy-two holes of medal play on record. He has already defeated the two world stars.

Some reporters acknowledged that the Vardon-Ray tour hadn't been the heavyweight slugfest it might once have been. In a separate piece in the *Constitution,* it was noted that "To date the Britishers have not met a super-abundance of worthy opposition in their exhibition matches. But at the rate Edgar has been toppling them over in the big tournaments this season, and Beckett's ability to shoot the Brookhaven course in about 76, the best pair of golfers in the world should meet some merry competition."

Two thousand people were expected to show up for the match. A dinner and dance would follow, with Tracy's Orchestra providing music in the main dining room, tea at five-thirty, and dinner at eight o'clock on the veranda.

Vardon committed a faux pax within minutes of arriving in Atlanta. He had barely gotten into the city limits when he was asked to comment on Bob Jones. "Bob Jones is a very good player," he said, assuming that such a response was more than adequate. It was not. Many Georgians failed to grasp the subtlety of British understatement. They wanted grand proclamations about their Wonder Boy's limitless powers to dominate the game. Nobody in town realized that to an Englishman, being called "a very good player" by someone like Vardon was praise of the highest order.

Harry realized his mistake and hustled off to a private room where he crafted a written statement designed to mollify his hosts. It read: "Bobby Jones is a golfer without a fault. He plays practically all his shots to perfection. I had heard that he was one of those unfortunate golfers prone to be slightly temperamental, but in my play with him in the qualifying rounds at Inverness, I watched him closely and saw him pull out of several holes that would have worried older campaigners. He failed completely to show any signs of a bad temper and played his game perfectly. I regard him as one of the best young golfers in America or anyplace for that matter."

This quieted the natives, and the match proceeded without further incident.

Doug and Beckett put up a game fight, remaining all square with Vardon and Ray through the first seventeen holes. Ray birdied the eighteenth to finish the morning session one-up. In the afternoon, though, Doug's putter abandoned him in the middle of the round, and Beck was unable to hold off the English charge. Ray was on a mission. He won eight out of thirty-six holes (every victory for his team) and while Doug won three holes on his own, it wasn't enough. Riding the coattails of the reigning

U.S. Open champion, Vardon got one back on Edgar. He and Ray won the match five-and-four.

Although all four players shook hands with their hosts before the crowds shuffled off for dinner and a waltz, there was little time to celebrate. Doug, Harry, and Ted had to hop a train for Chattanooga. They had another exhibition match the next morning, September 9, at Chattanooga Golf and Country Club.

Meg was none too pleased. While her husband was flitting around the exhibition circuit, she had come to a decision: she was going home, with or without him. The Atlanta experiment had failed. As Doug and a pro named Jim McKenzie dueled Vardon and Ray to a draw in Chattanooga, Meg wrote to her sister to inform her of the news:

> My Dearest Lilly,
>
> It's just so bloody hot, I don't know anything else to do but swear. Oh dear, it is hot. I wish you could see Douglas, Jr. He has learned to ride Rhoda's bicycle. You would scream. I just let them go as they please. They are real cowboys riding on the back of the bicycle, and climbing trees like monkeys, things I would never dream of letting them do at home.
>
> Well, again, I'm thinking seriously about making another attempt to get to England, but I'm afraid of all the strikes and troubles that are facing you all, and the food is so expensive, although we pay pretty high for food here. Perhaps Ada will hand me a few cheese crumbs and bacon cuttings over the counter once in a while, so I think I can manage.
>
> Douglas has been from home so much this year. Really there is nothing for me living in this desolate place, and he is not finished yet. He goes away about three weeks in October until the second week in November. He is very undecided as to whether he should go to England for Christmas, but I'm so determined I'm coming that I'm going to risk it alone. I'm so fed up. I want to come on the Celtic, which leaves New York for Liverpool on the sixth of November. Why I've picked that boat: Vardon and Ray are coming on that boat, so there will always be someone I know that I can speak to.
>
> I will let you know all the particulars by the next mail. Then Douglas will be quite sure what is going to happen on our side as well as your side.

The next mail turned out to be two weeks later, when she wrote to Lilly once more:

> Have you found a house for me yet, because I'm coming back to England as soon as Douglas gets his patent fixed up. This is the most gossipy place. I thought Gosforth was bad, but a few people I know have been inquiring how many and where I get all the smart costumes from, as they thought a golf pro could not have much wage to afford that. So, they are fussing.
>
> I've got my nigger making me a new set of golf clubs and I think that I can play pretty well, so I shall be able to take McShaw and you when I return. I'm having my own silk hat and the straw fixed up this week as the people here are wearing straw hats and silk dresses, white shoes and stockings. They don't mind the rain as long as it's warm.
>
> I've nothing much to say, but please give me the news of Gosforth.
>
> Goodbye,
> Love ever,
> Meg

One of the October events Doug played in was the Southern Open at East Lake, the longest golf course in the country to host a top-flight open event at just a few paces over seven thousand yards. The tournament was also one of the most popular, in part because Atlanta was the perfect place for golf in October, and also because the winner's check was a thousand dollars. Hutchison, Diegel, Barnes, and Burke all made the trip to East Lake. And, of course, there were the locals, Jones, Perry Adair, Willie Ogg, and Edgar.

Doug liked his chances, and not just because he had played East Lake often enough to know its many intricacies. The day before the opening round of the tournament he went out for a practice round with Darkie and shot deep into the 60s. When they finished, Darkie did a little calculating and said, *"Doug, did ye kna ye had eleven threes in tha' round?"*

Doug put his fingers to his lips and said, *"If ye tell a soul, I'll break yer bloody neck."*

He didn't want to keep the secret out of modesty or to minimize the pressure; he wanted to bet on himself. So sure was Doug that he was going to win that he contacted his regular bookie and wagered $700 that he would be the next Southern Open champion.

For a while this didn't seem like a good bet. The weather turned nasty on the first day of play, with winds howling through the pines at thirty miles an hour. Scores went up accordingly. Jim Barnes, the defending champion, led the way with a 75. Bob Jones was in second with a 78, Hutchison and a fellow named Harry Hampton shot 79s, and Edgar, along with a pro from Montgomery named W. J. Daman, and Willie Ogg lurked six shots back having posted 81s.

The wind still whipped on the second day, only this time it blew a steady drizzle into the players' ears. Slogging through the miserable conditions, Barnes shot an 81 of his own, which allowed Bob Jones, who came in with another 78, to tie him for the lead going into the thirty-six-hole final day. Doug shot 77 in the worst of the storm, a score that impressed those who braved the elements to see it. Even with nature conspiring against him, he seemed to be playing inspired golf.

Calm conditions greeted the players when they arrived on October 3 for the final two rounds. Clouds had blown eastward and the sun shone brightly as the seventy-four players shed their topcoats and cut loose on the soft and soggy course. The wet conditions made it play even longer than normal, but at least the wind had died down and the temperature had gone up to a comfortable high of sixty-nine degrees.

The scores tumbled as conditions improved. Leo Diegel shot one-under-par 35 on his first nine holes of the day. Doug and Bob Jones were right behind him, with opening nines of even-par 36. Barnes and Hutchison remained in the hunt by going out with 39s. Finally, the event was becoming a horserace.

At the lunch break, Jones, Barnes, and Edgar had all shot 74s. The young amateur and the defending champion were tied at the top, two shots ahead of the man who had put a month's salary down on himself to win. Doug would later say of the bet, *"It wozn't ego, mind you, though it might sound like it. Ah just knew tha' Ah woz ganna play well. Ah'd got control o' the ball. Ah knew that Ah could put it anywhere Ah wanted it te go."*

He put it exactly where he wanted to in the final round that afternoon. A four, three, three start set the pace. Just like that, Doug was tied for the lead. He posted two more threes and two fives on the front nine, turning with a birdie at the par five ninth to shoot 34, the best nine-hole score of the week, and good enough for the outright lead. He cruised in with one birdie and one bogey on the back nine for a two-under-par finale.

As the *Constitution* reported, "the most spectacular round of the entire tournament was the last by Edgar. On it, he won the championship, and believe me, it was some round, for it gave him a 70. This is miracle golf when it is considered the strain under which he played. Tied for third place when he started with several hundred dollars hanging on the difference between a few strokes one way or another, he displayed granite nerve in the thrilling rush he made. And when he got through the first nine it was evident that only super-miracle golf would beat him."

Jones came close to pulling off a super miracle. He played well throughout, but failed to hole crucial putts on the back nine. When he tapped in for par on the final hole, he had shot his second 74 of the day—a respectable round and a precursor of good things to come—but not good enough. Jones finished alone in second place, two shots behind Edgar.

The new champion posed for the cameras and held the trophy aloft for all to see. The gallery loved it, and they loved him. He also accepted the thousand-dollar winner's check as if it were the grandest sum of money he had ever seen. It would be some time before he would tell anyone that he had made far more than that from his bookie. For now, he was, once more, the Whistling Champion, the jolly golfer with the mischievous twinkle and the handsome smile.

Later that day, O. B. Keeler went through the scores and realized that Edgar had played seventy-two holes of championship golf on the longest competitive course in the land without posting a single six on his card. "Another record, I believe," Keeler said.

Doug was sure it would be one of many more records and victories to come. The patent for his "Gate to Golf" was within days of being approved and his book was already at the printer's. He would be wealthy and famous beyond his wildest dreams; he just knew it. He was playing so well, and had become so famous, what could possibly go wrong?

Good to her word, on the 6th of November, Meg Edgar held Harry Vardon's elbow and allowed him to escort her up the gangplank of RMS *Celtic*, a steamship bound for Liverpool from New York. She had bid Atlanta adieu. Whether or not her husband would follow was completely up to him.

Two weeks after Meg and the children set sail, Doug played in the Pinehurst Best Ball tournament where he and Perry Adair finished second to Tommy Armour and Leo Diegel. They brought home the "club trophy" to Druid Hills, since they were the low team from the same club, but despite his great play, Doug's heart wasn't in it. He and Darkie talked about the future, but Doug seemed to battle the old melancholy. Even his exhibitions became lackluster. He apologized to his members and sponsors, telling them he was suffering from poor health, but a few of his friends knew the real story. Doug remained a man-child, a person who wore responsibility like an ill-fitting coat. His personal life was a mess, and until he reconciled his intentions with his family, his professional career would suffer.

On December 14, Doug boarded RMS *Aquitania* to sail from New York to Cherbourg and Southampton. He would be home with his family for Christmas. Beyond that, he would have to see how things worked out.

CHAPTER 15

Thomas "Darkie" Wilson.

The tragic and untimely death of J. Douglas Edgar has shocked and grieved us profoundly. During the Open Championship here, he endeared himself to the members of the Inverness Club by all those qualities that win the high esteem and love of one's fellow men.

—OPEN LETTER OF TRIBUTE,
members of the Inverness Club,
Toledo, Ohio

Almost sixty hours after the fact, Comer still couldn't shake the blood: couldn't shake it from his conscience, couldn't shake it from his dreams, and couldn't shake it from his shoes. After fouling the crime scene by stepping in the sticky pool, he'd had his wingtips cleaned and shined. Then he put them away in one of his chests. He would never wear them again.

The knowledge that he would never rid his mind of Douglas Edgar filled him with trepidation, the same kind of anxiety he felt about going back into Patterson and Sons, an act he dreaded not because of the testimony he would give—he had reconciled himself to speaking the truth and enduring whatever came as a result—but because of the setting. The tools of undertaking—hooks, knives, double-sided picks and hammers, and large-bladed saws—looked to Comer like things out of a medieval torture chamber; and the room itself, with its spartan furnishings and bright, harsh lights humming like a swarm of summer hornets, brought on a disquieting sense of unease. That was before taking into account the wailing cries of mourners and the smells from those god-awful chemicals. Throw in the fact that Edgar lay not thirty feet away in one of the parlors, and it was easy to see why Comer would have rather plowed a cotton field than gone back into town.

He was up early again. The morning sun through the windows of his sleeping porch had disrupted his normal rest patterns for the third straight day. His negress had already prepared coffee and biscuits with sorghum, his favorite, and the morning paper lay folded on the dining table just to the right of the butter knife. Comer thought the *Constitution* staff had done a passing job covering all the fundamentals of the hearing, quoting Dr. Noble, Lester Shivers, Wilhoit, Miss Warren, and Darkie Wilson correctly, but failing to mention the leading nature of Coroner Donahue's questions. In the column next to the Edgar story, the headline read: "Medicine Liquor Gets Negro in Bad." According to the beat reporter covering such matters, one James Hall, negro, and his live-in negress, Ella Burns, were being held on $2,000 bond for having six one-gallon jugs of cane whiskey in the corner of their kitchen. Upon apprehension, Hall had said, "I thought I was allowed to have a little liquor in the house for medicine."

Well, that put things into perspective. Comer was about to lay bare his standing in the city, as well as his reputation within his own family, for a man he did not know—a golf player of all things!—but at least Atlantans were safe from whiskey-hoarding negroes and their shack-up mistresses.

When his father had been his age, working as an earnest cub reporter at the *Constitution,* he had gone to the tiny community of Allenwood, Georgia, for a political rally of some sort, and filed his story at the telegraph office in nearby Milledgeville. The next day, after spending a restful night in Allenwood, he took a coach back to Milledgeville in order to catch the train home. Because he had a few minutes to spare, he went back to the telegraph office to thank the dispatcher. *"Young feller, that'uz a durn fine story you writ,"* said the telegraph operator, a man with tobacco stains in his beard and on his overalls. *"Why, I done sent almost half of it to Atlanty."* Clark Howell always laughed before getting to the punch line of that story. Comer could imagine his father having all kinds of reactions to this current episode: laughter was not among them.

Even the biscuits and sorghum couldn't settle his stomach. He put the paper aside, finished his coffee, and headed to town.

H. M. Patterson and Sons Undertaking hadn't changed much in a day, although the number of spectators for this inquest had increased. Every newspaper in town had a staff writer in the back of the room or standing outside an open window. Darkie Wilson was there as well, even though he wasn't likely to be called again to testify. From the look on his face, he appeared to be there for answers. Comer hoped he found them.

The chairs looked as though they hadn't been touched, but Coroner Donahue seemed fresher than he'd been yesterday. He had a spring in his step as he joked with jurors while the crowd settled in.

"If everyone is present, I would suggest we get on with it," Donahue said in a voice loud enough to jar the room into silence. "Reconvening this coroner's jury in the question of the manner and cause of death of one James Douglas Edgar of Newcastle, England, and Atlanta, Georgia, the first witness of the day is Atlanta police detective J. W. Lowe."

Lowe had been standing near the door and marched to the seat nearest jury foreman Charles Girardeau. He had the physique of a middleweight boxer, but the long nights and many dead ends of this case had taken their toll. His chest appeared sunken, and his clipped walk carried a twitch of frayed nerves that accompanies a lack of sleep.

"Dectective Lowe, please recount your involvement in this case to the jurors, and if you don't mind, please give us the latest developments in your investigation."

That was as open-ended a question as Comer had ever heard. Either Donahue was losing his touch for steering witnesses, or he felt confident in what Lowe was going to say. Comer assumed it was the latter. Chief Beavers had been yelling "Traffic Safety" like a country Baptist preacher. Donahue had to assume that Detective Lowe was not going to run afoul of his boss.

To his credit, after explaining that he had been the detective on call the night of Edgar's death, Lowe went through the curious circumstantial evidence, including the three men seen standing on the street corner mere moments before Mr. Shivers left Edgar in front of his house. "None of the people I questioned at the scene knew anything about those men," Lowe said.

He left the mystery of the three men hanging. Then he moved on to finding the shoe in the hedge near the boardinghouse.

"Would not the impact of an automobile have knocked a man out of his shoes?" Donahue asked holding his hands up at his sides as if this were the most obvious thing in the world.

Lowe nodded. "That is certainly a possibility. The curious aspect is that the shoe was undamaged and remained completely laced and tied. I have investigated other instances where men have been separated from their shoes and even their stockings, including a boxcar tramp who was hit by a train, but in each of those instances the shoes have suffered serious damage to the point of uselessness. Mr. Edgar's shoe was in fine shape, as were his clothes, with the exception of a small gash in the leg of his trousers where the implement that killed him entered."

This sent Coroner Donahue into a momentary sputtering fit. When he collected himself, he questioned Lowe's expertise on persons being struck by enough force to send their shoes flying hither and yon. Lowe agreed he was not an expert, but he had seen it happen, something not many people in the room could say.

"How long was it before you concluded that Mr. Edgar had been struck by an automobile that failed to stop?" Donahue asked.

This was the equivalent of asking a man what time of day he preferred to strike his wife. But Lowe remained unfazed. He walked the jury through the evolution of the hit-and-run theory, starting with Comer banging on the boardinghouse door and yelling that a man had been struck by a car, and going through the testimony of Miss Warren and others who claimed to have heard a high-powered motorcar speeding down the street.

"And can you tell the jury about the progress you have made in the search for this motorcar and its driver?" the coroner asked.

"We have followed several leads, including an automobile that was reported as having been parked on the street near the scene of Mr. Edgar's death earlier in the evening. Those leads continue, including two men who might have information on the identity of the three men seen by Mr. Irvin Fisher from his streetcar. They are prepared to testify—"

Donahue waved his hands in front of him as if he were warding off some unseen dog that was about to jump on his trousers. "We don't want to waste the jurors' time with irrelevant testimony," he said.

Lowe moved on to other things, but Comer had to give the detective credit for at least glancing toward the mysterious three men on the street corner. After another hour of tedious testimony, Donahue wore Lowe down and forced him admit that, yes, even though he was not a doctor, a scientist, or a pathologist, it was his opinion that a sharp object protruding from the front of a speeding car *could* have caused the injury that killed Edgar.

"Are you aware of any further complaints from citizens concerning speeding automobiles?" Donahue asked Lowe.

That, of course, was far less relevant than what Lowe's two witnesses might offer, but this wasn't a courtroom. There was no opposing counsel to object.

Lowe nodded. "Complaints have been especially high among residents of Juniper Street between the hours of five and seven P.M.," he said. "But other complainants have mentioned all the main streets in Atlanta as being, at times, speedways for reckless drivers."

Donahue thanked Lowe and dismissed him. That left one last witness.

"Would Mr. H. Comer Howell step forward and be heard," Donahue said.

Comer pushed himself up from one hard chair and walked slowly to another. His heart raced, and he slowed his movements to try to hide his nerves. Once in the chair nearest the jurors, he nodded to Foreman Gi-rardeau.

"Good morning, Comer," Donahue said. "Even though you are well known to most of us here, please state your full name, age, and occupa-tion."

"Hugh Comer Howell," Comer said. "I'm twenty years old, a stu-dent, and a reporter at the *Atlanta Constitution.*"

"And you are the son of Mr. Clark Howell?" Donahue asked for the benefit of the transcript and history.

"I am," Comer said.

"Can you tell this coroner's jury how you came to be involved in this Edgar business?"

Comer began his tale with Wilhoit and Warwick seeking a ride home after closing the issue late Monday night. "We were going out West Peachtree at about midnight Monday night. We had gotten almost to Fifth Street when Wilhoit, who was in the rear, called my attention to a body which seemed to be lying near the curb. I had not observed it. I turned around at the intersection of West Peachtree and Fifth and running back on the other side of the street, passed the body, and, turning again, threw the lights on it. We got out and stopped a passing streetcar. All of us then went to where the body lay."

He could not speak of the terror they all felt, the high-pitched panic in Wilhoit's voice as he screamed "A man in the road!" or how they had all hesitated rather than sprinting forward to administer first aid.

"It was in a pool of blood and lay facedown, stretching out into the street from the curb." Comer did his best to keep his voice from quivering through this part of the recitation. "The hat was found in the street about ten yards back in the direction of town. One shoe was later found in the yard. It was a golf shoe and was entirely laced up."

"Were you not among the first people to conclude that Mr. Edgar had been struck by a speeding motorcar?" Donahue said with a smile, assum-ing Comer would leap at the chance to confirm the consensus theory, so his fellow citizens could get this matter behind them. "Was that not your first instinct?"

Comer had tried to imagine how he would handle this moment when it came, but none of the scenarios he had played out in his mind seemed to work. Donahue had come at him at the weakest point. Comer's first in-stinct had, indeed, been to assume the man in the road had been hit by a car. Answering the question honestly was a problem. But he refused to be bullied. He wouldn't let Coroner Donahue, who hadn't seen Edgar in the street, hadn't seen Darkie Wilson weep like a child, and hadn't watched the man take his last breath in a pool of his own blood, brush this event aside with the wave of a hand, dismissing it as some cosmic accident of bad driving and worse timing.

He took a deep breath and gave the only answer that made sense to him. "I made a terrible mistake," Comer said. And then before Donahue could interrupt, he explained: "I, like a great number of citizens, had been concerning myself with the increased frequency and severity of traffic accidents in the city, especially at that time, it, of course, being the onset of Traffic Safety Awareness Week. It was with those thoughts and concerns occupying my mind that I jumped to the rash conclusion that Mr. Edgar, who had not been identified to me at that time, had been struck by a car. This was a conclusion based not on evidence, but on the thoughts that had preoccupied my own mind in the time leading up to discovering Mr. Edgar."

Donahue recoiled as if he'd been punched in the face. This was not how things were supposed to go with the last witness. He had strategically placed Comer last as a cherry on top of this cream soda of a presentation. The Howell boy had, after all, been the first to call this a case of automobile recklessness. Now, he was soiling the process, muddying the waters for jurors who were easily led. This would not do. The coroner's face turned red, and he took an aggressive step toward Comer's chair.

"In point of fact, Mr. Howell, you did call out to Mr. Thomas Wilson that a man had been struck by a car. Were those not your words that night immediately upon discovery of the body? Was that not your first instinct?"

"It was the imprudent reaction of an impulsive young man," he said. "I would hope you and the jurors, indeed, the citizens of Atlanta, would forgive me this failing of youth."

For a moment Comer was back in school debating some esoteric point or another with a group of friends while smoking cigarettes and sneaking sips of corn from a Mason jar. It would be at this point that his friends would fall over with laughter. Donahue, however, was far from amused.

"How could you have been so sure, in the moments immediately following the discovery of Mr. Edgar's body, that he had, in fact, been struck by a motorcar, and yet now be so sure that you were mistaken?" he asked. "Could this change of heart not also be youthful impudence?"

"There were no skid marks," Comer continued, his voice getting louder. "Nothing that we could see at the time or in the light of day that would indicate a man had been dragged or thrown any distance. The small puncture wound in his leg was not immediately visible that night, but it was evident that there was no trauma to the rest of the body or the clothing. There was no 'mangling' as it were. His face was quite recognizable and completely without blemish of any sort. The only trauma appeared to be in the one area of the lower extremities."

Somebody killed this man, he wanted to yell. Isn't anybody interested in knowing who or why?

Donahue sighed, and said, "Mr. Howell, you have heard the testimony of Doctor Noble and Detective Lowe, as well as your colleague at the *Constitution* and passenger that night, Mr. Wilhoit. Given what you have heard and learned, do you or do you not believe the wound that killed Mr. Edgar could have been caused, as has been postulated here, by a metal object protruding from the front or side of an automobile?"

Comer paused, but only for a second. "I do not," he said. "Given what I have seen and heard, I find it to be highly improbable and unlikely. Mr. Edgar most definitely died from the puncture wound to his leg, but I think the causation of that injury remains an open question."

Donahue shook his head and paced the room with a smile. Then he thanked Comer with a wave of his hand as if dismissing a child. With that, the proceedings were closed.

Patience had never been one of Comer's strongest virtues, a point his mother reminded him of with painful regularity. Outside Patterson and Sons, the smells of bleach, antiseptic, formaldehyde, and death caught somewhere between his nostrils and his throat, Comer paced the gravel parking area like a cornered bobcat. He didn't stop moving until Darkie Wilson offered him a cigarette.

Darkie commented on the weather, and the proceedings. Then he filled Comer in on all the particulars of the book *The Gate to Golf* where Doug had laid out the specifics of his Movement. In it Doug wrote, "Why the movement is the key to golf may seem at first sight rather difficult of explanation. Just so! Why are short stirrups the best for jockeys? I imagine that when riding all 'tucked up' the rider can throw his weight forward where the horse finds it easiest to carry him. So the golfer, swinging with the Movement, can throw his weight into his stroke in the most effective manner. In fact, he can get the maximum power and control with the least exertion. Or again, just as a boxer in a certain position can get in his heaviest blow, so a golfer in a certain position can get in his most powerful swing."

He also wrote that "The effect this game has on the minds of the sanest and strongest men is almost uncanny."

What effect the game and its trappings had on Edgar would remain a mystery. But as Darkie told Comer as they kicked gravel and blew white smoke into the hazing summer air, *"He seemed lost for a time. There woz talk tha' he woz gannin te tour in Florida wi' Barnes an' Hagen. Then Ah read tha' he planned te stay in England. The Royal Canadian Golf Association expected him te defend his title, but he hadn't sent in his application. Ah divin't think he knew what he woz dein' until he did it. Tha' woz Doug. He woz finally happy, though. Ah think he died tha' way."* Then he smiled, although his eyes remained sad, and said, *"All the 'Gate te' Golf' did woz get every pro in England narked at him. That damn thing cost them a fortune in lessons."*

They both laughed, and Darkie shared stories about going out with his friend in the weeks prior to Prohibition. *"He enjoyed his drink,"* Wilson said. *"He thowt Prohibition woz a fool's law. He swore it wad never last."*

The stories carried on for several more minutes. Then Detective Lowe joined them. He nodded to indicate that he had news. "The jury adjourned without rendering a verdict," Lowe said with a hint of admiration in his voice.

"Wot's tha' mean, then?" Darkie asked.

"It means they dismissed without rendering a verdict on the cause of death," Lowe answered.

"It means they find doubt in the theory that Edgar was struck by a speeding car," Comer said with a smile. "They have left the question open, which is what should have been done."

He had done it. The case was not closed. The men of the coroner's jury had listened and chosen the right path. As small as his efforts might have been in the grand scheme of things, Comer had stood up for Edgar—for the truth—and his fellow Atlantans had listened. He had in no way solved the case; he hadn't even named any suspects—that was up to the police—but because of him, the question of who killed Douglas Edgar remained open. Politics, for once, had failed, and the pathway had been cleared for an unbiased investigation.

Comer felt confident that the truth would eventually come out.

The funeral was at four o'clock that afternoon at the Patterson chapel, a sanctuary with pews and a pulpit adjacent to the embalming room and bereavement parlors. The Druid Hills Club shut down at noon and remained closed for the rest of the day so all the members could go to the service. Most did. A delegation of the British Society of Atlanta also attended, although Dr. Alexander Williamson Stirling, former British consul to the city and father of Edgar's star pupil, Alexa, was still in New York and could not make it.

Anglican priests were in short supply in Georgia, but one was drummed up to officiate, and a Union Jack was draped over the casket in honor of Doug's war service. There was the traditional opening prayer, a couple of hymns, the Twenty-third Psalm, "Amazing Grace" (sung with gusto by Asa Candler, tears streaking his hard face), and the Committal. Then they adjourned to Westview Cemetery where beautiful women wearing large, stylish hats wept openly at the graveside scripture reading. Lester Shivers, the man who'd had the last meaningful conversation with Edgar, was one of the pallbearers along with Howard Beckett, Willie Ogg, the pro from East Lake, and three other members from Druid Hills.

Four thousand miles from his home, in the hot red clay of a city his wife despised and in a land where he found the kind of trouble that so easily befell a man of his nature, a flag-covered cherry casket was submersed beneath a gray headstone that read:

J. Douglas Edgar
Sept. 30, 1886 – Aug. 9, 1921
A Native of England
One of the Greatest Golfers of the Age

Three days later the *Atlanta Constitution* ran a paragraph about Edgar's death beneath the headline, "Heavy Toll Paid to Carelessness in 'Safety' Week."—"The principal events of the week came when J. Douglas Edgar, famous golfer, was killed presumably by a speeding car in front of his home on West Peachtree and Fifth." Two paragraphs later, the final accident of the week was described. A man in a Model T had rear-ended a negro driving a mule-drawn watermelon cart down Spring Street. The paper was intentionally slow latching on to the implications of the jurors' decision.

But at least Wilhoit had used the word "presumably," Comer thought. Edgar deserved that much.

PART THREE

Follow-Through

CHAPTER 16

From left: Mrs. Ted Ray, Ted Ray, Meg Edgar,
Harry Vardon sailing back to England
in the fall of 1920.

Detectives have obtained information of great importance linking a chain
of circumstantial evidence pointing to the guilt of one of a small number of
persons. The unusual circumstances of the supposed murder have made
police work difficult, and several times they have been blocked by an im-
passe which compelled them to disregard previous suspicions and com-
mence work again from the beginning.

—*Atlanta Journal*,
August 1921

Newspapering was hard work, the kind of business that required an objective eye and the ability to fairly present the facts in a concise, accurate, and interesting way. Prior to Edgar, Comer Howell had believed he possessed all of those skills and more. He had been earnest in his efforts, even when he felt his newspaper assignments were beneath his abilities. But Edgar had changed all of that. From the moment he turned his Cadillac around on West Peachtree on the night of August 8, Comer had been a part of the Edgar story, too close to remain objective, too young to be unaffected, and too idealistic to let a political whitewashing go unquestioned. Stepping forward hadn't had any immediate repercussions, but he could sense that his time at the paper might have already passed. Men like his father and brother could remain detached from the stories they covered, no matter how outrageous or horrific; Comer no longer could.

At least he had done what he could in the Edgar case. After the coroner's inquest, he felt confident that police would discover the identities of the three men who had been lurking near the scene moments before Edgar's death. He also thought Lowe and his colleagues would develop an ample list of suspects—bookies, bootleggers, gamblers, jilted boyfriends or wronged husbands—and that the case would be on a path toward resolution. Unfortunately, that was not to be. The case of J. Douglas Edgar remained an unsolved mystery, one that continued to baffle detectives.

The last time Comer spoke with Lowe, the detective appeared to be on the right track, but he didn't seem confident that an arrest would come soon. He didn't come right out and say it, but Comer sensed that the jealous lover theory was bearing more fruit than any other. That would lead to some uncomfortable questions for people in Atlanta unaccustomed to wallowing in such muck. Little wonder Lowe didn't go out of his way to be chatty.

Atlantans liked to think of their city as the "New York of the South," but in many ways it was a small town stretching the seams of its britches. And Comer was very much a part of it. He still donned his tailored suits and attended parties where the name Douglas Edgar was occasionally whispered once loose tongues slipped into gossip mode. Comer did not shy away from those discussions. Sex, murder, and a foreign-born golfing champion could have been a subplot in *The Magnificent Ambersons,* not the kind of things respectable men in Atlanta would welcome, but Comer soon realized that his friends loved gossiping about Edgar, raising tantalizing speculation with each new fantastic tale. But legitimate news still came through long, tedious investigative work, the kind of work Comer no longer had the stomach to attempt.

He hadn't visited Edgar's grave often, but the rolling hills of the Westview Cemetery, with its yawning oaks and a tall, proud Confederate sentry guarding the gravestones at the Battle of Ezra Church Memorial, always seemed like a good place to clear one's head. Crisp air filled the October sky as Comer walked past the stone water tower, constructed in 1850 to look like a cylindrical donjon. He had needed to get out of the city for a few hours, and this was as fine a spot as any. The town was buzzing about President Warren Harding's visit. The president was being given a lunch at Druid Hills that afternoon where a young girl in a white dress would present him with a lovely bouquet of roses under the club's porte cochere. Harding had been elected on a campaign of "restoring normalcy" after the trauma of the world war, and no place needed to be normalized more than Atlanta. Unemployment continued to rise, and Klan membership continued to explode. The hooded knights were seen as a stabilizing force in a world that had lost its compass. America needed clarity from its leaders. A lot was riding on Harding's moral character.

Mrs. Harding had come to town as well, and was being entertained at the home of Chamber of Commerce president Lee Ashcroft (a short distance from Druid Hills) by Mrs. Ashcroft and a gaggle of Atlanta women, all of whom would talk about their lunch with the first lady for the rest of their lives.

The president's train had arrived at one o'clock from Columbus where he had been inspecting the troops at Fort Benning. The motorcade route from the train station to Druid Hills was swarmed with enthusiastic onlookers. According to O. B. Keeler, "The way to Druid Hills Golf Club was bordered with humanity. Groups stood at corners of Ponce de Leon Avenue and waved at the first of the official cars in which sat the nation's chief executive, and he waved back and lifted his hand and smiled."

A sentry from the Senegambian Confederation (a loose West African alliance between Senegal and Gambia), in full native garb, opened the car door for the president and walked backward bowing as he led him inside.

Once there, Walker Lee, the mayor's secretary, introduced the president, since the mayor himself had forgone the state luncheon to attend a Penn State–Georgia Tech football game in New York.

Mr. Lee said, "One of your first utterances, Mr. President, was the statement that you desired to render a service to the South in meeting its great and perplexing difficulties. You have done so, and we wish to acknowledge our grateful appreciation. We believe in you, Mr. President, and we are relying on you."

Clark Howell was one of the 250 guests at the luncheon who got to hear Harding say, "The gospel I have preached is one of understanding— understanding between the different sections of the republic, and understanding between the different nations of the world. Where a perfect understanding exists and where conscience abides, there is little room for conflict or controversy."

Comer chose to miss it all. He would rather spend the afternoon at Westview.

It had been one week since another sorry bit of news hit the golf world. Louis Tellier, the Frenchman who had first been the pro at the Country Club in Brookline and then at Brae Burn in Boston, a fine player and a great friend of Edgar's, had hanged himself from the center beam of one of the houses on club property. According to accounts in *Canadian Golfer* magazine, "The two leading entrants at the Canadian Open Championship at Rivermead, Ottawa, in 1920 were Douglas Edgar of Atlanta, Georgia, and Louis Tellier of Brae Burn, Boston. Edgar was killed this summer, and now comes word from Boston that Tellier has committed suicide. Ill health is given as the cause."

His English wife, herself a fine player whose brother was the pro Wilfred Reid, said that Louis had never come to terms with Edgar's death. He killed himself on his thirty-fifth birthday, the same age Edgar had been when he died.

"Tellier was a Frenchman with a delightful style," *Canadian Golfer* reported. "He was really a very little chap, but got capital distance from the tee and was really a very high-class golfer and instructor. That he was immensely popular throughout the States is amply demonstrated by the tributes that have been paid his memory by professional and amateur golfers from all over the country. It would appear that he took very seriously to heart the death of Douglas Edgar. They were great pals. Mrs. Tellier tells rather weird stories of how Tellier often imagined Doug was still with him and carried on conversations with him in a most animated manner. It was a sad ending to a brilliant career. Incidentally, this is the first time on record that a prominent golfer has taken his own life. The game is generally the great antidote to morbidness and shattered nerves and other run-down conditions usually to be found in suicides."

Comer parked the car and buttoned his coat before venturing out to the gravesite. The first frost had come a week before, and it had rained earlier in the day. Gold and orange leaves covered the ground like a sparkling carpet. He looked down as he walked, watching his step in the damp ground cover. The hill wasn't too steep, but in slick conditions he didn't want to end up on his backside.

He stopped walking when he heard a faint whimper ahead. Someone was standing by Edgar's grave: a petite figure in a black topcoat, a woman who appeared to be crying. When the sun broke from behind a cloud Comer saw a stunning Oriental woman, fair and young, the kind of tall beauty that would turn heads wherever she went. She was dabbing her nose and eyes with a silk cloth, the collar of her coat turned up as if she were attempting to hide inside her clothes. The jet black hair glistened like an onyx, and for a second, Comer thought he recognized her. It took a couple of minutes, but when he finally realized who the woman was, it all made sense.

After Howard Beckett had come to him with the tale of the Jap florist and his mystery wife, Comer had done a little investigating and found that the Druid Hills florist was a local white woman and her two negro helpers. With that information, he wrote Beckett's story off as another in a long list of unfounded rumors. But the old Brookhaven pro had been right all along, just wrong about the timing. The current florist was an older woman, but the person previously contracted to provide floral arrangements for the club was a man named William K. Abbey, the Japanese owner of the Nikko Inn.

While he had never made the connection, Comer had heard rumors about Abbey. For starters, everyone assumed that William Abbey was not the man's real name. Like most Japs, he had tried to Americanize himself by taking a name locals could pronounce and spell. He was reasonably young, twenty-nine, and, from what Comer had picked up in the newsroom, a provider of all things illicit in Atlanta's Jap community. The Nikko Inn was, according to what Comer had heard, the place an Oriental man would head if he was looking for a game of cards or dice, along with a stiff drink and a comely woman. As was common, the police let such things slide. Japs were not troublemakers per se, although most Atlantans steered clear of them. They were a godless lot, unrepentant in their intentions to remain so, which was a sin far more damning than drinking, gambling, or fornicating. Like a majority of white Americans, Comer's neighbors ignored the Japs in their midst, and paid little attention when rumors of the Yakuza, Jap bootleggers and bookies who also ran protection rackets in their neighborhoods, swirled through the room at dinner parties.

Still, as he watched the woman from a distance, tears running from her almond eyes along her high, perfect cheekbones, Comer found her just as intoxicating as she had been when he had first seen her, at some Chamber of Commerce function she had attended with her husband, William K. Abbey.

He hadn't spoken to Mrs. Abbey that first day he had met her, and he would not speak to her today. He was content to watch in silence as this beautiful creature wept quietly, running her hand over the top of Edgar's tombstone.

A good reporter, someone who wanted to build a career in the business of news, would have walked up and asked a few questions: Are you not Mrs. William Abbey? How did you come to know the late Mr. Edgar? And why are you out here alone?

Comer stayed on the hill, watching from a distance for another minute or two. Then he turned and walked back to his car, careful not to rustle the leaves as he left.

CHAPTER 17

Friends in the game:
Douglas Edgar and Harry Vardon.

In an effort to appraise this country's opinions on the Japanese question, through gathering from all States representative expressions by public men and the press, an abstract of the symposium of opinions just made public covers answers from Americans from all walks of life all over the country. . . . In terms of percentage, fifty-seven percent (considerably more than half of those consulted) feel antipathy toward the Japanese. Twenty-two percent are neutral and eleven percent are pro-Japanese. It will be seen from these figures that the percentages of those antagonistic to the Japanese is considerably greater than the number of neutrals and pro-Japanese added together.

—*New York Times,*
June 19, 1921

Just how deeply entwined William Abbey was in the Asian underworld of the 1920s remains unknown. What is known is that the Nikko Inn he owned and operated at the intersection of Forsyth Street and Carnegie Way in Atlanta was, in addition to a restaurant and boardinghouse, an occasional casino, speakeasy, and bordello, one of several spots in Atlanta where an Asian man could place a wager and get a sweet vegetable and fruit chu-hi cocktail during Prohibition.

The goings-on of the Nikko Inn went largely unnoticed until the evening of October 25, 1924, when a local seventeen-year-old boy named Dillard Moore and six of his buddies ate dinner there. After finishing their meal, Moore and his friends got up to leave. The details of what happened next were murky. Some accounts said that Abbey shouted in Japanese, but Moore, unable to understand, ignored him and ran out. This seemed unlikely since Abbey spoke English and had local customers in his restaurant quite often. Other accounts stated that Moore and his cohorts had every intention of skipping out on the bill, while others said Moore hurled racial epithets at Abbey while he was fleeing the inn.

What happened next was undisputed. Abbey, age thirty-two at the time, fired several rounds from a Type-4 Nambu automatic pistol, one of which hit Moore in the chest. The boy died on the sidewalk. Abbey fled the scene, but was found in a nearby hotel. He claimed to have been trying to fire warning shots through the window of the restaurant to stop Moore and the others from escaping without paying their bill, and to alert police. He also claimed to have fled out of fear. Abbey was charged with murder and held without bond in the Atlanta Penitentiary.

One day after the shooting, the detective in charge of the investigation, R. J. Hunt, made a shocking revelation. According to the *Atlanta Constitution,* "[Hunt] announced that the police intend to revive the sensational and mysterious killing of J. Douglas Edgar, popular Druid Hills golf professional on West Peachtree Street several years ago, to see if Abbey can be connected with the old slaying. Mr. Edgar was found dying in the street in front of his home. Many wild rumors were current at the time linking the names of Mr. Edgar and Abbey, who conducted a flower shop at Druid Hills club, the reports being to the effect that ill-will between Edgar and the Jap existed." No mention was made of Abbey's marital status, or the whereabouts of his wife.

Six weeks later, Judge George H. Howard called his courtroom in Fulton Superior Court to order and the Abbey trial got under way after much preliminary turmoil. Four extra panels had to be brought in before twelve jurors could be selected. Problems arose on several fronts. Many of the potential jurors knew Abbey or the Nikko Inn by reputation and were, therefore, released for cause. Others were dismissed after admitting their strong prejudices against the Japanese, a line of voir dire questioning that gave some hint as to the defense strategy.

Abbey had hired a legal dream team. In Atlanta, few courtroom practitioners were more respected than John and Ralph McClelland, Joe Ewing, and Paul Carpenter. They would tag-team witnesses with Ewing, a lanky and distinguished legal fixture with a chiseled chin and a penetrating baritone voice, arguing that, while the series of events in question was tragic, the entire trial was racially motivated. Ewing would put forth the claim that if Abbey had been a white man, no charges would have been filed; that a man had a right to stop thievery, which is what walking out without paying for a meal amounted to; and that an accidental shooting was just that: accidental.

Harold Allen, the assistant solicitor for the state, opened the trial by saying, "This case is clear-cut, as clear a case of cold-blooded murder as has ever been tried in the courts of this state. In fact, I have never seen so little evidence to justify a killing."

Paul Carpenter started to plant the seeds of the race defense, stating that "The only trouble with this case is the unfortunate nationality of the defendant." He went on to say, "I would implore you, good men of this jury, to decide the fate of Mr. Abbey just as if he were one of your own color and race."

The McClellands then regaled jurors with tales of Moore and his compatriots as "whiskey-heads" and "automobile thieves, who threatened and intimidated Mr. Abbey." During the interrogation of a kid named Charlie Lancaster, one of the other boys in the restaurant that night, John McClelland squared his shoulders and yelled, "Did you not hear Dillard Moore tell Charlie Jones [another of Moore's young dinner companions] as he was getting out of the automobile that you all were going to pull a job?"

Lancaster said he had not, but the answer didn't matter. Moore was being portrayed as the leader of a gang of hoodlums hell-bent on robbing a poor Japanese man. Even Moore's mother could not rehabilitate the boy's reputation. Through sobs, she stated that Dillard had no intention of robbing anybody, and that he had left home with two dollars in his pocket, which was gone when she retrieved his belongings at the morgue.

Abbey took the stand around noon. A missionary named William Clark was sworn in as his translator if circumstances overwhelmed him and he could no longer continue in English. As courtroom theatrics went, this was perfect. Abbey wore a dark suit and white tie, looking as humble and Southern as any average Atlantan, and by his side sat a man of God who had devoted his life to saving souls around the world.

Abbey had no trouble recounting his version of events in English. "On the morning of October twenty-fifth about one o'clock, I had let my cook go and was all by myself waiting to close my place," he said, although the time of the events had already been established as a full hour earlier. "Ten or twelve young men came in." The number was actually seven. "They looked rough and I told them I was preparing to close. They insisted on having something to eat.

"I was afraid, and when one of them asked me to get him some cigarettes, I went to a store, hoping to find a policeman. I could not find one and went back where I said, 'Well, gentlemen, what will you have?' One of them replied, 'There is no gentleman in this bunch.' When they had finished eating, two of them asked me for coffee. I went back to the kitchen. Then I heard my cash register ring and knew that somebody was opening it. I ran to the door and saw the boys running down the stairs. At the same time, I noticed the cash drawer was open and that a ten-dollar bill and some five-dollar bills were missing.

"I grabbed my pistol and called for them to stop. I could easily have shot any one of them from the top of the stairs, but I didn't want to hurt them. I went to the window and tried to shoot in the air, but the gun wouldn't work. It was jammed. While I was working to release it, it suddenly went off. I held it in the air until it stopped, and then ran in the street and told an officer what had happened. While I was talking to him, somebody said that one of the boys had been shot. I then ran in a room in a nearby hotel, where the police found me.

"I am very sorry that the boy was shot. I have great sympathy for the mother as I have a dear mother myself, but I am not guilty of this crime—that is my statement."

The English became much worse on cross examination, and several times the missionary had to translate. No, Mr. Abbey could not say exactly how much money was missing from his cash register, and, no, he wasn't sure about the exact number of boys who had entered his establishment. No, he could not remember how many times the Nambu mysteriously went off as he held it in the air, his hand nowhere near the trigger, and, no, he had never heard of a jammed handgun going off multiple times, but it was a Japanese gun.

The jury adjourned to chambers at ten-thirty. At eleven, they asked the judge to clarify the definition of robbery, and asked if a man was within his rights to shoot a robber who was attempting to escape. Judge Howard said he was unable to answer that question. So a few minutes before one A.M., the jury returned with a verdict of not guilty.

Mrs. Moore had to be restrained by her husband as she tried to go after Abbey in the courtroom. "He can't murder my boy and get away with it like that," she yelled. "He shot him down in cold blood and he must pay. He must pay for it! He must!"

By the spring of 1925, Abbey had sold the Nikko Inn and moved to Miami. Once a quarter for the next five years, Atlanta detective J. W. Lowe would phone the Miami Police Department where he requested an informal update on Abbey. Then, in the early spring of 1930, William K. Abbey died suddenly at the age of thirty-seven from an unspecified ailment.

Lowe notified Meg Edgar of Abbey's death. One month later, Mrs. Edgar passed away at the age of forty-nine after battling uremia and acute nephritis. She died at peace, having received an answer to the last remaining question in her life.

After Abbey's death, Lowe put the Edgar file away and never touched it again. It remains classified as an "Unsolved Death" to this day.

CHAPTER 18

The grave, Westview Cemetery,
Atlanta, Georgia.

An English professional of whom a great majority of British golfers have never heard was a player who might have been the greatest of the twenties, greater than Bobby Jones and Walter Hagen. Ironically, he may also have been the man who showed the Americans the way to world domination in golf. But violent death nipped his career in the bud one warm August night in Atlanta, Georgia, in 1921. . . . There were suspicions of course, and clues, and possible clues, and clues that should have been clues but weren't. There were rumors which always follow the violent death of a "Ladies Man." The investigation slowly ground to a halt and went into the files of the Georgia Bureau of Vital Statistics. So, the golf instructor without peer, the man who taught the Americans how to play golf, whose book had only just hit the book-stands, lived fully and died violently: "One of the Greatest Golfers of the Age."

—*Golf Monthly,*
August–September 1978

Meg Edgar and her children never returned to America. For the rest of her living days after Douglas's death, Meg kept a fresh rose in a pink crystal vase on the shelf of her home in Gosforth. After Meg's death in 1930, Rhoda kept the vase in a prominent place in her home for the rest of her life, passing it on to her son, Michael Newrick, after she died.

Rhoda married a man a year younger than her father who had also served with honor in the First World War. Her memories of her father remained happy if not vague. She also reclaimed her faith in God as an adult, faith she had lost when informed so cruelly about her father's death. The only times she displayed anger was when anyone brought up her father's philandering. It was a subject she rejected out of hand.

Doug Jr. was another story. He never spoke of his father, and would become visibly angry whenever the elder Edgar's name came up. He did, however, follow in his father's footsteps, serving as the golf pro at Theydon Bois Golf Club in Essex, England, for twenty years. J. Douglas Edgar III (the spitting image of his grandfather) also became a golf professional, playing competitively in Europe in the 1970s and 1980s and following his father as the pro at Theydon Bois before purchasing an executive course, the Wheathampstead Golf Club, outside London. In February of 2008, the clubhouse at Wheathampstead was broken into by thieves who made off with thousands of dollars in equipment, and one priceless heirloom: a Waltham watch presented to Doug upon winning the 1919 Canadian Open.

"I couldn't insure it as it was impossible to value," Douglas III said. "Twenty years ago, I turned down an offer of $35,000. I just can't believe it. It was the only time I had ever left my briefcase with the watch inside in the club. The rest of the stolen equipment is insured, but the watch is irreplaceable."

Oddly enough, two of Doug's grandsons, Michael Newrick and J. Douglas Edgar III, suffer from degenerative hips and knees. Heredity has been listed as a primary cause.

Not long after Edgar's death, President Harding appointed Clark Howell to the National Coal Commission. It was one of many national posts he would hold. Calvin Coolidge appointed him to the National Transportation Commission, and when Franklin Roosevelt, a longtime friend of Howell's, came into office, the president offered him several ambassadorships, which he turned down before finally accepting a post as chairman of the Federal Aviation Administration where he became good friends with Charles Lindbergh.

He was also one of the founding members of the Associated Press. Even as he served in his many national roles, Howell remained the consummate newspaperman. In 1929, Fourth Ward alderman Ben T. Huiet came forward with a claim that certain city councilmen had requested a $3,500 kickback to approve wiring being installed in Atlanta's new City Hall building. An outraged Clark Howell wrote an editorial demanding a grand jury investigation. The paper continued to pound the drum day after day, reporting on each witness brought before the grand jury and exposing a web of corruption that would end with twenty-six indictments. Howell and the *Constitution* won a Pulitzer for their coverage of what became known as the "Atlanta Graft Ring."

Six years later, after a two-month illness, Clark Howell passed away at his home. He was writing a letter to Franklin Roosevelt congratulating him on his reelection when he died.

Comer Howell worked one more year at the *Constitution* after Edgar's death. But after his own mother, Anne Comer Howell, died in 1922, Comer left the family business to pursue other interests, including an unsuccessful attempt at running a car dealership in Atlanta, and stock brokerage. He married Mildred Asquith and the two traveled extensively, never having children, but sending postcards home from South America, Panama, and Australia. They also lived in New Orleans for a brief period.

After retiring as a stockbroker, Comer and Mildred moved to Miami, which is where Comer died on March 3, 1972. Funeral services were held at Philbrick's Funeral Home in Miami and his remains were cremated.

He never got over the Edgar affair. It bothered and baffled him for the rest of his life, and he would often recount the events of that time to friends in a way that sounded as if retelling it to friends would somehow make it all make sense. One thing is certain: until now, Comer never received the credit he deserved for standing up and doing the right thing.

• • •

Tommy Wilson stayed in Georgia. He became the pro at Ansley Golf Club in Atlanta, and in his later years he moved to Brunswick Country Club, a classic old Donald Ross–designed course in the sleepy coastal community of Brunswick, Georgia, an hour's drive from Savannah to the north and Jacksonville, Florida, to the south. He retired and died in Brunswick, where his daughter and grandchildren still live.

Howard "Pop" Beckett also stayed in Atlanta, and in fact, never left the Capital City Club. He retired there and died just a few short miles from the club.

Long Jim Barnes won the U.S. Open by nine shots one month after Edgar's death. The margin of victory was a U.S. Open record that stood for eighty years until Tiger Woods beat it in 2000. Barnes was (and remains) the only player to be awarded the U.S. Open trophy by a president. Harding was on hand to watch the golf and asked if he could present the trophy to the winner.

Long Jim went on to win the British Open in 1925, and was elected into the World Golf Hall of Fame in 1989.

Walter Hagen won the PGA Championship the year of Edgar's death, the first of five such titles. He also won the British Open four times between 1922 and 1929. His total of eleven wins in what constitutes the modern professional majors ranks third all-time behind Jack Nicklaus and Tiger Woods.

He had a total of fifty-two professional wins, and was the first professional to make a living as what would now be known as a "tour player." Gene Sarazen said of him, "Walter made professional golf what it is." And when the World Golf Hall of Fame was created in 1974, Hagen was the first member installed.

No such luck befell Jock Hutchison. "Hutch" won the last British Open that Edgar played in. It was his second straight year of winning a major championship. He also finished in the top ten in the U.S. Open eight times, including two runner-up finishes. In 1937 he won the inaugural Senior PGA Championship at Augusta National, and a decade later, he won that event for the second time.

Bob Jones thought so highly of Hutch that he invited him to be the honorary starter at the Masters, a job he held until 1977 when he died at age ninety-three. Yet, for all his successes, Jock Hutchison failed to be inducted into the Hall of Fame, a travesty that the guardians of the game should rectify.

Alexa Stirling didn't win another major after Edgar's death, being defeated five-and-four in the finals of the 1921 U.S. Women's Amateur by Marion Hollins, a woman who would go on to found the Cypress Point Club in Monterey and Pasatiempo outside San Francisco, both Alister MacKenzie–designed masterpieces. Hollins had lost to Alexa in the second round of the U.S. Women's Amateur in 1919.

The 1921 loss was the first of many disappointments. Alexa's game became more deliberate after Edgar's death, especially the finesse shots that require far more touch than mechanics. She did win the Met Women's Championships in 1922 and 1923, but that was it for her playing career. She moved to New York and took a securities job.

Then, during the 1923 Women's Canadian Open at Rivermead Club in Ottawa (the club where Doug won his second Canadian title), Alexa met Dr. Wilbert Crieve Fraser. They hit it off immediately. He hunted and fished and did all the things she loved. They were married in 1925 in a spectacular ceremony at East Lake in Atlanta, an event attended by the entire Howell clan, including Comer. Alexa was twenty-eight.

The Frasers sailed to Europe for a monthlong honeymoon, and then settled in Ottawa. In 1928, they had a daughter, Sandra, and five years later, a son, Glen. Their third child, a boy named Richard, was born in 1939. While not reclusive, the Frasers didn't travel much. Alexa was a member at Royal Ottawa Golf Club where she won the ladies' club championship thirteen straight times, and they belonged to the Ottawa Hunt Club where she hunted pheasants more often than she played golf.

In 1950, Alexa came back to Atlanta for the fiftieth anniversary of the U.S. Women's Amateur, which was being played at East Lake. She reunited with Bob Jones for the first time in a quarter century, and was shocked by his condition. Jones was already suffering from the devastating effects of syringomyelia, a congenital disorder that disconnects the body's motor nerves from the brain. By 1950, he walked like an eighty-year-old with arthritis. Alexa stayed at her friend's side throughout the week.

On April 14 of that year, she wrote to O. B. Keeler,

Dear Mr. Keeler:

I am writing you as an old friend, to thank you for your share in selecting me for the "Hall of Fame." You and the other judges have done me a great favor, and I appreciate it most sincerely.

The announcement in the papers here has caused quite a stir, and coming as it has after a long period of inactivity in the golfing world has been most exciting. All during the War, I was very tired with my growing family and lack of domestic help. So my golf went fully well into discard, and I now play but little I'm afraid, and only for pleasure in any event.

Our family now consists of one girl and two boys. Our daughter is in the midst of studying for the third-year exams at Carlton College. There she expects to get her B.A. next year. She is 21. Glen, the eldest boy, is now 17 and is at the moment down in New Hampshire skiing at Mount Washington. He is in his third year at Glebe Collegiate (high school). Dickie, the youngest, is at home and is doing the things that most little boys of 10 usually do. They are a trio and no end of fun.

I tell you these things so that you have some idea of the interests which surround us. We go as most people hereabouts do, to our summer place for July and part of August and during the fall do a bit of partridge and duck hunting.

It's a good life and we have lots of fun in a quiet way. If you care to, I would be glad if you would get word to the other judges who voted about the "Hall of Fame" and let them know how I appreciate having been chosen.

Let me hear what goes on with you—and again many thanks.

Very Sincerely Yours,
Alexa Stirling Fraser
12 Lakeview Terrace
Ottawa Ontario

Keeler never responded. While the Amateur was played at East Lake, he was admitted to Emory Hospital and died on October 15, 1950.

Alexa did not return to Atlanta again until 1976 when the Atlanta Athletic Club hosted the U.S. Open. The USGA had intended on making this Jones's last hurrah, but he had died in December of 1971. By then the club had abandoned East Lake for the sprawling northern suburbs of Atlanta, a town called Duluth. Jerry Pate, a rookie, won the tournament with a spectacular five-iron shot from the rough on the seventy-second hole, a shot most golf historians recall with great clarity. Fewer remember the eloquent speech Alexa gave on what it meant to her and to the memory of Bobby Jones to have the tournament return to their home club (although neither ever played the Duluth course).

Not long after returning to Ottawa, she was diagnosed with lung cancer. Alexa Stirling Fraser died on April 15, 1977, at home in Canada and was buried in Pembroke.

She was again honored in Georgia when she was inducted into the Georgia Sports Hall of Fame in 1978. Alexa's children were invited down, and they wondered why they were being treated so royally. As Alexa's daughter, Sandra, recalled, "We had no idea what our mother had done. We just assumed they were making a fuss because Southerners are hospitable." When she realized all that her mother had accomplished, Sandra cried, saying that her mother had never told them any of it. They knew she played golf, but they had no idea.

Alexa was inducted into the Canadian Golf Hall of Fame in 1986 and the Georgia Golf Hall of Fame in 1989. But perhaps the greatest honor came when Patty Berg was asked to name the greatest champion in women's golf. Most assumed that Berg would call out Mickey Wright or Babe Didrikson Zaharias. Instead she said, "Alexa [Stirling] is the finest competitor, and the finest lady the game has ever known."

Edgar's other star, Bob Jones, went on to win thirteen major championships, including the British Open, British Amateur, U.S. Open, and U.S. Amateur in 1930, a feat known as the Grand Slam. He then retired from competitive golf at age twenty-eight. He practiced law as one of the founding partners in Jones, Bird and Howell, which would later become Alston & Bird, one of the world's largest and most prestigious law firms. And he formed Augusta National Golf Club, which began hosting an invitational tournament for a few of Bob's friends. It would later become known as the Masters.

Jones remains the greatest amateur golfer in history. His Grand Slam has never been matched, and his impact on the game never equaled. Almost lost to history is the fact that during a critical stage in his golfing life, Jones "learned through observation" from one of the greatest golfers of the age: J. Douglas Edgar.

Acknowledgments

Sometimes stories come to you when you least expect them. This one came to me from my dear friend Furman Bisher, who, at ninety-one years old, is still one of the best sports columnists in the business. Furman and I were at the Tour Championship, a PGA Tour event at historic East Lake Golf Club, the course where Bob Jones played his first and last rounds. As we were sipping coffee in the media center and solving some major world crisis, Furman picked up the latest edition of the media guide, and turned to the Records section. After a minute of searching, he said, "Well, Douglas Edgar's record is still intact."

I shrugged and said, "Who the hell is Douglas Edgar?"

By the time Furman finished telling this story my jaw was on the floor. I said something like, "Furman, that's unbelievable."

He responded with, "Ah, everybody knows that story. I wrote that story."

"When did you write it?" I asked.

"Either nineteen sixty-three or -four," he said.

After assuring him that a fair number of people might have missed it, I asked if he would mind if I took another stab at it. "No," he said. "Come over to the house. I'll give you all my notes."

One advantage to having a ninety-one-year-old friend with a mind like a thirty-year-old's is that he remembers everything; another is that newspapermen from that generation never threw away anything. Furman still had all his old notes, transcripts of interviews with Bob Jones,

Tommy Wilson, Tommy Armour, and Howard "Pop" Beckett, as well as first-person accounts from people who knew Edgar and had seen him play. It was a solid foundation on which to begin this tale.

From there it was off to London, Newcastle, Toronto, and Atlanta where I had the great fortune of meeting Doug Edgar's grandchildren. His grandson on his son's side could not have been friendlier or more helpful, but, as is the case with most families, it was Doug's daughter who saved everything. Mick Newrick still lives in Newcastle, a ten-minute cab ride from Northumberland Golf Club. He provided a treasure trove of memorabilia, letters, clippings, passports, ship manifests, notes, and photographs, and he read and reread the manuscript numerous times and offered great details throughout, all of which added color and depth to the story. I also found Tommy Wilson's daughter, retired and living near her children on St. Simon's Island just south of Savannah. She was able to provide a wealth of stories of her father. After that, it was a hard chair and long days in the Atlanta History Center and the Emory University Manuscript and Rare Book Library, along with hundreds of out-of-the-blue phone calls, and thousands of questions passed back and forth with my researchers, Jan and Barry Young.

A special note of thanks goes out to Peter Dawson, secretary of the Royal & Ancient Golf Club at St. Andrews, and a member at Northumberland Golf Club, who introduced me to golf in High Gosforth Park, as well as to Jamie Forteath, the secretary at Northumberland Golf Club, who proved to be a gracious host and patient listener. Also, the staff and members at Druid Hills Golf Club in Atlanta were tremendously helpful. Thanks also to David Randall of the *London Independent,* legendary sportswriter and commentator Ben Wright, and author, attorney, and Bob Jones historian Sidney L. Matthew, who gave great insight and support throughout. Karen Hewson at the Royal Canadian Golf Association provided invaluable information, as did my old friend Julius Mason at the PGA of America. Finally, a note of thanks to Mark Tavani at Random House for seeing the potential in this story and believing that someone of my limited skills might actually be able to pull it off.

This is as close a re-creation of the events as I could put forth. I hope I have done justice to Edgar's life, and the times in which he lived.

Index

Page numbers in italics refer to illustrations.

ABOUT THE AUTHOR

STEVE EUBANKS is an award-winning sportswriter and former PGA golf professional. He has coauthored books with Arnold Palmer, NASCAR champion Jeff Gordon, world champion rodeo cowboy Ty Murray, and former Notre Dame coach Lou Holts, as well as authoring two sports novels. Steve lives with his wife and family in Peachtree City, Georgia.